Mastering
Organisational Behaviour

Richard Pettinger

First published 2000 by
MACMILLAN PRESS LTD
Houndmills, Basingstoke, Hampshire RG21 6XS and London
Companies and representatives throughout the world

ISBN 0–333–79279–3

A catalogue record for this book is available from
the British Library.

This book is printed on paper suitable for recycling
and made from fully managed and sustained forest sources.

10 9 8 7 6 5 4 3 2 1
09 08 07 06 05 04 03 02 01 00

Typeset by Best-set Typesetters Ltd

Printed in Great Britain by
Creative Print & Design (Wales) Ltd, Ebbw Vale

◾ ⓥ Contents

⚟ Preface

Understanding the ways in which people behave in organisations, and why they behave in these ways, is a prerequisite of being a fully effective supervisor or manager. Yet of all the different areas that are covered during the study and practice of management, organisational behaviour is the one that is neglected the most.

This is a critical omission, for all aspects of organisation management require a basic understanding of the principles that govern human behaviour, both from the individual point of view, and also in prescribed, regulated and directed – organised – places of work. These principles apply equally to effective, successful and profitable sales and marketing management, production and operations management, and the organisation and direction of project teams. They apply equally to all sectors of industry and commerce, as they do to the direction and management of public services and the not-for-profit sector. They apply equally to anyone at all levels within organisations, whether supervisor, charge hand, junior, middle, senior manager or director. Moreover, the effects on people's behaviour of policy and direction initiatives need to be understood by those who take these decisions.

There are two main reasons why the subject is not given the position of importance that it deserves. First, because they themselves have not studied human behaviour, practising managers tend to dismiss it as 'soft' or 'touchy-feely', declaring themselves having more important things to do. This is a fatal error. In all parts of organisations, performance is adversely affected when there is insufficient attention to the human aspects of enterprise. Sales are lost because prospective customers and clients have no confidence in the sales force, rather than a lack of confidence in the products. Strikes and disputes occur overwhelmingly because of communication breakdowns, misunderstandings or ignorance of people's expectations and aspirations. People leave organisations because they are bullied, or not respected or not valued; when people say that they hate their job, they nearly always mean that they hate the style of management or general human interaction, rather than the work itself. People may leave organisations because they are bullied, not respected or not valued; but they join, and stay with, organisations where they are respected and valued. And each of these factors adversely affects financial performance, productivity, sales and output targets.

Second, those who have studied and taught organisational behaviour have somehow managed to cloak the subject in a shroud of mystique. This is actually quite unwarranted; there is no reason why anyone who wishes to become an effective and expert manager should not be able to learn, understand and apply effectively the basic principles of organisational and human behaviour.

This book introduces these principles in simple and direct terms. The main aim is to cover the basic aspects of human behaviour, and how this is affected when people come to work in organisations. The book is produced in such a way as to break down the barriers and mystique with which the subject has been surrounded in the past.

It is aimed primarily at those studying business and management for the first time, and is of especial value to those studying through professional bodies and associations, and those following Certificate in Management and Certificate in Supervisory Management programmes. It is also an essential introductory reader for those on HNC/HND and first-year undergraduate courses in business and management. It will also be of use to practitioners seeking to gain a better understanding of the human aspects of enterprise as they pursue career paths and continuous professional development programmes.

University College London   RICHARD PETTINGER

▼ ▮ Introduction

1.1 Introduction

Organisational behaviour is concerned with the study of the behaviour and interaction of people in restricted or organised settings. It involves understanding and predicting the behaviour of people, and the means by which their behaviour is influenced and shaped.

Organisations are bodies or entities created for a stated purpose. They may consist of one or more people. Sole trader or single operators need to build relationships with suppliers, contractors, customers, clients and the community. For those that consist of more than one person, internal as well as external relationships have to be created and maintained. Organisations therefore consist of individuals; groups; and relationships. Objectives, structures, systems and processes are then created to give direction and order to activities and interactions.

Organisational behaviour is thus of great concern to anyone who organises, creates, orders, directs, manages or supervises the activities of others. It is also of concern to those who build relationships between individuals, groups of people, different parts of organisations and between different organisations, for all of these activities are founded on human interaction.

Organisational behaviour is concerned with:

- the purposes for which organisations are created;
- the behaviour of individuals, and an understanding of the pressures and influences that cause them to act and react in particular ways;
- the qualities that individuals bring to particular situations;
- the creation of groups, collections of people brought together for given purposes;
- the background and context within which activities take place;
- relationships and interactions with the wider environment with other organisations and groups;
- the management and ordering of the whole and its parts into productive and effective work relationships.

1.2 The background of organisational behaviour

Organisational behaviour is not a natural or absolute science, and neither is it a distinctive field of study. It draws on a range of disciplines and is viewed from a variety of perspectives. Rather than provide an absolute or perfect body of knowledge and expertise, each of these offers a different point of view on the whole, so that as complete an understanding as possible may be built up. Consideration of organisational behaviour from each standpoint indicates both the broad context, and also some of the specific areas of concern.

Moreover, each discipline and perspective is incomplete and imperfect. Each is in itself an ever-developing and enlarging field. However, this at least indicates why a full understanding of organisational behaviour has not yet been achieved and provides the context in which studies in the field are to be seen.

■ Disciplines

The main disciplines that contribute to the study of organisational behaviour are as follows. In summary, they are concerned with the capabilities and potential of people; influences on capabilities; the attitudes and behaviour of people; influences on behaviour; the organisational context; organisational processes and the execution of work; and interaction with the environment.

1 **Psychology:** concerned with the study and understanding of human personality and behaviour, the traits and characteristics of individuals; their perceptions, attitudes, values, beliefs and motives; their goals and priorities; their capabilities and potential.

2 **Sociology:** concerned with the study of behaviour in groups; influences on this behaviour; interactions between groups; the extent to which people organise themselves, and the ways in which they do this; processes of socialisation (the ordering and limiting of individual behaviour by groups and the environment); the creation of norms, rules and regulations.

3 **Anthropology:** concerned with the study of large groups, nations and cultures; global beliefs, customs, ideas and values; the wider processes of socialisation (for example, through religious activities, caste systems, aristocracies, technocracies).

4 **Economics:** concerned with the study of the ordering, use and distribution of the world's resources; of gathering and using these to best effect in particular situations and in the pursuit of stated aims and objectives.

5 **Ethics:** concerned with the establishment of absolute standards; these relate, above all, to the nature of interpersonal relationships and interactions; which includes standards of honesty, integrity, probity, value, esteem and respect.

6 **Mathematics and statistics:** concerned with the need to prove absolutes and facts wherever possible; to give a basis of certainty to particular situations; to provide the means by which logical and demonstrable conclusions from bodies of knowledge and research can be drawn.

Each of these disciplines offers a different point of view and contributes to understanding; none, however, offers the complete picture. The major problem is the inability to arrive at absolute facts and conclusions. This is in direct contrast to the study of physics, mathematics, mechanics, chemistry and biology, each of which is capable of:

- absolute and logical reasoning;
- the combination of components and variables to produce certain and predictable results;
- consistent relationships between variables through time and space that are incapable of being reinterpreted due to differences in nationality or location;
- validation and demonstration through experimentation.

Each of the disciplines indicated earlier has none of this certainty, predictability, validity or reliability. People do not behave in consistent or rational ways. Every situation is unique and so it is impossible to recreate the conditions under which one experiment took place in order to repeat it. Rather than controlled experimentation, organisational behaviour investigations rely on observed experiments, case studies, the analysis of documentation and the use of qualitative investigations and questionnaires to provide the information on which researchers may base their conclusions.

1 Observations and observed experiments are subject to perception and interpretation; the use of the senses; and the ability to take in enough of a particular situation to form a sufficient understanding on which judgements can be made.
2 Observed experiments are limited by the ability of researchers to design hypotheses and devise means for testing these in ways that are capable of being validated.
3 The study of case histories and examples are subject to perception and judgement, except where cause and effects can be directly related (for example, where £10.00 was made because 10 items were sold at £1.00 each).
4 The analysis of documentation is subject to the knowledge, quality and judgement of those who originally produced the documents, as well as being subject to the interpretation of those currently using them.
5 Questionnaires: the use of questioning and questionnaires is limited by the capabilities of the researchers to define their purpose, ask the right questions, interpret and analyse the responses and draw conclusions from the information and material gained. Limitations are also produced by situational factors, individual priorities and perspectives. These are continuously being influenced by their environment and can quite legitimately provide a different set of answers to the same questions within moments if their circumstances suddenly change.
   (a) People's responses are influenced by the ways in which they are questioned.
   (b) The response to written questionnaires is affected by their length; the number of questions; the nature of questions asked; the ways in which these are asked; the length of time required to complete the questionnaire; the length of time at the disposal of the individual; the responses of others if these are known; the language used; the extent of interest of the individual in the material; the visual presentation of the questionnaire (or the interviewer); the amount of space or time given for each answer.
   (c) The response to oral questioning is also influenced by: the media used

(face-to-face or telephone); whether it is an individual or group situation; time constraints; attitude of questioner; personality of questioner; importance of subject matter to interviewer and interviewee; extent of mutual respect; appearance, manner, dress; speech patterns and emphases on different words.

(d) Responses are also conditioned and limited through the responders not knowing the answer to questions or only knowing a part of it; they may also tell the interviewer what they think the interviewer wants to hear, or what they think the answer should be; they may lie; they may give no answer; they may give an answer at variance with their own views or understanding because they perceive that this is expected of them; or they may just make something up.

(e) Responses are also conditioned by wider situational factors and constraints; matters of confidentiality; the use to which the information is going to be put; any opportunities or threats that are known or perceived to arise as the result of giving particular answers.

This has all then to be interpreted and analysed by others. Because there is no absolute basis or certainty, reception is subject to the expertise of the receivers and also matters of familiarity, credibility and acceptability, all of which are highly subjective.

This is the context in which the disciplines used in researching and investigating organisational behaviour are used. The picture is further complicated by the range of more general points of view from which organisations may be seen. These are as follows.

1 **Structures and edifices:** the analogy here is with buildings. Indeed, the physical premises often represent the hierarchical and value structure (for example, top managers on the top floor or away from the noise and bustle of production).

2 **Aims and objectives:** this is where relationships are drawn or inferred between the design of the organisation and the purposes for which it was designed.

3 **Stability:** this is where the future of the organisation is viewed in terms of its past history, its traditions, long-standing areas of activity, achievements and reputation. This also often includes a role, as provider of regular and constant employment in the particular locality or with certain skills and expertise.

4 **Dominance-dependency:** this concerns the general state of relationships between the organisation and its employees and also between particular groups. These relationships may be based on each or all of the following:

(a) authority: the ability of one group (for example, supervisors) to get others (for example, workers) to carry out work because of their position;

(b) function: the ability of one group to get others to work in particular ways because of their particular expertise;

(c) economic: the ability to persuade people to work because of their need to earn money and support themselves;

(d) social: the ability to persuade people to a particular point view because it is held to be right or important.

5 **Restriction:** this concerns the ability to guide, order and organise people in the pursuit of stated purposes (that is, restrict their freedom to act as they might otherwise choose to do). It refers to the extent and perspective by which rules and procedures are drawn up and applied.

6 **Creativity:** this refers to the fact of continuous development that individuals (and therefore their organisations) are forever enlarging their knowledge, skills, capabilities and experiences, and that organisations have this ever-increasing fund at their disposal if they so wish. It also includes the approaches used to address issues and solve problems, and the presence or otherwise of inventiveness and imagination.

7 **Interaction:** this concerns the totality of the relationships that exist. It includes relations between and within individual groups, departments, divisions and functions; between different positions in the hierarchies; between different types and levels of expertise. It also refers to the interactions between work and non-work, between the people and work, between the organisation and other organisations, and the organisation in its wider environment.

8 **Psychological contract:** this concerns the extent to which a psychological bond (as well as a contract of employment) is deemed or perceived to exist between organisations and employees. It has implications for wider concerns for individual welfare, loyalty, identity and commitment.

9 **Stakeholders:** this refers to everyone who has a particular interest in the well-being of the organisation. Stakeholders are: staff, potential staff, former staff (especially those dependent on the organisation for references or a pension), suppliers, customers, clients, shareholders, other backers, directors, governors, the community, influential figures.

10 **Effectiveness:** this refers to the need to maximise and optimise resources and to pursue aims and objectives successfully. This is concerned with the tangible (providing goods and services for sale at a profit and, in public service terms, meeting demands in full); and the intangible (generating levels of expectation, satisfaction and confidence among customers and clients so that they will return in the future).

11 **Managerial:** this refers to the ability to plan, organise, coordinate and control activities in the pursuit of effective performance. It refers to the ability to get things done through other people, arranging and ordering equipment, processes and materials, and designing work and organisational forms for this purpose.

12 **Means and ends:** this refers to the relationships between what is done and why, and the ways in which things are done and why. This concerns the nature and standard of the relationship between an organisation and its people, managers and staff, and levels of understanding, compliance and acceptance of purposes. It has implications for organisational policies, ethics and integrity. It also normally directly relates behaviour and performance effectiveness.

13 **Employment:** this refers to the basis of the employment relationship. The main strands of this are hiring people because there is work to be done which they can do, and giving opportunities for progress, enhancement, variety

and development (in personal, professional, occupational and economic terms). In the past, some organisations sought to offer lifetime employment, guaranteeing that there would be no lay-offs or redundancies. Others tried to create complete stability and certainty based around permanent technology, skills, output and quality. Currently, both positions are untenable.

14 **Conflict:** this refers to the adversarial or confrontational view taken of employment relations. It is based on a combination of mistrust and occupational status and personal differentials. It normally implies a proliferation of rules and regulations, administrative processes and the means of institutionalising and formalising conflict.

15 **Cooperative:** the cooperative perspective takes the view that success and effectiveness are most likely to come about where people are encouraged and directed to work with each other for the good of the organisation and, by implication, for the good of each other and themselves. This can only be achieved through the creation of a harmonious environment, equality of opportunity and treatment, clear communications and well understood aims and objectives.

16 **Case histories:** this refers to lessons learned and conclusions drawn from extensive studies of organisations and situations. These are then used as the basis for evaluating success and failure and may hold (or be perceived to hold) wider lessons for other organisations and situations.

1.3 Conclusions

Understanding the behaviour of organisations arises from combining the elements of the sciences or disciplines indicated with a number of more general and overtly subjective assertions. The total picture is incomplete, ever-changing and constantly developing. The drive is therefore towards as complete an understanding as possible rather than absolute enlightenment. This understanding is based on the application of methods of research and inquiry that are capable of contextual evaluation. This also concerns the validation and reliability of results and conclusions, especially when the divergent and conflicting nature of the different perspectives is considered. Ultimately, conclusions and predictions about human, and therefore organisational, behaviour are always subject to measures of uncertainty and interpretation

2 The organisation and its environment

2.1 Introduction

Organisations are created on the basis that more can be achieved by people working in harmony and towards a stated purpose than by individuals acting alone. It is also more efficient and effective to specialise in seeking to serve or fulfil a given set of wants or needs. Resources – technology, expertise, information, finance and property – can then be commanded and ordered for the stated purpose. Activities can be determined, coordinated and controlled.

The result of this is that society is more or less founded on a highly complex and all-pervading network of organisations, each of which serves a given purpose and all of which serve the entire range of purposes required. Organisations pervade all aspects of life: economic, social, political, cultural, religious, communal and family. They serve needs and essentials (food, shelter, health, education, water, energy and communications) as well as wants and choices (cola, cinema, football). They serve these needs and wants from before the cradle, through every aspect of life until after the grave.

An organisation is any body that is constituted for such a given purpose, and which then establishes and conducts activities in pursuit of this.

Organisations may be considered from a variety of different points of view. These are:

- legal status and formal regulation;
- primary beneficiaries (those for whom the organisation is especially important for some reason);
- approach and attitude to staff;
- psychological contract, or the nature and level of mutual commitment between organisation and staff.

■ Legal status

The main forms are as follows.

1 **Sole traders**, in which an individual sets herself up as a going concern and puts her own resources into it. People who do this are entitled to receive any profits or surpluses accrued, and are also responsible in full for any losses.

2 **Partnership**, in which two or more people establish themselves as a going concern as above.

3 **Limited company**, in which the organisation is based on the private sale of shares which provides it with a financial and capital base. The company is given its own life and entity in this way and it receives any profits made and is responsible for making good any losses. The liability of shareholders for any losses is limited to the extent of their share ownership.

4 **PLC or corporation**: the same as for a limited company but where shares are offered for sale to the general public on a recognised stock exchange.

5 **Friendly or mutual society**, in which the benefits accrued by activities are distributed among members as agreed between them.

6 **Cooperative**, usually constituted as a company or partnership in which everyone involved has a stake (financial, physical or psychological).

7 **Public bodies and public corporations**, central, regional and local government functions to provide essential public services and ensure adequate infrastructure, transport and communications for the society at large.

8 **Quangos** (quasi-autonomous non-governmental organisations) are autonomous entities funded by government grant and constituted for a particular purpose.

9 **Charities**, funded by donations and other receipts for stated purposes; these funds are then distributed to the areas with which the charity is concerned. Charities must be registered with the charity commissioner in order to carry out activities in this way.

■ Primary beneficiaries

Primary beneficiaries are those people for whom the organisation is especially important or for whom it was constituted. A primary beneficiary approach requires organisations to be looked at as follows.

1 **Business organisations**, where the primary beneficiaries are shareholders and staff, and where the benefits accrue from providing products and services required by customers and clients.

2 **Utilities**, where the primary beneficiary is society at large. Utilities include gas, electricity, water, transport, post and telecommunications organisations.

3 **Public service organisations**, where the primary beneficiaries are particular client groups drawn in because of their characteristics and which include provision for the homeless destitute, elderly, disabled and handicapped (some of these functions are also carried out by charities).

4 **Cooperatives**, where the primary beneficiaries are all those who work in them and which coordinate their business from the point of view of this mutual commitment and identity.

5 **Convenience organisations**, where the primary beneficiaries are those that avail themselves of the organisation's products and services on the basis of convenience. This includes village shops and amenities (a form of this is also

to be found in those organisations that take a 'just in time' approach to the purchase of raw materials).

6 **Institutions**, where the primary beneficiaries are those who avail themselves of the institutions services and facilities, or who are sent there (for whatever reason) by society. Examples include schools, colleges and prisons.

7 **Mutual benefit associations**, where the primary beneficiaries are the members; these include trade unions, churches, political parties, clubs, friendly societies and cooperatives.

8 **Service organisations**, where the primary beneficiaries are the clients who come to use its services for stated reasons, or when they need them on particular occasions. Examples include hospitals and the fire service.

9 **Bodies for the regulation of society**, constituted by government and given the means and wherewithal to act in the interests of the members of the society. The main examples of these are the police and the military.

10 **Common general organisations**, where the primary beneficiaries are the general public. These include police services and also education, health and social services.

■ Approach to staff

Organisations may also be viewed from the standpoint from which they regard their staff: some examples are given below.

1 **Unitary**, in which the aims, objectives, hopes, fears, aspirations and ambitions of the individual must be harmonised and integrated with those of the organisation, and where necessary subordinated so that the overall purpose of the organisation remains the main driving force.

2 **Pluralist**, in which the organisation recognises the divergence and often conflicting aims, objectives and drives of the people who work for it. Organisations that take this view normally include opportunities for personal and professional (as well as organisational) fulfilment. The basis is that by recognising this divergence and attending to all needs, organisation needs will be satisfied.

3 **Cooperative**, in which the organisation establishes a psychological and behavioural basis of partnership and involvement based on the value of the contribution that everyone is to make.

4 **Confrontational** – an adversarial approach to staff. This is based, at best, on the recognition that harmony of objectives is impossible leading to the creation of systems and processes for the containment and management of conflict. At worst it is based on mistrust and coercion, often stemming from a lack of genuine respect for staff.

■ Psychological contract

Organisations may be viewed from the nature of the psychological contract that they engage in with their staff. This is the result of implications and expectations that arise from particular organisational, occupational, professional and personal relationships in specific situations. They vary between all organisations and situations and may be summarised as follows.

1 **Coercive**, whereby the relationship between organisation and staff, and also organisation and customer, is founded on a negative. An example of this is prison, because the prisoners are there against their will. It is also present where sections of the community are forced or pressurised into using a monopoly or near-monopoly for an essential commodity or service; examples include electricity, telecommunication, petrol and fuel. It also can be present in institutions such as schools and colleges where the children or students attend because they are required to do so by society.

2 **Alienative**, whereby the relationship between staff and organisation is negative. This has traditionally applied to large and sophisticated organisations and especially to those staff working on production lines and in administrative hierarchies where they have no or very little control over the quality and output of work.

3 **Remunerative**, whereby the relationship between staff and organisation is clearly drawn in terms of money in return for efforts and attendance. It is normally to be found as the dominant feature where there is also a low level of mutual identity between staff and organisation.

4 **Calculative**, whereby the staff have a low commitment to organisation goals and high commitment to current levels of earning and satisfaction. It is again a key feature of the wage-work bargain for production and administrative staff. For those with high levels of professional and technical expertise, the calculative relationship is based on the ability to practise, the need to find an employer and outlet for those skills and individual drives to serve and become expert.

5 **Normative**, whereby the individual commitment to organisational purpose is very high. This is found in religious organisations, political parties and trade unions. It is also increasingly found in some business organisations when a normative (that is, committed quarrel) approach is taken to the wage-work bargain as well as an economic. It is effective as long as the wage work bargain itself is sound and the organisation accepts a range of obligations and responsibilities to ensure that it is maintained.

Viewing organisations from a variety of positions in these ways indicates the background against which aims and objectives are to be drawn up. It also indicates the source of some of the limitations and constraints that have to be taken into account when considering the capabilities of organisations and the nature and relationship of these with the purposes that are to be pursued.

2.2 Organisational goals, aims and objectives

However constituted and from whatever point of view they are considered, all organisations have purposes: goals, aims and objectives, their reason for being.

These provide the essential foundation on which the organisation is to be built. Some essential features of aims and objectives should therefore be defined.

■ Clarity

Aims and objectives should be specific and capable of being understood and accepted by all those who are to be engaged in their pursuit.

■ Measurable

Aims and objectives provide the measures against which success and failure are to be evaluated. The clearer the means of measurement, the more accurate the assessment; and the easier it is to establish why something has been successful or why it failed (as well as the fact of the matter).

■ Capability

Organisations combine resources – human, technology, financial and other equipment – to pursue their goals. The purpose is to maximise and optimise usage of those resources. Inadequacy of resources leads to loss of capability. Surfeit of resources leads to waste and profligacy. This may also lead to incapability caused by a loss of drive or urgency: if too many resources seem to be available, those concerned may feel no need to maximise/optimise performance.

■ Time scales

These act as a general discipline on the organisation as specific performance indicators on groups and individuals.

■ Efficiency and effectiveness

P. F. Drucker defined these as:

- efficiency is doing things right;
- effectiveness is doing the right thing.

Efficiency is therefore concerned with performance during the task and attention to best use of resources. Effectiveness is concerned with the end result; it may also be concerned with resources, especially where these constitute the building blocks of the eventual outcome.

■ Organisational performance

Organisational performance may be classified under the following headings.

1 **Steady-state:** the conduct of day-to-day activities, routines and tasks; the creation of structures, systems, rules and procedures to ensure that these continue; the creation of stability and confidence.

2 **Innovative:** the drive to continuously improve all aspects of the organisation and its work; the drive to seek improvements in efficiency and effectiveness; the drive to seek new products, opportunities and markets; the drive to seek new and better means of staff management, organisation and development.

3 **Pioneering:** the drive for radically new activities and markets; the drive for radical new technology, its uses and applications; the drive for radically new means and methods of organisation, staffing and management.

4 **Crisis:** the handling of emergencies, problems and dramas when they occur; the structuring of activities and resources to ensure that there is a balance between being able to meet crises when they do happen or taking steps to ensure that these occur as infrequently as possible; the avoidance of crisis management (lurching from one emergency to another); the recognition and addressing of the likely and actual components of crises in the given situation.

5 **Strategic and directional:** concerned with the organisation, its purposes, goals and overall aims and objectives; the monitoring, review and evaluation of these and of the activities organised and structured in their pursuit; attention to the success and effectiveness – and profitability – of performance; taking remedial action where required. Strategic and directional performance also includes attention to the nature and mix of steady-state, innovative, pioneering and crisis aspects indicated above.

This can then be related to the different headings under which objectives are classified. In general, these are a combination of:

- *strategic:* concerned with overall direction of the organisation and the focus for all other activities;
- *operational:* concerned with the effectiveness of day-to-day activities in pursuit of the strategic;
- *behavioural:* concerned with the human aspects of the organisation, management and supervisory style and the aura of general well-being;
- *ethical:* concerned with particular standards of operation and interaction, the ways in which staff, customers, the community and the environment are treated and the general level of respect which they are accorded;
- *attitudes and values:* the psychological focus of the organisation and requirements and expectations placed on staff and customers;
- *superior and subordinate or supporting aims and objectives:* the inter-relationship, harmony and unit of purpose and drive between overall aims and the goals set for departments, divisions, functions and individuals.

■ Other boundaries

Other boundaries around overall purposes, aims and objectives are as follows.

1 Policies, representing the ways in which the organisation seeks and determines to operate, and the standards (especially of honesty and integrity) that it sets for itself. These normally refer to:

(a) attention to staff and staff relations;
(b) attention to customers and customer relations;

(c) attention to community and community relations;

(d) attention to the environment and waste disposal;

(e) standards of image, marketing and public relations;

(f) the promotion of equity and equality;

(g) the extent of commitment to product and service quality, and customer satisfaction

2 Specific operational constraints, the interaction with suppliers, distributors and customers; any legal constraints; the effects of internal and external pressure groups and vested interests.

3 The preferences and drives of shareholders and other stakeholders, especially in terms of the nature of the results required and the deadlines for these.

4 The nature of expertise required. Where persons of high professional or technical qualifications are employed, there is often a potential conflict between their commitment to the organisation and to their profession or occupation.

5 Ethical and social constraints. These are based on the norms, values and standards of the wider society and communities in which activities are to be conducted; and concern the extent to which the organisation itself is, or seeks to be, a good citizen.

6 The need for discipline, guidance and motivation on the part of staff and the creation of support functions, procedures and processes of supervision and management for these reasons.

7 Competitive pressures: the need to compete for business, work and customers; and the need to compete for staff and resources. Competition for staff and resources may have both external and internal constraints.

8 Cooperative pressure: the extent of dependency on other bodies and organisations (that is, suppliers, distributors; also banks and other sources of finance; any other particular expertise required); the extent to which other bodies are allowed to influence the direction and purpose of the particular organisation.

9 Relationships between means and ends, and the priority that is placed on each; the extent to which people and groups are rewarded for hard work (means) as distinct from effective or productive work (ends); the views taken by the organisation of success and failure.

These constitute the main constraints within which organisations have to set their aims and objectives if they are to be effective. It is impossible to work in isolation from these except in the very short term and where a monopoly on the particular product or service is held.

2.3 Limitations

Limitations on effectiveness are as follows.

1 The drive for volume of work rather than quality or effectiveness. This is exacerbated where rewards are given for volume rather than quality. This is

satisfactory only as long as competitive position can be maintained on the basis of volume and as long as some level of profit is achieved. It is invariably unsatisfactory in the long term unless accompanied by drives for quality and effectiveness.

2 Lack of attention to supposedly non-quantifiable aims and objectives, especially for managers, administrators and support functions.

3 Attention becomes focused on length rather than effectiveness of attendance, and volume rather than quality or purpose of work.

4 Operational and political influence of interest groups increases at the expense of their productive output.

5 Concentration on compliance and conformity rather than effectiveness.

6 Compliance is not achieved, either because the required attitudes and standards are not recognised or valued, or because those working in the organisation place no value on the overall purpose.

2.4 Decision-making

Decisions are taken at all levels: strategic and policy; operational, divisional and departmental; managerial and supervisory; and individual. Whatever the level, there are certain fundamental considerations to be considered if the process is to be effective and successful. There are also different stages that have to be understood and followed (see Figure 2.1).

■ Problem or issue definition

This is the starting point of the process. Once this is defined, the likely effects and consequences of particular courses of action can begin to be understood. Failure to do this may lead to considerable waste of time, effort and resource.

■ Process determination

Much of this depends on culture, structure, environmental and other pressures on the organisation or department involved. It also depends on ways of working and the personalities and groups involved. There may also be key groups – staff, customers, vested interests, pressure groups – who must be consulted on particular matters. Failure to consult, in spite of the fact that the decision may be 'right', is likely to minimise or even nullify the whole effect.

■ Time scale

Time is involved heavily in process determination. There is also a trade off between the quality and volume of information that can be gathered and the time available to do this. The longer the time scale, the better the chance of gaining adequate information and considering it and evaluating it effectively. However, this also increases the cost of the eventual course of action. On the other hand,

1. PROGRESSION

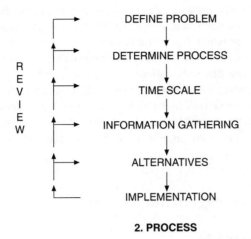

2. PROCESS

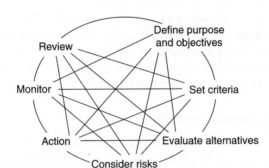

Figure 2.1 Decision-making: model and process

a quick decision may involve hidden extras at the implementation stage if insufficient time has been spent on the background.

■ Information gathering

Very few decisions are taken with perfect information; conversely, decisions made without any information are pure guesswork. Both quality and volume of information are required; and means for the understanding, evaluation and review of that which is gathered are also essential.

■ The alternatives

The result of the process is that alternative courses of action become apparent. At the very least there is always the choice of doing nothing.

■ Implementation

This is the point of action. It arises as the result of working through each of the previous elements. The choice made affects future courses of action; as well as the choice, the reasons for which it was made should be understood.

This is an attempt to provide a rationale for courses of action that often have to be taken in ways that are not fully logical. Part of the purpose is therefore to recognise where the non-rational elements lie and, in recognising these, how they can best be accommodated. It is not a prescription for providing perfect decisions. It is, instead, the means by which opportunities and consequences of following particular courses of action may be understood, assessed and evaluated.

2.5 Decision-making: other factors

■ Risk and uncertainty

Uncertainty occurs where no information exists. This in itself underlines the need to gain as much knowledge and understanding as possible, in advance of choosing a particular course of action. However, there is an element of risk in all decision-taking. This is reduced by the quality and volume of information available, and the accuracy of its evaluation.

■ Participation and consultation

This is necessary where a wide measure of support from among the workforce community or public at large is required. The purpose here is to generate understanding and acceptance of courses of action.

It may also be necessary to consider:

- legal constraints, affecting all aspects of business and organisation practice;
- public interest, public pressure, lobby and special interest groups;
- economic, social and political groups, including consumer groups, environmental lobbies, local and public authorities, public agencies and statutory bodies, industrial lobbies and staff representative bodies;
- committees and other formally constituted boards.

■ Organisational adjustment

This is where the process is limited or constrained, based on each of the factors indicated. The normal result is that the organisation alters, adjusts or limits its activities in some way as the result.

Sufficient time and resources must be set aside to deal with these, if what is proposed is to be supported and accepted.

Effective decisions are therefore arrived at through a combination of the preferred and chosen direction, together with recognising and accommodating a means by which this chosen direction can be made successful. A large part of the consultation, participation, staff and public communication processes are directed at generating understanding and acceptance of particular courses of action. Organisations must accept that everyone is much more likely to follow a course of action if this is understood. If they do not understand what they are being asked to do, people tend either to reject the matter outright, or else view it with suspicion and uncertainty.

2.6 Failure

As stated above, a key ingredient of performance failure is insufficient attention to establishing a clarity and understanding of purpose at the outset. Other features are now identified.

1 Insufficient attention to the behavioural aspects of operations, above all in creating effective and suitable conditions and support systems as the basis for carrying out the work. This also includes insufficient attention to the need to motivate and value the staff engaged in the work.
2 Insufficient attention to the quantifiable performance requirements of management and to the establishment of proper aims and objectives in managerial, administrative and support functions.
3 Prioritising short-term results at the expense of the long-term future together with the over-consumption of resources in this way. This normally occurs because the organisation can see easy results if it pursues the short term. It also occurs because of the need for triumphs on the part of a key figure or particular department.
4 Artificial constraints and deadlines, driven by budget systems and reporting relationships, require energy and resources to be used in non-productive and often counter-productive activities, rather than as a check on continuous performance.
5 Establishment of priorities for reasons other than performance effectiveness and especially for reasons of publicity, kudos, status, and the demands of key figures for their own purposes.
6 Setting unreasonable deadlines for the achievement of particular objectives.
7 Casting plans, aims and objectives as 'tablets of stone': once they are written they are never to be changed or modified.
8 Failure to recognise that which cannot be controlled and which may nevertheless have great effects on organisational activities. This includes changes in customer demands and expectations; legislative changes; the activities of competitors; loss of sources of supply; change in relationships with distributors; and so on.
9 Complacency, often based on a long history of success, continuity and achievement in the past, which tends to lead to feelings of infallibility and immortality. This leads to loss of commitment to purpose, loss of focus and what constitutes truly effective performance.
10 Attention to means rather than ends and the confusion of hard work with productive work. Sheer volume of work therefore becomes the measure of

performance rather than the purpose for which it is being conducted. Or, to quote a former Chief Executive (CE) of the Cadillac Car Company: 'Any fool can learn to stay within budget. But I have met only a handful of managers in my life who could draw up a budget that is worth staying within.'

2.7 Systems

A system is a collection of inter-related parts and components that form a whole. Typical organisation systems are production, communication and electronic data systems. Systems may first be defined as either closed or open.

■ Closed

This refers to systems that are self-contained and self-sufficient, and which do not require other interactions to make them work. There are very few systems that are genuinely closed. Some domestic central heating systems are more or less closed. In these cases the components are assembled, the system is switched on and must then operate continuously or else break down. Even this depends upon the system being fed a constant supply of energy to ensure continuity of operation. They are also dependent upon maintenance, to prevent breakdowns and to carry out repairs when faults occur.

■ Open

Open systems are those that require constant interaction with their environment to make them work (see Figure 2.2).

■ Formal

Formal systems may be devised and developed by the organisation with specific purposes in mind and with the view that effective operations are dependent upon those which are put in place.

■ Informal

Such systems are devised by individuals and groups to facilitate their own place and well-being in the organisation and to fill those gaps left by the formal approach.

■ Networks

The combination of the formal with the informal, networks are normally based on human interaction and information exchange (and sometimes information hoarding and trading). Their purpose is to support both the operations of the organisation and also to ensure the continuity and stability of the position of individuals and groups.

Inputs (External)	Process The System	Outputs
Expertise Supplies Components Resources Energy Demands	Technology Expertise Energy	Products Services Waste Exhaust

The characteristics are:

(a) the need to provide inputs and energy to make sure that the process – the system – is able to operate (inputs and energy come from elsewhere in the environment);
(b) the discharge of outputs – production waste and energy residue and exhaust – into the environment;
(c) the operation of the system itself as the conversion process.

Figure 2.2 An open system

Input	Process	Output
Raw materials Energy Expertise Components Information Demand Ideas Inventions	Technology Applied expertise Applied information Coordination Planning Control Supervision	Finished goods Services Waste Exhaust

Figure 2.3 Organisation systems

Organisation systems may now be shown as follows (Figure 2.3). They convert human activity, energy, information resources, components of raw materials into products and services, usable information, by-products and waste.

2.8 Main systems

Main systems are those devised to ensure that the organisation can pursue its core purposes successfully. They are normally the production service and information systems essential to well-being and success. They may be largely:

- human or social, where achievement of the core purpose depends greatly on interactions between people;

- technological, where achievement of the core purpose depends greatly on the output of large volumes of items;
- socio-technical, in which the interaction between the two is critical (see Figure 2.4).

■ Maintenance systems

These are devised in order to prevent any blockages occurring and to put them right where they do happen. Maintenance systems require attention to both social and technical aspects. A part of organisation and individual development is concerned with maintaining the human resource. This includes attention to morale and commitment, as well as skills, knowledge and expertise.

■ Crisis systems

These are devised and put in place on the basis that they are seldom to be used but, nevertheless, when they are required they can be speedily energised. Emergency systems are clear examples of this. So also are systems for the handling of operational input and distribution breakdowns and hiatuses, and in these cases they will normally consist of hot-line arrangements for emergency supplies, activities and distribution.

■ Managerial systems

At their best these start with the performance of others. They are created to provide a process for evaluation of performance, organisation adaptation, coordination of activities and taking decisions.

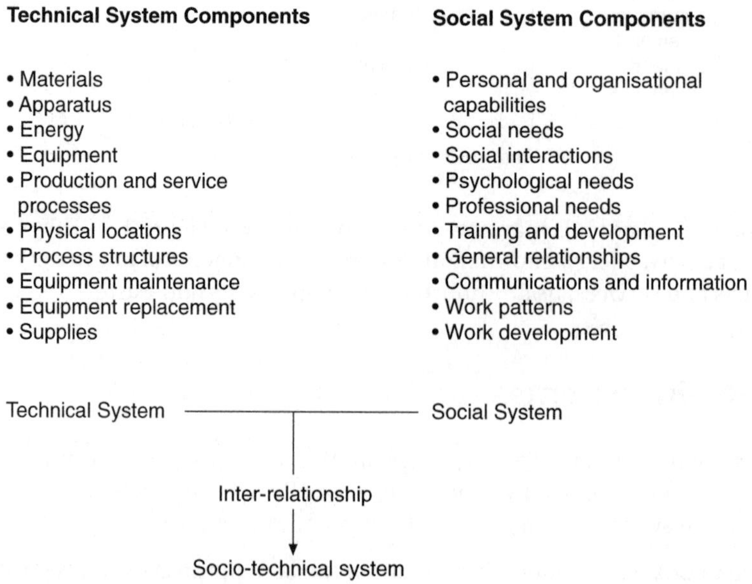

Technical System Components	Social System Components
• Materials	• Personal and organisational
• Apparatus	capabilities
• Energy	• Social needs
• Equipment	• Social interactions
• Production and service	• Psychological needs
processes	• Professional needs
• Physical locations	• Training and development
• Process structures	• General relationships
• Equipment maintenance	• Communications and information
• Equipment replacement	• Work patterns
• Supplies	• Work development

Technical System ———————┬——————— Social System

Inter-relationship

↓

Socio-technical system

Figure 2.4 Socio-technical systems

1 Evaluation of performance: the actual performance of the system will be evaluated through constant monitoring and review, and the results achieved analysed to show why success has been achieved and where and why any failures have occurred. This will also indicate general areas for attention, capabilities for improvements and progress; it will also include establishing the reasons for success so that these may be built on for the future in other areas.

2 Adaptation and change: this is concerned with the future of the organisation, the development of structures, attitudes, values, skills, knowledge and expertise for the purpose of achieving aims and objectives and planning for longer-term strategies and directions.

3 Coordination and control: this is the harmonisation process, the ordering of the disparate and divergent elements, conflict resolution, balancing and ordering of priorities and resources.

4 Decision-making: this is attention to the processes by which effective decisions are made and the elements that contribute to this.

For effective performance in each of the processes to take place, a systematic approach is required. This should ensure that sufficient attention is paid, and an examination of each area takes place on the basis of depth and breadth of knowledge, so that in turn a full basis of judgement, analysis and assessment is achieved and ensured.

2.9 Organisations in their environment

As no organisation exists in isolation from its environment, the nature and extent of the relationship and interactions must be considered (see Figure 2.5). Organisations are subject to a variety of economic, legal, social and ethical pressures that they must be capable of accommodating if they are to operate effectively. In some cases there are strong religious and cultural effects, and local traditions which must also be capable of effective harmonisation. More specifically, organisations need access to workforces, suppliers, distributors, customers and clients; and to technology, equipment and financial resources.

Relationships between organisations and their environment may be simply summarised as:

- environment domination, especially overwhelming legal, social and ethical pressures and also those that relate to any strong local histories and traditions;
- organisation domination, where the environment is dependent on the organisation for the provision of work, good and services.

This has then to be seen in the context that the best organisation–environment relationships are generated where measures of general responsibility are attached to each. If the environmental pressures are too great, or somehow otherwise unacceptable to the organisation, it will eventually relocate elsewhere. If the organisation takes an expedient or cavalier view of its involvement in a particular area, it will be rejected by those who live there. The picture is further

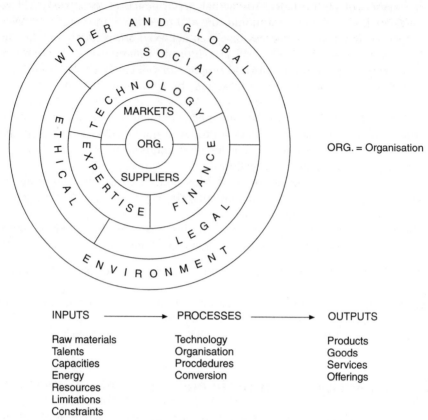

INPUTS ⟶ PROCESSES ⟶ OUTPUTS

INPUTS	PROCESSES	OUTPUTS
Raw materials	Technology	Products
Talents	Organisation	Goods
Capacities	Procdedures	Services
Energy	Conversion	Offerings
Resources		
Limitations		
Constraints		

Figure 2.5   Archetype model of the organisation and its environment
Source: Katz and Kahn (1978).

complicated by the fact that all organisations interact with other organisations that are also part of their own environment; they influence these, and are influenced by them in turn.

2.10 Contingency approaches

Contingency approaches indicate the context in which effective organisations are devised and designed. Burns and Stalker (1961) defined the contingency approach as 'the most appropriate system for a given set of circumstances'. While this may appear a statement of the obvious, it does at least indicate the important relationship between appropriateness and circumstances; effective (appropriate) organisations cannot be designed in isolation from their situation.

It is necessary to recognise the related concepts of divergence and integration. Divergence and integration can be seen at three levels: between organisation and its environment; between different organisations; and within organisations (see Figure 2.6). Some parts of the relationship between organisations and environment are based on the reconciliation of conflicting demands. Other parts are based on a stated or implied mutuality of interest. The problem is therefore to recognise where the mutuality lies and the extent of this as the basis by which the points of conflict can then be addressed. Some factors may be distinguished.

The more dynamic and diverse the environment, the greater the degree of differentiation and specialisation required within organisations to cope with its demands. High degrees of integration are also required (a) to build up effective working relationships with each part of the environment, and (b) to harmonise differing and often divergent efforts within the organisation itself.

Less dynamic and more stable environments require high degrees of interaction to ensure that the stability is preserved. A major cause of conflict is lack of communications and understanding, caused in turn by lack of attention to continuing relationships.

The more dynamic and diverse the environment, the greater the likelihood of misunderstandings and conflict occurring. In these situations, a proportion of organisation resources is therefore likely to be required to ensure that these can be tackled effectively when they do arise.

2.11 Conclusions

Some conclusions and inferences may be drawn.

1 There is clearly no best way to organise; as the environment changes, so systems, aims and objectives must be flexible and responsive.
2 The environment changes in both predictable and unpredictable ways; and it changes in ways that can be controlled and influenced and in ways that cannot be controlled and influenced. The problem for managers lies in the

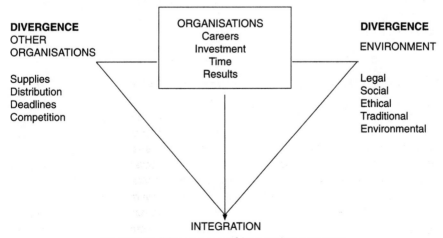

Figure 2.6 Divergence and integration pressures

extent of their understanding of their environment and in their ability to anticipate the unexpected by building systems that are capable of accommodating these pressures.

3 Because of the nature of the relationship with the environment, organisations require to spend time on external issues, assessing and understanding the environment, and the changes and turbulence within it.

4 Each input-process-output cycle changes the nature of the organisation's social and technical resources, presenting an opportunity to strive for optimisation and improvement.

5 Above all, the environment is dynamic and not static or rigid, allowing for limitless opportunities for change to occur; investment in environmental adaptation and transformation are as essential to success as investments in capital, equipment and staffing. The more complex and turbulent the environment, the more essential this form of investment becomes.

6 Environmental, technological and social changes are the primary causes and inspiration for organisational improvement.

7 Legal and ethical constraints constitute the main limitations placed on the activities of organisations. These require that specific approaches are adopted to all aspects of activities in order to meet standards prescribed by law or laid down by the prevailing values and morals of society.

The purpose of this chapter has been to summarise and indicate the various forms of organisation, the different points of view from which they may be considered and the wider context in which they operate. No organisation operates in isolation from, or without reference to, its environment. The environment provides staff, customers, resources, technology and equipment, and also confidence and expectations: in short, the context in which successful and effective activities take place.

⊠ **3** Perception

3.1 Introduction

Perception is the process by which all people limit their views of the world. Perception is essential because of the amount of information, signals and cues with which the senses are constantly assailed. The total is not capable of assimilation because it is constantly changing and developing and because of the constant nature of human activity. A process of some sort is therefore clearly necessary by which this is first limited and then transformed into something that is useful and usable.

The process by which individual perception is developed is both learned and instinctive. Some of it comes from the senses: sight, hearing, touch, taste and smell. Some of it also plainly comes from instinct, since one's view of what is edible is clearly coloured by how hungry one is.

That which is learned comes from a combination of civilisation and socialisation. This gives rise, above all, to moral and ethical codes by which behaviour is regulated. It also gives rise to the formation of norms, expectations, customs and etiquette. It forms the basis for concepts of fashion and desirability and the need for achievement (see Figures 3.1 and 3.2).

■ Perceptual errors

The sources of error in person and situational perception include:

- not collecting enough information;
- assuming that enough information has been collected;
- not collecting the right information; collecting the wrong information;
- assuming that the right information has been collected;
- seeing what we want and expect to see; fitting reality to our view of the world (rather than the reverse);
- looking for in others what we value for and in ourselves;
- assuming that the past was always good when making judgements for the future;
- failure to acknowledge and recognise other points of view;
- failure to consider situations and people from the widest possible point of view;
- unrealistic expectations, levels of comfort and satisfaction;
- confusing the unusual and unexpected with the impossible.

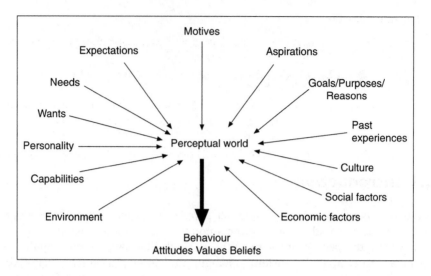

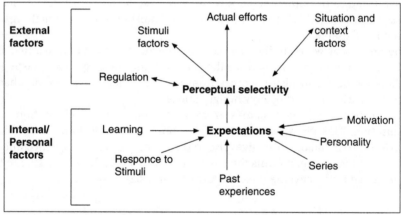

Figure 3.1 Relationships between perception, behaviour, attitudes and values
Source: from Huczynski and Buchanan (1993).

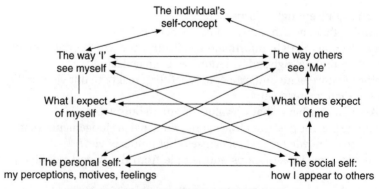

Figure 3.2 The basis of interpersonal perception
Source: Rogers (1947).

The remedies are:

- understand the limitations of personal knowledge and perception, realising that this is imperfect and that there are gaps;
- decide in advance what knowledge is required of people and situations and set out to collect it from this standpoint;
- structure activities where the gathering of information is important (for example, this should apply to all interviews, research activities, questioning, work organisation, use of technology);
- avoid instant judgements about people, however strong and positive, or weak and negative the first impression may be;
- avoid instant judgements about organisations, whether as customer or employee;
- build expectations on knowledge and understanding rather than halo effects, stereotypes and self-fulfilling prophecies;
- ensure exchanges and availability of good quality information;
- ensure open relationships that encourage discussion and debate and generate high levels of understanding and knowledge exchange;
- develop self-awareness and understanding among all staff;
- recognise and understand the nature of prevailing attitudes, values and beliefs, as well as prejudices;
- recognise and understand other strong prevailing influences, especially language, nationality, culture and experience.

■ Comfort and liking

Comfort and liking occur when elements and features accord and harmonise with each other. Instant rapport is achieved when initial perceptions – strong characteristics, halo effects – coincide, meet expectations and lead to an initially productive relationship. This is developed as people become more familiar and knowledgeable about each other and about situations and circumstances. Discomfort and dislike occur when the elements are in discord. This is usually found in strong and contradictory initial and continuing impressions.

Some illustrations of perception can be seen in Figure 3.3.

■ Inference

People infer or make assumptions about others and about things, situations and circumstances based on the information available and their interpretation and analysis of it. Simple forms of this are found in stereotyping and the halo effect.

3.2 Halo effect

This is the process by which a person is ascribed a great range of capabilities and expertise as the result of one initial impression of an overwhelming

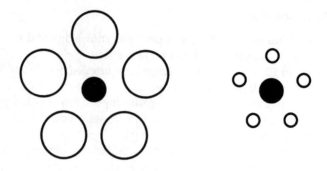

(a) Which black spot is larger?

(b) Old lady or young girl?

Figure 3.3 Perception: illustrations
Source: C. Escher/Cordon Art © 1995.

characteristic. As stated above, the person who has a firm handshake is deemed to be decisive. A person with a public school education is deemed to be officer material. The person who can play golf is deemed to be an expert in business.

The converse of this is the horns effect (the halo apparently comes from heaven; the horns clearly originate elsewhere). This is where a negative connotation is put on someone or something as the result of one (supposedly) negative characteristic. Thus the person with the soft handshake and lisp is perceived to be soft and indecisive. Anyone who wears fashions from a past era is deemed to be eccentric or old fashioned.

Excellent examples of this clearly abound. Kim Philby was able to act as a Soviet spy for 20 years with ease because nobody in the British establishment believed that anyone with his impeccable credentials could possibly be anything other

(c) Water flowing up and down?
Source: C. Escher/Cordon Art © 1995

Figure 3.3   Continued

than a pillar of the aforesaid establishment. Richard Branson is perceived to by dynamic and iconoclastic partly because of the clothes that he wears and the style with which he presents his company in the media. Apples sold at Marks & Spencer must be good because they are shiny and bruise free.

It is also worth drawing attention to the dedication to the book *Recruitment and Selection* by Clive T. Goodworth. This book is dedicated as follows: 'To all those who can spot a good chap as soon as they walk into the room. And to all those who suffer as the result.'

3.3 Stereotyping, pigeonholing and compartmentalisation

It is a short step from the halo effect to developing a process of stereotyping, pigeonholing and compartmentalisation. This occurs at places of work whereby because of a past range of activities somebody is deemed to be that kind of a person for the future. This may both enhance and limit careers, activities and organisational progress dependent upon the nature of the compartmentalisation. In any case it gives specific and limited direction. The person who has worked overseas for a multinational corporation for a long time may have difficulty getting a job back at Head Office because he has been pigeonholed as 'an expatriate' and may be perceived to have difficulties should he be required to conform to the Head Office norms and practices.

3.4 Self-fulfilling prophecy

Self-fulfilling prophecy occurs when a judgement is made about someone or something. The person making that judgement then picks out further characteristics or attributes that support her view and edits out those do not fit in. The following are examples of self-fulfilling prophecy.

1 If you want people to be trustworthy, trust them. If you want people to accept responsibility, give them responsibility (Semler, 1992).
2 People will behave as they expect those in charge would behave in the same situation. *The Herald of Free Enterprise* sank because the staff perceived that it was important to set sail in spite of the fact that the bow doors were not closed. When the ship turned over the hunt was for scapegoats, not mistakes (*Brass Tacks*, BBC2: 1989).
3 Universities have adopted systems of numbered exam papers. This is so that those who mark the papers see what is actually written rather than what they expect to see written by particular students to whom they can put a name and therefore a set of perceptions.

3.5 Perceptual mythology

This occurs where myths are created by people as part of their own processes of limiting and understanding particular situations. A form of rationale emerges, usually spurious.

Thus, for example, people will say such things as 'I can tell as soon as someone walks in the door whether they can do this job' or 'I always ask this question and it never fails' or 'I never trust people in white shoes/white socks/with moustaches/with tinted glasses', in order to give themselves some chance of understanding and therefore mapping the person who stands before them.

People also use phrases such as 'in my opinion' and 'in my experience' for the same general reasons, and to support uninformed views of the world's stereotypes.

■ Personal mapping and constructs

In this process people, situations, activities, images and impressions are being fitted into the perceived map of the world in ways which can be understood, managed and accommodated. The information thus gathered is broken down into constructs or characteristics that may be categorised as follows.

1 **Physical:** by which we assume or infer the qualities of the person from their appearance, racial group, beauty, style, dress and other visual images.
2 **Behavioural:** whereby we place people according to the way they act and behave or the ways in which we think they will act and behave.
3 **Role:** whereby we make assumptions about people because of the variety of roles they assume; the different situations in which they assume these roles; their dominant role or roles; and the trappings that go with them.
4 **Psychological:** whereby certain occupations, appearances, manifestations, presentation and images are assumed to be of a higher order of things than others (part of this is also sociological). This reflects the morality, values and ethics of the society of the day as well as the environment and organisation in question.

This part of the perception process aims to build up a picture of the world with which the individual can be comfortable. Comfort is achieved when people and situations are perceived to have complementary characteristics or constructs. Discomfort occurs when characteristics and constructs are contradictory: for example, there is no difficulty placing an individual who is kind and gentle in the perceptual map, but there is difficulty in being comfortable with an individual who is both kind and violent.

■ Closure

Closure occurs where an individual sees part of a picture and then completes the rest of it in his mind; or hears part of a statement or conversation and then mentally finishes it off.

■ Proximity

Proximity is based on the desire to understand and be comfortable with that which is close at hand – to be at ease in the immediate environment. Matters that cause discomfort therefore assume importance, often out of proportion to their actual effect.

Proximity also concerns the tendency to group people or items that are physically close into groups. Those who work in the same office, for example, are viewed as a group, and if one or two continually raise grievances, the whole may come to be seen as a collection of trouble makers.

■ Intensity

Perception is affected by extremes of heat, cold, light, darkness, noise, silence, colour, taste, touch and smell. People who wish to stand out from the crowd wear bright or other eye-catching colours. People who move from the city to the country notice the contrast between the noise and bustle of the one and the peace and quiet of the other.

■ Attribution

Attribution is the explanation put by individuals on behaviour or activities. Attribution may be:

- rational – 'you burnt your hand because the plate was hot';
- pseudo-rational – 'he is a bully at work because he has a difficult home life';
- empathised – 'in her place I would have done the same thing';
- mythological – 'this was how we always used to do it and it worked then'.

Whether rational or not, attribution gives people a point of reference for their actions and for those of others. It also helps in the attaining of comfort and satisfaction, enabling people to explain – to themselves at least – why they continue to work in particular occupations, ways, situations, or with particular people.

3.6 Other influences on perception

The following more general influences may also be distinguished.

■ Repetition

The repetition of a message or an event gives currency, familiarity and validity. This may subsequently become a barrier to change.

■ Familiarity

This is the outcome of repetition and also of continued exposure and involvement in given situations. The most positive form is comfort; the negative is complacency. It is a general bonus, however, in the generation of organisational format (such as for memos, reports and letters). It has great importance in the development of a house style for general communication purposes.

■ Authority, responsibility and position

These relate to the person giving the message. This influences the propensity of the receiver to accept or reject it. The person who understands well the strength or weakness of her own position in this regard is always likely to be a more effective communicator than one who does not.

■ Emotions

Feelings of anger, antagonism, mistrust and disregard emphasise the tendency to reject. At the very least, therefore, any such feelings present or potentially present in a given situation are to be recognised at the outset and neutralised where possible.

The greatest of all emotional barriers in organisations is pride. Nobody likes to lose face or to have it made plain that they were wrong. Neither do others wish to be associated with someone who is forced to be seen as defeated, to back down, or to climb down from a given position.

■ Visibility

Much is made of visibility as an instrument of the generation of effective organisational behaviour throughout this book. Visibility is the cornerstone of so much. It is a prerequisite to effective communication. It greatly helps in the generation of confidence, familiarity and interaction. It underlines levels of honesty, trustworthiness and straightforwardness. It helps develop both professional and personal relationships between those involved. There are therefore both general and specific benefits to be gained from an effective face to face relationship.

The converse is also true. Lack of visibility is both a perceptual barrier in itself and also compounds others that are present, such as general feelings of disregard, distrust and dishonesty, for example. Misunderstandings occur least often and are most quickly and easily sorted out face to face. Where this is not possible, such misunderstandings invariably take longer to resolve and may quickly become disputes and grievances.

■ Comparison

Comparison is a part of the process of perceptual mapping. Some comparisons are precise and exact: this glass is fuller than that; she is better qualified than he is, for example. Others are less so and may be based on a range of opinion (informal or otherwise), expectation and prejudice. Some comparisons are valid, others not.

Comparisons also have the added value of helping to meet the expectations of people in certain situations. If one company has a bigger percentage pay rise than another, staff tend to be happy. If the pay rise is lower, staff tend to be unhappy. Organisations therefore tend to seek out and emphasise those comparators that present them in their best light.

The standpoint from which the comparison is made must also be considered: for example, the statement that bankers earn more than teachers is valid only if a simple comparison of earnings is being considered; it does not prove or disprove that one job is better or worse than the other. For other aspects, therefore, other equivalent comparators have to be identified and addressed.

It is also usual to put weightings on different comparators when trying to arrive at satisfactory, complex and valid comparisons. The process at least recognises the difficulties involved and proposes steps towards addressing them, even if it is unlikely that they can be entirely resolved.

■ First impressions

First impressions count: this is received wisdom throughout the Western world. It applies everywhere, but first impressions are plainly misleading: prima facie you must know less about someone after 30 seconds than after 30 minutes. Yet overwhelmingly the converse is highly influential and this should be understood.

Above all, the first impression gives a frame of reference to the receiver. The appearance, manner, handshake and initial transaction are like the writing on a blank sheet. Before there was nothing, now there is something on which to place measure and assess the other. The impact is therefore very strong. It is essential to recognise this. The consequence of not doing so is that a one-dimensional view of the individual is formed and everything which is contrary to that dimension or which indicates complexities, other dimensions and qualities are edited out (see Figure 3.4).

■ Expectations

People go into every situational transaction with a purpose. The fulfilment of this is their expectation. Expectations are measured in hard material terms; soft behavioural terms; and a combination of the two:

People	Service
• appearance, dress, hair handshake • voice, eye contact • scent, smell • disposition (positive, negative, smiling, frowning) • establishing common interest/failure to do so • courtesy, manner • age	• friendliness (or lack of) • effectiveness • speed • quality • confidence • value • respect • ambience • appearance
Objects	Organisations
• design • colour/colours • weight • shape • size • materials • purpose, usage • price, value, cost	• ambience • welcome • appearance • image and impression • technology • care • respect for others • confidence • trust

This is a useful (but by no means perfect or complete) means of compartmentalising the cues and signals that are present when coming into any situation or into contact with someone for the first time. There are certain to be contradictions and contra-indications. It is essential to recognise and understand this in order to understand, in turn, the impact and influence of first impressions.

Figure 3.4 First impressions

- hard: goods for money;
- soft: courtesy, honesty, trustworthiness, value;
- combination: value for money; a combination of the measurable (the money with the unmeasurable (value).

The following approaches to expectation may be distinguished.

1 Expectation as a customer: of value for money; of utility and reliability of products and services; to be treated with courtesy and accuracy.
2 Expectation as a shareholder or stakeholder: of the longevity, stability and profitability of the organisation; of steady and increasing returns on investment; of strength of positive reputation.
3 Expectation as a staff member: to be treated well and fairly; to be paid well and on time; to have prospects for advancement; to have pay and rewards increased; to participate in the success of the organisation; to be treated with respect; to receive accurate and up-to-date information.

Fulfilment of expectations is a key feature of the motivation of the individual.

■ Exceeding expectations

Generally expectations are exceeded in the very short term only. It occurs when the outcome of a particular situation, performance or product, or result of a transaction is more positive or brings a greater level of satisfaction than was anticipated at the outset. The invariable result of this is the setting of a new level of expectation in regard to the particular activity in question. This becomes the norm by which these events will be measured in the future; if there is then a reversion to the original level of performance or output, dissatisfaction will be engendered.

■ Perceptual defence mechanisms

People build perceptual defences against people or situations that are personally or culturally unacceptable, unrecognisable, threatening or incapable of assimilation. Perceptual defence normally takes one or more of the following forms.

1 Denial – refusal to recognise the evidence of the senses.
2 Modification and distortion – accommodating disparate elements in ways which reinforce the comfort of the individual.
3 Change in perception – from positive to negative or from negative to positive, often based on a single trait or characteristic becoming apparent which was not previously so.
4 Recognition but refusal to change – where people are not prepared to have their view of the world disrupted by a single factor or example. This is often apparent when people define 'the exceptions to the rule'.
5 Outlets – where the individual seeks an outlet (especially for frustration or anger) away from its cause. For example, browbeating a subordinate offers a

sense of relief to someone who has previously been browbeaten himself by his superior.

6 Recognition thresholds – the higher the contentiousness or emotional content of information, the higher the threshold for recognition (that is, the less likely it is to be perceived readily).

■ Adaptation

Adaptation is 'perception as a continuous process'. Our view of the world is influenced directly by the circumstances and surroundings in which we find ourselves. Part of the process also relates to priority levels, both what is important now, and what is important for life, work, leisure, and so on.

Adaptation is therefore the process by which our view of the world and our relationships with it and within it, and its people and its organisations, establishments and events, constantly change. It is based on a combination of expectation and anticipation, knowledge, actions, previous experience and the continuing development of particular situations. It is accentuated by the other perceptual effects indicated above.

Adaptation is positive and negative as well as constant. It is accentuated by priorities, crises and constantly changing circumstances.

For example, an individual who is waiting for a train may become agitated if the train is late, especially if she has to get somewhere else quickly at the other end. When the train finally arrives, it is crowded, dirty and noisy and she has to stand. She therefore starts thinking of alternatives: the car, the coach. The train makes up time on its journey and arrives 20 minutes early. She has therefore time for food and drink before going on to her appointment. The overall feeling becomes one of satisfaction because the speed of service and time of arrival were the highest priority. The other factors simply contributed to the nature of the situation at the particular point of time.

3.7 Conclusions

Perception is the basis on which we form our understanding of the world. People make interpretations of others that they meet, and places and situations that are encountered by combining each of the elements indicated to produce their own individual picture, which they can then understand and be comfortable with.

Perception is affected by repetition and familiarity. Something or someone who is always present acquires the illusion of permanence. Routines and habits are formed by organising activities and interactions into regular patterns based on a combination of expectation and near certainty.

Perception is affected by the context in which individuals are placed. There is a great range of responses to the request 'please do this for me'; this depends on who has made the request and under what circumstances (for example, whether it was a manager, subordinate, child, spouse, customer, waiter, barman), and whether the person to whom the request was made was feeling well, ill, good or bad tempered, calm or stressed; the tone of voice in which the request was made;

whether it was a work or social situation; and what had gone on immediately beforehand.

Perception is affected by the characteristics of perceiver and perceived. The greater the knowledge of perception on the part of people and organisations, the greater the mutual understanding likely to be generated; and where problems do arise, the greater the potential for addressing these effectively. Personal characteristics affect the type of characteristics likely to be seen in others, their levels of importance and whether these are or should be negative or positive. Those being perceived greatly influence the views of the perceiver through their visibility (appearance, manner, dress, speech), and their status and role (either in the given situation or in a wider context). The simplest form of this is a conversation between two people; this becomes much more complex where the conversation is between more than two people, and more complicated still where this is in a new or unknown situation.

▼ 4 Attitudes, values and beliefs

4.1 Introduction

Attitudes are the mental, moral and ethical dispositions adopted by individuals to others and the situations and environments in which they find themselves. They can be broken down into the following components.

1 **Emotional:** feelings of positivity, negativity, neutrality or indifference; anger, love, hatred, desire, rejection, envy and jealousy; satisfaction and dissatisfaction. Emotional aspects are present in all work as part of the content, working relationships with other people, reactions to the environment, and the demands placed on particular occupations.
2 **Informational:** the nature and quality of the information present and the importance that it is given. Where this is known or widely understood to be wrong or incomplete, feelings of negativity and frustration arise.
3 **Behavioural:** the tendency to act in particular ways in given situations. This leads to the formation of attitudes where the behaviour required can be demonstrated as important or valuable; and to negative attitudes where the behaviour required is seen as futile or unimportant.
4 **Past experience:** memories of what happened in the past affect current and future feelings.
5 **Specific influences:** especially those of peer groups, work groups and key individuals, such as managers and supervisors. These also include family and social groups, and may also include religious and political influences.
6 **Defence:** once formed, attitudes and values are internalised and become a part of the individual. Any challenge to them is often viewed as a more general threat to the comfort of the individual.

4.2 Values

Values are the absolute standards by which people order their lives. Everyone needs to be aware of their own personal values so that they may deal pragmatically with any situation. This may extend to marked differences between individuals or between an individual and demands of the organisation. Conflicts of value often arise at places of work; anything to which people are required to ascribe must recognise this and, if it is to be effective, must be capable of harmonisation with the values of the individual. These values may be summarised as follows.

- **theoretical:** where everything is ordered, factual and in place;
- **economic:** making the best practical use of resources; results orientated, the cornerstone of people's standards and costs of living;
- **aesthetic:** the process of seeing and perceiving beauty; relating that which is positive and desirable or negative and undesirable;
- **social:** the sharing of emotions with other people;
- **integrity:** matters of loyalty, honesty, openness, trust, honour, decency; concern for the truth;
- **political:** the ways and choices concerning the ordering of society and its subsections and strata;
- **religious and ethical:** the dignity of mankind; the inherent worth of people; the morality – the absolute standards – of human conduct (this includes specific beliefs and the requirements of particular religions).

4.3 Shared values

A clear set of values or direction offered by an organisation to its people, its customers and environment gives a clear sense of identity. The adoption of shared values is central to the generation of high levels of commitment and motivation among those who work in organisations. Recognising that people bring a diverse range of qualities to an organisation is essential. Giving a clear corporate purpose that is both above individual aspirations, and also accommodates them, is a major function of the articulation of shared values. This is also instrumental in structuring particular ethical and moral stances that are taken.

Attitudes and values are affected by:

- past experiences and interactions with a given person, or people, or situation;
- continuing experiences and interactions;
- perceptions and levels of general understanding;
- the presence of, and understanding of, the particular rules, regulations and other limitations with which these are bounded;
- particular mental and physical aspects;
- levels of identity with the others involved and with the situation;
- the extent to which the people/situations are known or unknown;
- aspects of risks and uncertainty;
- levels of active or passive involvement;
- positive aspects – the extent to which something good and productive is certain or expected to come out;
- negative aspects – the extent to which something negative and unproductive is certain or expected to come out;
- any strong or prevailing moral, ethical or social pressures;
- general degrees of comfort – usually based on levels of knowledge and understanding.

Attitudes are not easy to define precisely. The attitude of one person is capable of being inferred over periods of time and from certain patterns of behaviour or from particular interactions – it is not possible to prove.

■ Formation of attitudes

The elements indicated are adopted by individuals in their own unique ways to form their own distinctive attitudes. The main processes that are involved are outlined below.

1 Their propensity to accept rather than reject those of the group (including the organisation) to which they seek to belong; they have a high degree of potential compliance.
2 Their perception of the future relationship as being productive, effective, profitable and harmonious; people do not willingly enter a situation if they have no expectational perception of this. However, they are more willing and likely to enter situations, the greater the likelihood of this being achieved, and people will avoid situations where these elements are neither present nor apparent.
3 Relating past experience to current and future situations, relationships and environment: positive experiences tend towards the formation of positive attitudes; negative experiences tend towards the formation of negative attitudes.
4 Availability and completeness of information; availability includes access and clarity; completeness includes reference to key and critical gaps (and also to the value and usefulness of that which is available).
5 The general state of organisational well-being, the general state of the individual and the relationship and interaction between the two.
6 Other pressures, including the views of peers, co-workers, superiors, subordinates, family, friends; and economic, social, legal, moral and ethical pressures. These are likely to include sweeping generalisations, prevailing received wisdom, opinions and prejudices (opinions formed without full reference to available facts); again, from the variety of sources indicated.
7 Any myths and legends present in the particular group or situation. For example, the statement that 'the person who holds job X or sits in office Y always gets promoted first/never gets promoted at all' puts behavioural and psychological pressures on each situation.

Each part of the process is present in the promotion and development of all attitudes, though the mix varies between particular situations and individuals. The mix also changes as people come into and go out of organisations and their groups. Also, by seeking to move, individuals may require (or perceive themselves to require) to change their attitudes in order to stand any chance of being successful. These attitudes may change again, depending on whether or not they were able to make the move and, if they did, whether or not this was successful.

■ Adjustment of attitudes

This is the development of attitudes (positive and negative) in a given situation. The processes by which adjustment is achieved are similar to those above. However, they tend to reinforce what is already present – for example, the perception if the future is well understood; the availability of information is regarded as satisfactory.

Problems occur when a radical adjustment is either required, or else is to be imposed. The first response to such an adjustment or shift is often simply to shut it out: those affected do not believe the evidence before them.

Adjustment therefore works best where the prevailing attitudes are being developed rather than radically transformed (see Table 4.1). Where a radical change of attitude is required, it is much better from the point of view of generating effective organisational behaviour and interpersonal and inter-group relations if it is tackled as a major change.

Table 4.1   Influences on attitudes: summary

Positive	Negative
• Equality of opportunity and treatment	• Inequality of opportunity and treatment
• Saying what is meant, meaning what is said	• Expediency
• Identifying and solving problems	• Victimisation, scapegoating
• Clarity of purpose	• Lack of clarity
• Unity of purpose	• Fragmentation of purpose
• Reward for achievement, loyalty and commitment	• Rewards based on favouritism and infighting
• Openness of management style	• Remoteness and distance of management style (both physical and psychological)
• Particular standards set at outset	
• Absolute standards for everyone	• Standards allowed to emerge
• High and equal value placed on all staff	• Different standards for different groups, departments, divisions and individuals
• Recognition of every contribution	
• Pride in the organisation	• Different levels of value placed on different staff groups
• Identity with the organisation	
• High levels of esteem and respect for staff	• Lack of recognition
• Clarity of communications	• Lack of pride in the organisation
• Harmony	• Lack of identity; rejection of identity
• High quality information	• Low levels of esteem and respect; variations in levels of esteem and respect according to occupation, department, division and function
• Open personal relationships	
• Open operational and professional relationships	
	• Lack of clarity of communications
	• Hostility
	• Low quality information

4.4 Beliefs

Beliefs are the certainties of the world. They may be:

- **absolute:** based on such things as mathematical fact, night following day, mortality and taxation;
- **near absolute:** based on seasonal changes, continuous development of knowledge and awareness, continuous technological and social development;
- **acts and articles of faith:** based on the certainty of God, and often under-pinned by religious allegiance and the following and adoption of the teachings of those who pronounce in the name of God (this may also extend to the adoption of social and political creeds);
- **other strong ethical and moral standpoints:** relating to honesty, trustworthiness, right and wrong;
- **strong illusions and perceptions of order, permanence and stability:** often founded on long steady-state factors.

Beliefs are the psychological cornerstone of the lives of people. They provide the foundations and framework upon which people order and structure the rest of their lives. They are internalised to the heart and soul of the individual, providing the basis for other attitudes, values and chosen behaviour.

4.5 Socialisation

Socialisation is the process by which individuals are persuaded to behave in ways acceptable to their society, family, social groups and clubs. This also applies to work organisations and their groups, departments, divisions and functions. Effective socialisation results in compliance and conformity with the values, beliefs, attitudes, rules and patterns of behaviour required.

For this to occur, the group's attitudes, values, beliefs, behaviour and rules must be capable of being accepted by the individuals that seek to join or who are required to join. They tend therefore to reflect the prevailing customs of the wider society and be in harmony with general ethical and social pressures.

On the other hand, socialisation should also leave enough space, latitude and freedom for individuals to express themselves in the given setting. Too great a restriction leads to frustration. At the other extreme, a lack of clear understanding of these standards leads to lack of focus and purpose leaving the individual in a void, which can be just as harmful and stressful as over-restraint.

Socialisation takes place from the moment of birth. It is conducted in the early years by parents and family, schools and colleges, religious institutions, sports and leisure clubs. By the time individuals arrive in work, therefore, they have been subject to a great variety of pressures and influences. The problem for organisations lies in their ability to build on this and create conditions that are both acceptable to individuals, and which also ensure that productive and effective work can take place (see Table 4.2).

This problem is greater with mature employees who may arrive at an

Table 4.2 Social needs

Organisation	Individual
• Productive effort	• Comfort
• Effective workforce	• Warmth
• Effective individuals	• Belonging
• Effective groups	• Contact
• Continuous development	• Success
• New talents and energies	• Fulfilment
• Work harmony	• Achievement
• Expectations	• Professionalism
• Job proficiency	• Expectations
• Professionalism	• Rewards
• Success	• Training and development
• Value	

The lists represent two sides of the same coin. Organisation socialisation is designed and devised to bring them together, to match up and harmonise the pressures. Some of these pressures are convergent, others divergent; all must be integrated and inter-related as far as possible.

organisation after experience in many others. They will therefore have formed their own ideas about high standards, best practice and optimum ways of working, and this in turn leads to the need for effective orientation at the outset of the new job.

This underlines the importance of adequate and effective induction and orientation programmes. Too many organisations and their managers still neglect this, believing it to be a waste of time, cutting into their other priorities; or else they have simply never learned to see it as an investment, the return on which is a committed and effective employee; and, if this is really successful, much of the process is achieved over a relatively short period of time.

4.6 Learning

Learning is the process by which skills, knowledge, attitudes and behaviour are formed and developed. It takes place as the result of education, training, socialisation and experience. Learning also occurs as the result of conditioning and restriction, whereby the individual is persuaded to adopt, and ultimately accept, guidance, regulation, conformity and compliance in particular situations.

Individuals learn at different rates, times and stages in their lives. Some people acquire new knowledge, skills and qualities easily, while others struggle to learn the very basics of the same things. This is based on a combination of the following elements:

● the desire and motivation to learn brought about by the individual's own needs and drives, usually in the expectation that this will bring success, rewards, enhanced potential and expertise, marketability; and also increased esteem, respect and status;

- the quality and suitability of the learning and teaching methods (including the quality of instruction);
- pressures to learn placed on individuals by others – including organisations – to enable them to acquire the knowledge, skills and qualities required by them in the individual; and also to adopt the attitudes, values and behaviour required in order to be comfortable in the particular situation;
- specific drives and requirements such as the onus placed on individuals in particular occupations to keep abreast of new developments and initiatives in their field;
- the nature of the individual's attitude and disposition to acquire new skills, knowledge and qualities.

The result is to increase the range, depth and interactions of thoughts, ideas and concepts, as well as skills, knowledge, attitude, behaviour and experience; to increase the ability to organise and reorganise these; and to order them in productive and effective activities (whatever they mean in the particular set of circumstances).

The cycle illustrates the importance of the relationship between behaviour, action, and experience. It also emphasises (testing and experience) the need to reinforce abstract learning with practice and performance (see Figures 4.1 and 4.2).

■ Retention

The ability to retain and internalise that which has been taught and learned is based on a combination of the following factors:

- the ability to practise and use, and become proficient in that which has been taught and learned;
- its actual value once it has been taught and learned (as distinct from its perceived or anticipated value before it was learned);
- the regularity and frequency with which it is to be put to use;
- the rewards that are to accrue as the result;
- the punishments and threats that occur if learning does not take place (this is especially important in the acquisition of attitudes, values and behaviour, and in conforming to rules and standards).

This is usually called learning reinforcement. Reinforcement may be:

- continuous, in which case the learning is soon internalised;
- intermittent, in which case it is likely to become important from time to time only and may lead to the need for revision, retraining and refresher courses;
- occasional, in which case the learning is likely to have been of general or marginal value only.

More generally still, learning, acquiring and becoming proficient in new skills and qualities normally leads to enhanced feelings of personal confidence and

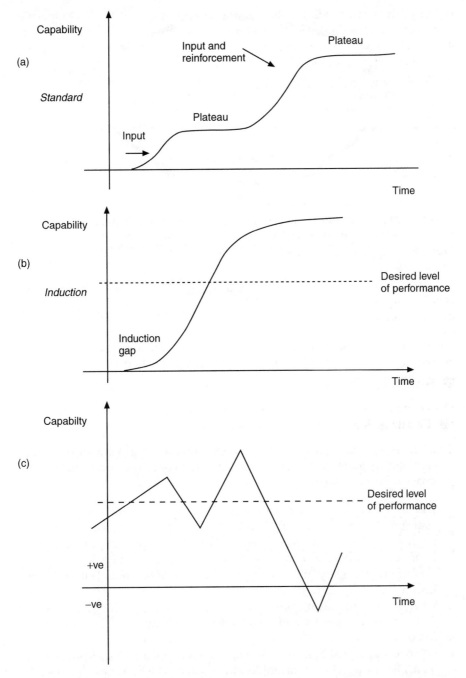

(a) Theoretical, based on rational and ordered input, familiarisation, practice and reinforcement.
(b) The theory of induction: time taken at the outset leads to long-term high levels of performance.
(c) The theory of non-induction and non-training, based on trial and error, and leading to haphazard behaviour and performance.

Figure 4.1 Learning curves

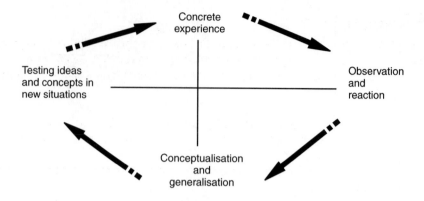

Concrete
experience

Testing ideas
and concepts in
new situations

Observation
and
reaction

Conceptualisation
and
generalisation

The cycle illustrates the importance of the relationship between behaviour, action and experience. It also emphasises (testing and experience) the need to reinforce abstract learning with practice and performance.

Figure 4.2 Learning cycle
Source: Kolb (1985).

self-respect. It enhances flexibility of attitudes and approaches. It is also increasingly likely that it will bring greater general perceptions of worth and value to the organisation.

■ Feedback

Feedback is essential on all aspects of performance leading to enhanced general levels of understanding, confidence and support. Related specifically to learning, feedback is best as follows:

1 When it is positive rather than negative, in that it enhances the general concept of progress to which learning is supposed to contribute. The negative is best as a 'nuclear deterrent' (that is, it is present, but is never to be used). It is normally to be applied to persistent failure to accept and conform to necessary rules, rather than because of failure to learn skills and knowledge.
2 When it concentrates on processes as well as results so that the individual both knows his results and also understands why he has succeeded or failed.
3 When it is delivered as near to the conclusion of the learning as possible and then followed up with opportunities to apply that which has been learned; this should also be incorporated into the feedback process.
4 When it is continuous in general, so that any problems with what has been learned which subsequently become apparent (or any later decline in performance) can be quickly rectified.

■ Learning styles

Individuals have preferred learning styles. For some this may be very marked: they can only learn in one particular way and other methods have little effect.

Honey and Mumford (1986) identify four preferred learning styles as follows (Figure 4.3).

1. **Activist:** concentrating on learning by doing and via direct experience, and through considering the results of trial and error so that performance may be improved next time.
2. **Pragmatist:** concentrating on that which is possible and practical and of direct application to given situations.
3. **Theorist:** concentrating on why things are as they are and investigating theories and concepts that form the background to this.
4. **Reflector:** concentrating on assessing and analysing why things have turned out in particular ways and using this as the basis on which to build understanding.

Honey and Mumford designed a questionnaire, the purpose of which was to identify under which of these four headings an individual's preferred learning style fell. The results would then be used to ensure that the individual understood why she tended to learn some things better than others; to seek out those activities that were best suited to her preferred learning style; and to develop her lesser and least preferred areas of learning to enhance their total learning capability.

Other aspects of preferred learning style may be identified:

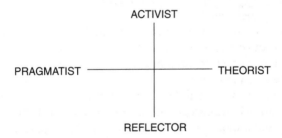

This spectrum was devised by Honey and Mumford to identify the preferred learning style. By completing a questionnaire and plotting the results the respondent would:

(a) identify those activities likely to be most and least beneficial;
(b) identify those areas which needed working on, so that full benefit from all activities could be gained.

Figure 4.3 Preferred learning styles

- the influence of rewards and outcomes;
- economic factors, such as career and payment enhancement;
- peer, professional and social group expectations;
- the nature of the material and the means by which it is taught/learned;
- the quality of the teacher;
- time factors.

There are also some absolutes. For example, eventually someone who wishes to know whether he can drive a car will have to sit in a car and drive, however much of a theorist he may be. Similarly, it is not possible to be an effective leader of people if there is no basic understanding of why people behave in different ways in different situations (and different ways in the same situation), however much of a pragmatist he may otherwise be. This underlines the need to broaden the preferred learning style into an individual learning style that can accept effective input and information from as wide a variety of sources and means as possible.

4.7 Individual development

Both in organisational terms, and also for the benefit of the individual, the primary purpose of individual development is to enhance skills, knowledge, qualifications and expertise so that a productive and fulfilling life can be lived, both in work and also in society at large. If this is to be achieved, the following elements must be present:

- aims and objectives, and measures of success/failure;
- positive motivation of both trainers and trainees;
- rewards must be perceived and available;
- benefits in terms of personal, professional and organisational performance and objectives must be met;
- it must be capable of reinforcement of the workplace;
- it must be current and relevant;
- it must have organisational and managerial support;
- it must be planned and integrated into the workload of the individual and have priority and importance at the time when it takes place;
- it should be part of a total package and process of continuous learning and development;
- it should be evaluated afterwards by all interested parties, in both the short term and the long term.

If this is to be achieved, organisations must also consider individual development from the point of view of:

- organisation requirements, the need and drive for enhanced current and future performance;

- professional and expertise requirements, the need for the individual to enhance and improve her general skills, knowledge and expertise;
- personal drives and preferences.

Other points may usefully be made.

1 Individuals must be motivated to learn. This motivation arises from a combination of personal and professional or occupational circumstances, drives and needs and the requirements of the organisation.
2 Learning and development are part of the general commitment to each other made by organisation and individual. The organisation is entitled to expect the individual to learn; and the individual is entitled to expect training and development.
3 Whatever is learned must be capable of recognition and measurement so that performance standards can be set and identified.
4 The better understood the activity, the stronger the motivation and drive to learn. It is often necessary to break complex tasks and practices down into smaller parts to avoid facing the trainee with too much to grasp at one time.
5 Feedback is essential to reinforce understanding, expertise and commitment. Current or immediate feedback is much better than delayed feedback: the greater the delay, the greater the loss of meaning and impact.

4.8 Conclusions

Forming and nurturing the required attitudes and values clearly requires a broad knowledge and understanding of all the factors and elements indicated. If this is to be effective, the following must be present.

1 Identification of the required attitudes and values, together with the reasons why these are desirable and methods of ensuring that these are capable of being supported and adopted by all those concerned.
2 Positive steps must be taken to reinforce them in the ways in which the organisation and its departments, divisions and functions operate, and any shortfall should be penalised.
3 The effects of all training and development activities on attitudes and values should be recognised, whatever the training and development is overtly concerned with. Attitudes and values are shaped, developed and reinforced by all learning activities, as is the general mutual relationship and commitment between organisation and individual.
4 It is also necessary to recognise that attitudes, and especially negative attitudes, emerge whether or not they are shaped and influenced by the organisation. Where the organisation has no influence on attitudes, these are formed by other pressures, especially peer, professional and social groups.
5 Positive attitudes help to provide a harmonious and open working environment, and increase general levels of motivation and morale. Negative attitudes tend to reinforce any stresses and strains (poor working relationships, lack of trust and value).

6 Attention to workplace attitudes, especially at the induction stage, helps employees to adopt and find the place required of them in their environment. It helps to provide a clear mutual understanding between organisation and employee, and is one of the cornerstones of the working environment. Above all, as organisations strive for ever-greater levels of flexibility and responsiveness, building these characteristics as positive and valuable attitudes is essential.

▼ 5 Motivation

5.1 Introduction

Motivation is a reflection of the reasons why people do things. All behaviour has a purpose (often several). All behaviour is therefore based on choice: people choose to do things that they do. Sometimes this choice is very restricted (sink or swim, for example). Sometimes again, it is constrained by the law (for example, stopping the car when the traffic lights are red). And again, it is constrained by the norms and processes of society: people tend to wear smart clothes to a party where they know that everybody else will be well dressed. In each case, however, there is a choice, though the propensity and encouragement and direction to choose one course of action rather than the other in the examples given is strong, if not overwhelming.

The following key features need to be understood.

1 **Goals and ambitions:** these must be present, and both realistic and achievable if satisfaction is eventually to occur. Problems arise when the goals set are too low (leading to feelings of frustration), or too high (leading to constant lack of achievement). They must also be acceptable to the individual concerned – in terms of self-image, self-worth, and self-value – so they are likely to be positive and based on the drive for improved levels of comfort, capability and well-being. They must also be acceptable (or at least not unacceptable) to the society and environment in which the individual lives and works, and capable of being harmonised and integrated with them.

2 **Recognition:** a critical part of the process of developing self-esteem and self-worth lies in the nature and levels of recognition accorded to the achievement of particular goals. The need for recognition itself therefore becomes a drive. Individuals tend to pursue goals that will be recognised and valued by those whose opinion and judgement is important to them, such as family, friends, peers and social groups, as well as work organisation. Dissatisfaction occurs when this recognition is not forthcoming.

3 **Achievement:** the components of achievement are the anticipated and actual rewards that the fulfilment of a particular goal brings. High levels of achievement occur where these overlap completely. High levels also normally occur where real rewards exceed those that are anticipated. Low levels occur where the anticipated rewards are not forthcoming; this devalues the achievement. High or complete achievement is normally seen and perceived as successful. Low achievement or failure to achieve is seen and perceived as a failure.

From this, in turn, other aspects of motivation become apparent.

1 **The need for success:** people tend to aim their sights at what they know they can do, or think they can do or think that they may be able to do, so that success is forthcoming. Genuine successes, victories and triumphs enhance feelings of self-esteem and self-value; failures diminish these.
2 **The need to be recognised and valued by others:** this is a combination of pursuing things that people know or perceive will be valued by those around them (as stated above) and also of seeking out those who will value the achievements for themselves.
3 **The need to develop and improve:** this is a positive statement of need. If satisfaction is not forthcoming in one field, individuals are likely to lose interest and find something else to pursue. As well as matters of comfort and well-being, it includes broadening and deepening experience and variety of life (including working life). It also includes developing new skills, capabilities and interests with the view to pursuing personal potential as far as possible.

These are social and behavioural needs, wants and desires; they are influenced, developed and conditioned by societies and organisations, and groups within them. They are based on more fundamental human needs.

1 **The need and instinct for survival:** when an individual is hungry or thirsty, his prime motivation is for food or drink. When an individual is cold, his instinct is to find warmth and shelter. When the life of an individual is under threat (for example, from war or disaster), his instinct is to take actions that preserve life.
2 **The need and instinct for society and belonging:** this is a reflection of the need for esteem, warmth and respect. More fundamentally, it is the need to belong, to interact and to have personal contact with those with whom the individual has identity, respect, liking and love. It also includes being drawn to those who have similar hopes, aspirations, interests and ambitions.
3 **The need to be in control:** this is the ability to influence the actions and feelings of others; and the ability to influence the environment, to make it comfortable and productive in response to the particular needs, wants and drives. Control is a function of purpose, the organisation and arrangement of particular resources (including other people) for given reasons.
4 **The need to progress:** this is a reflection of the capacity to develop, to enhance knowledge, skills and capability. It includes:

   (a) economic drives for better standards of living, quality of life and enhanced capacity to make choices;
   (b) social drives to gain status, respect, influence and esteem as the result of enhanced capability and economic advantage;
   (c) personal drives reflecting ambition and the need to maximise/optimise the potential to achieve;
   (d) opportunistic drives, the identification and pursuit of opportunities that may become apparent and attractive to the individual;
   (e) invention and creativity, the ability to see things from various points of view and create the mean by which quality of life can be enhanced.

Development, adaptation and creativity are also features of the needs for survival, society and control. They are a reflection of the extent to which individuals are able to influence their ability to survive, belong and control their environment.

Except at the point of life and death, when the instinct for survival is everything, these needs constitute parts of the wider process of adaptation and interaction. At given moments, therefore, some will be stronger than others; there is no linear progression from one to the next.

5.2 Major theories of motivation

■ Achievement Motivation Theory: D. C. McClelland

Much of the background on which the nature of motivation is based was organised and summarised by D. C. McClelland. Working in the 1950s and 1960s he identified the relationship between personal characteristics, social and general background and achievement.

Persons with high needs for achievement exhibited the following characteristics:

- task rather than relationship orientation;
- a preference for tasks over which they had sole or over-riding control and responsibility;
- the need to identify closely, and be identified closely, with the successful outcomes of their action;
- task balance: this had to be difficult enough on the one hand to be challenging and rewarding, to be capable of demonstrating expertise and good results, and gaining status and recognition from others; on the other hand, it needed to be moderate enough to be capable of successful achievement;
- risk balance: in which the individual seeks to avoid as far as possible the likelihood and consequences of failure;
- the need for feedback on the results achieved to reinforce the knowledge of success and to ensure that successes were validated and publicised;
- the need for progress, variety and opportunity.

Need for achievement is based on a combination of:

- intrinsic motivation – the drives from within the individual;
- extrinsic motivation – the drives, pressures and expectations exerted by the organisation, peers and society.

It is also influenced by education, awareness, social and cultural background, and values.

One potential problem was identified in relation to the appointment of high achievers to highly responsible managerial and supervisory positions. Because the higher achievement tended to be task- rather than relationship-driven, many did not possess (or regard as important) the human relations characteristics necessary to get things done through people.

■ Rensis Likert: System 4

Likert's contribution to the theories of workplace motivation arose from his work with high performing managers: that is, managers and supervisors who achieved high levels of productivity, low levels of cost and high levels of employee motivation, participation and involvement at their places of work. The work demonstrated a correlation between this success and the style and structure of the work groups that they created. The groups achieved not only high levels of economic output and therefore wage and salary targets, but were also heavily involved in both group maintenance activities and the design and definition of work patterns. This was under-pinned by a supportive style of supervision and the generation of a sense of personal worth, importance and esteem in belonging to the group itself (see Figure 5.1).

The System 4 model arose from this work. He identified four styles or systems of management, as explained below.

System 1:
Exploitative Authoritative, where power and direction come from the top downwards and where there is no participation, consultation or involvement on the part of the workforce. Workforce compliance is thus based on fear. Unfavourable attitudes are generated, there is little confidence and trust, and there are low levels of motivation to cooperate or generate output above the absolute minimum.

System 2:
Benevolent Authoritative, which is similar to System 1 but which allows some upward opportunity for consultation and participation in some areas. Again, attitudes tend to be generally unfavourable; confidence, trust and communication are also at low levels.

In both Systems 1 and 2, productivity may be high over the short run when targets can be achieved by a combination of coercion and bonus and over-time payments. However, both productivity and earnings are demonstrably low over the long run; there is also manifestation of high absenteeism and labour turnover.

System 3:
Consultative, where aims and objectives are set after discussion and consultation with subordinates; where communication is two-way and where teamwork is encouraged, at least in some areas. Attitudes towards both superiors and the organisation tend to be favourable, especially when the organisation is working steadily. Productivity tends to be higher, absenteeism and turnover lower. There are also demonstrable reductions in scrap, improvement in product quality, reduction in overall operational costs and higher levels of earning on the part of the workforce.

System 4:
Participative; in this system three basic concepts have a very important effect on performance. These are (a) the use by the manager of the principle of supportive relationships throughout the work group referred to above; (b) the use of group decision-making and group methods of supervision; and (c) the setting of high

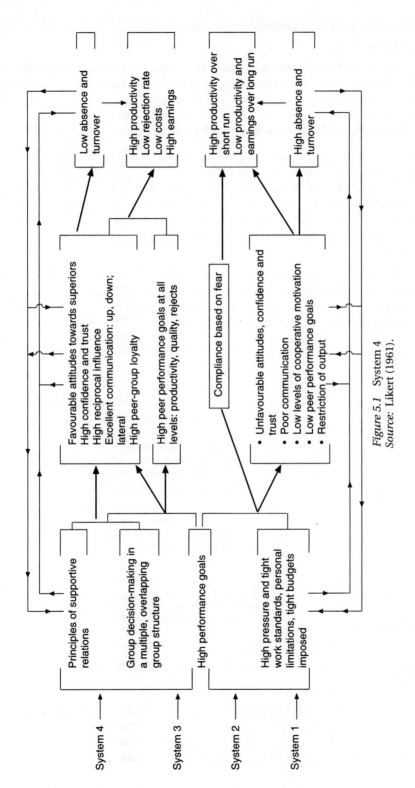

Figure 5.1 System 4
Source: Likert (1961).

performance and very ambitious goals for the department and also for the organisation overall.

System 4 was Likert's favoured system. His research has demonstrated that the principles and attitudes prevalent in System 4 could and should be applied to all types of organisation.

■ Abraham Maslow: a hierarchy of needs

Abraham Maslow depicted a hierarchy of needs which explained different types and levels of motivation that were important to people at different times. This hierarchy of needs is normally shown as a pyramid. The hierarchy of needs works from the bottom of the pyramid upwards showing the most basic needs and motivations at the lowest levels and those created by, or fostered by, civilisation and society towards the top of it (see Figure 5.2). The needs are as follows.

1 Physiological – the need for food, drink, air, warmth, sleep and shelter; that is, basic survival needs related to the instinct for self-preservation.
2 Safety and security – that is, protection from danger, threats or deprivation and the need for stability (or relative stability) of environment.

Figure 5.2   A hierarchy of needs
Source: Maslow (1960).

3   Social – that is, a sense of belonging to a society and the groups within it: for example, the family, the organisation, the work group. Also included in this level are matters to do with the giving and receiving of friendship; basic status needs within these groups; and the need to participate in social activities.
4   Esteem needs – these are the needs for self-respect, self-esteem, appreciation, recognition and status both on the part of the individual concerned and the society, circle or group in which they inter-relate; part of the esteem need is therefore the drive to gain the respect, esteem and appreciation accorded by others.
5   Self-actualization – that is, the need for self-fulfilment, self-realisation, personal development, accomplishment, mental, material and social growth and the development and fulfilment of the creative faculties.

Maslow then reinforced this by stating that people tended to satisfy their needs systematically. They started with the basic, instinctive needs and then moved up the hierarchy. Until one particular group of needs was satisfied, a person's behaviour would be dominated by them. Thus hungry or homeless people will look to needs for self-esteem and society only after hunger has been satisfied and they have found a place to stay. The other point that Maslow made was that people's motives were constantly being modified as their situation changed, and in relation to their levels of adaptation and other perceptual factors. This was especially true of the self-actualisation needs since, having achieved measures of fulfilment and recognition, people nevertheless tended to remain unsatisfied and wished to make further progress.

Maslow's work was based on general studies of human motivation and as such was not directly related to matters endemic at the workplace. However, matters concerning the last two items on the pyramid, those of self-esteem and self-actualisation, have clear implications for the motivation (and self-motivation) of professional, technical and managerial staff in organisations.

■ Douglas McGregor: Theory X and Theory Y

McGregor identified two distinctive sets of assumptions made by managers about employees. From this he articulated two extreme attitudes or views and called these Theory X and Theory Y. His thesis was that in practice most people would come somewhere between the two except in certain circumstances.

❐ Theory X

This is based on the following premises.

1   People dislike work and will avoid it if they can. They would rather be directed than accept any responsibility; indeed, they will avoid authority and responsibility if possible. They have no creativity except when it comes to getting around the rules and procedures of the organisation. Above all, they will not use their creativity in pursuit of the job, or the interests of the organisation.
2   People must be forced or bribed to apply the right effort. They are motivated

mainly by money, which remains the over-riding reason why they go to work. Their chief anxiety concerns personal security, which is alleviated by earning money.

3 People are inherently lazy and require high degrees of supervision, coercion and control in order to produce adequate output.

❒ Theory Y

This is based on the premise that work is necessary to everyone's psychological growth. People wish only to be interested in work, and under the right conditions they will enjoy it. People gain intrinsic fulfilment from it. They are motivated by the desire to achieve and to realise potential, to work to the best of their capabilities and to employ the creativity and ingenuity with which they are endowed in the pursuit of this.

People direct themselves towards given accepted and understood targets; they will seek and accept responsibility and authority; and they will accept the discipline of the organisation in the pursuit of this. People will also impose self-discipline on both themselves and their activities.

Whatever the conditions, management should be responsible for organising the elements of productive enterprise and its resources in the interests of economic ends. This would be done in ways suitable to the nature of the organisation and the workforce in question; either providing a coercive style of management and supervision or arranging a productive and harmonious environment in which the workforce can, and will, take responsibility for directing their own efforts and those of their unit towards organisational aims and objectives.

■ Frederick Herzberg: two-factor theory

The research of Herzberg was directed at people in places of work. It was based on questioning people in organisations in different jobs, at different levels, to establish:

- those factors that led to extreme dissatisfaction with the job, the environment and the workplace;
- those factors that led to extreme satisfaction with the job, the environment and the workplace.

The factors giving rise to satisfaction he called motivators, and those giving rise to dissatisfaction he called hygiene factors (see Figure 5.3).

The motivators that emerged were: achievement, recognition, the nature of the work itself, level of responsibility, advancement, and opportunities for personal growth and development. These factors are all related to the actual content of the work and job responsibilities. Where present in a working situation, these factors led to high levels and degrees of satisfaction on the part of the workforce.

The hygiene factors or dissatisfiers that he identified were as follows: company policy and administration; supervision and management style; levels of pay and salary; relationships with peers; relationships with subordinates; status; and security. These are factors that, where they are good or adequate, will not in

Factors on the job that led to extreme dissatisfaction but not satisfaction

Factors on the job that led to extreme satisfaction but not dissatisfation

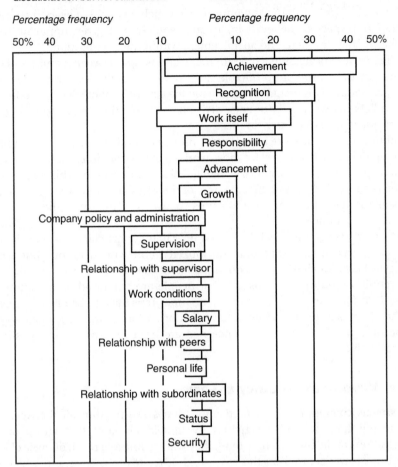

Figure 5.3 Two-factor theory
Source: Herzberg (1960).

themselves make people satisfied; by ensuring that they are indeed adequate, dissatisfaction is removed but satisfaction is not in itself generated. On the other hand, where these aspects were bad, extreme dissatisfaction was experienced by all respondents. Organisations that failed to provide adequate hygiene factors tended to have high levels of conflict, absenteeism and labour turnover and low general morale.

The work of Herzberg encourages concentration on the following.

1 A management style, attitude and approach to staff that is based on integrity, honesty and trust, whatever the nature, limitations or technology concerned in the work itself.

2 The working environment should be comfortable, functional and suitable in

human terms, again whatever the operational constraints and limitations may be.

3 General factors of status and importance which ensure that every member of staff is respected, believed in, treated equally and given opportunity for change, development and advancement within the organisation.

4 Effective and professional operational relationships between members of staff that, in turn, promote profitable and successful activities across the entire organisation. This includes recognising the existence of barriers and potential conflicts between departments, divisions and functions and taking steps to provide effective counters to these.

5 Administrative support and control processes and mechanisms should be designed to make life easy for those working at the front line, while at the same time providing the necessary management information. This particularly refers to the nature and effectiveness of the roles and functions of corporate headquarters and the relationships between these and the front-line operations indicated.

6 The work itself, and how it is divided up. There is particular reference here to those parts of the work that are looked upon with disfavour but which nevertheless must be carried out adequately and effectively (see above).

7 Security of tenure. This ensures that people are employed on a continuous basis as far as is possible. At the same time steps have to be taken to ensure that there is a steady and open flow of information, so that when changes do become necessary the staff concerned are both forewarned and positively responsive.

■ V. Vroom: expectancy theories

In essence, this approach to motivation draws the relationship between the efforts put into particular activities by individuals, and the nature of the expectations of the rewards they think they will recome as a result of these efforts.

This is clearly centred on the individual. It relates to the ways in which the individual sees or perceives the environment. In particular, it relates to his view of work, his expectations, aspirations, ambitions and desired outcomes from it, and the extent to which these can be satisfied at the workplace or carrying out the occupation in question. For example, the individual may have no particular regard for the job that he is currently doing but will nevertheless work productively and effectively at it and be committed to it because it is a stepping stone (in his view) to greater things; these are the expectations that he has of it and so these constitute the basis of his efforts and the quality of these efforts. This is compounded, however, by other factors: the actual capacities and aptitudes of the individual concerned on the one hand, and the nature of the work environment on the other. It is also limited by the perceptions and expectations that the commissioner of the work has of the person who is actually carrying it out. There is a distinction to be drawn between the effort put into performance and the effectiveness of that effort: hard work, conscientiously carried out, does not always produce effective activity; the effort has to be directed and targeted. There must also be a match between the rewards expected and those that are offered, since a reward is merely a value judgement placed on something offered in return for effort, and if this is not valued by the receiver it has no effect on her motivation (see Figure 5.4).

There has consequently to be an understanding of the nature of the motives and expectations of the individual, related to an ability to satisfy these on the part of the organisation if it is to address effectively the issue of motivation. The approach required is therefore to take both an enlightened and specific view of what constitutes job satisfaction (rather than assuming that it exists or exists in certain occupations at least); and an understanding of the processes of perception and the nature of reward in relation to the aspirations of those conducting the work.

The components of the expectation–effort–reward mixture are as follows.

1 **Personal ambition:** the inner drive to make progress and the rewards that this progress brings with it.
2 **Professional ambition:** the drive and desire to make it to the top of one's chosen occupation.

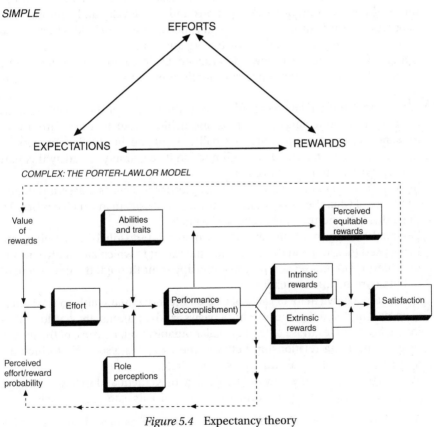

Figure 5.4 Expectancy theory
Source: from Luthans (1986).

3 **Situation:** the ability of the situation to provide the rewards expected and anticipated.

4 **Performance:** in which individuals gravitate towards those tasks that are seen to produce a greater level of desired rewards.

5 **Perception:** understanding that most of the drive comes from within the individual rather than being imposed or directed; the highest levels of individual motivation are achieved in workplaces where conditions are created that enable this to take place.

■ Motivation, achievement and rewards

An alternative view of the expectation, effort, reward mixture consists of restating this as motivation, achievement, rewards. Drives for particular goals are enhanced by the capability to achieve them and the rewards that are to accrue as the result.

These rewards are a combination of the following foctors.

1 **Economic:** monetary pay for carrying out the job, for special achievement for responsibility and accountability, which is expected to continue and improve in line with the relationship between organisation and individual, both in terms of current and future occupations and also loyalty and commitment. Economic rewards meet the needs and expectations of individuals, and also reflect the value placed on them by the organisation.

2 **Job satisfaction:** intrinsic rewards attained by individuals in terms of the quality of their work, the range and depth of expertise used and the results achieved.

3 **Work content:** the relative contribution to the output of the organisation as a whole and the feelings of success and achievement that arise from this. As stated elsewhere, operating a small part of the production process or administrative system tends to be limited in its capability to satisfy this part of the requirement for achievement.

4 **Job title:** certain job titles give images of prestige as well as a description and summary of what the work is, and the respect and esteem in which it is held by the individual and their peers and social circles.

5 **Personal development:** the extent to which the individuals' capabilities are being used (or limited in their use); and the extent to which alternative means of achievement and reward may become apparent through the development of both current and new expertise.

6 **Status:** the relative mark of value placed on the individual's rank, role, which is expertise and job by those whose views and opinions they value. This invariably includes those of the particular organisation, because of the nature of the continuing relationship between the two. It is also likely to include, again, the views of social and professional circles.

7 **Trappings:** these are the outward marks of achievement and success, material and visible benefits by which others can recognise its extent. They include:

(a) benefits, such as cars (both the fact that a car as been issued and also the value of the car itself); other business technology; business trips;

sabbaticals; course and seminar attendance; health care (they are marks of achievement when presented in professional and social circles);

(b) autonomy – the ability of the individual to set their own patterns of work; to come and go as they see fit, to work from home; to attend the place of work at weekends or other quiet periods in order to be able to work without interruptions (as distinct from having to attend during the same time as everyone else); to make work arrangements based on sole individual judgement without reference to higher authorities; to exhibit absolute, professional or technical expertise and judgement;

(c) secretaries, personal assistants and personal departments: normally integral to the nature of the work, they also constitute a trapping insofar as they are an outward representation to the rest of the organisation of the value and importance of the individual's work;

(d) accessibility: in many organisations, the inability to get to see someone, either because of their rank or because of their workload, constitutes a mark of achievement (often perverse).

The problems associated with these do not lie in their validity. This is not an issue since they are based on perceptions, expectations, the wider situation and the individual drives that accumulate from the achievement and possession of these. Instead, they indicate the organisation's capacity to recognise the extent to which its employees need and want them, and its ability to satisfy them in these ways.

■ The Hawthorne Studies

The Hawthorne Studies were carried out between 1924 and 1932. They took their name from the Hawthorne Works of the Western Electrical Company at Chicago where the research was conducted. The original objective was to ascertain the relationships between the physical working environment and operational productivity. However, the main findings were in terms of the social environment of work: membership of groups, both formal and informal; relationships between workers and supervision; relationships between workers and organisation; and the degree of attention and interest shown by the organisation to its staff.

The work was carried out by George Elton Mayo (1880–1949), an Australian academic. He was Professor of Industrial Research at Harvard Business School, and an authority on industrial fatigue, labour turnover and accidents, and health and safety. He was called in by the Western Electrical Company to advise on the results of a study that had already been carried out by the company into the effects of lighting on productive output and staff morale. One group – the core group – had the lighting levels in which it had to work varied; the other – the control group – had constant lighting levels. The output of both groups rose consistently over the period of the experiment (1924–7). The output of the core group rose whether the lighting levels were increased or diminished. The output of the control group, where the lighting levels remained constant, also rose.

Four aspects were addressed: employee attitudes; group attitudes; personal factors; and physical conditions. The findings were as follows.

❐ Employee attitudes

Employee attitudes overall were formed on the basis of an assessment of relative satisfaction and dissatisfaction of work, and this, in turn, was based on:

- social organisation of the company, both formal and informal, including the formation and membership of cliques and other groups;
- organisational policies and directives;
- the position, work content and status of the individual;
- outside demands and commitments placed on employees.

❐ Group attitudes

These can be summarised as follows:

- the need to be part of the work group is very strong;
- the pressures to conform to the norms and standards of the group (as distinct from those of the organisation) are very strong;
- attitudes are shaped and influenced by the group, both between members and also in relation to the work;
- these pressures and needs are strong motivators, especially in the ways of working and its organisation (the individual is more responsive to peer pressure than organisational and managerial incentives and exhortations).

❐ Personal attitudes

Various forms of motivation were found to be significant, including:

- to seek out particular types of work, the determination to follow a particular career, to work in particular sectors, occupations, trades, professions and crafts;
- to apply for specific jobs, with specific employers, to complete the application process and to subject oneself to the recruitment and selection processes;
- to accept job offers, to accept the salary/occupation/prospects mixes of particular organisations;
- to turn up for work on the first day;
- to turn up for work on the second day and to continue turning up on a daily basis; and to start and continue to produce effective and successful work on behalf of the organisation.

❐ Physical conditions

The response to the physical conditions was much more complex. Whenever the lighting levels were adjusted, productivity went up. This was also the case when other changes were made, including the introduction and withdrawal of breaks (productivity even rose when breaks were withdrawn by the experimenters). In one particular case, the conclusion was drawn that those involved were responding to special treatment. They were the centre of attention; they had a good relationship with the researchers; and, by being placed in separate accommodation, they felt special and distinctive, with consequent increases in morale and self-worth. So long as they understood the changes in the physical conditions, they were happy.

Beyond this, the experimenters found that people working in any situation tended to operate in ways that were both comfortable as well as productive.

*   *   *

Both from the findings of the Hawthorne experiments, and also in relation to wider studies of motivation, there are lessons to be drawn which have direct applications for the effective management of people.

■ Job and work design

When considering job and work design from the point of view of human behaviour and motivation, it is essential to try to reconcile the organisation's often conflicting operational, technical and professional requirements into sets of activities (jobs and occupations) that are effective, productive and satisfying, both from an occupational and a personal point of view (see Figure 5.5).

This may be reinforced by the use of job titles, which may be either demeaning and dissatisfying, or else a reflection of status or expertise. It is a key organisational responsibility to address the issues – both positive and also negative – that these matters raise.

It is then necessary to empathise: if those responsible for the design and ordering of work know themselves that what is proposed will be repetitive, boring and dissatisfying, then the likely output is loss of morale.

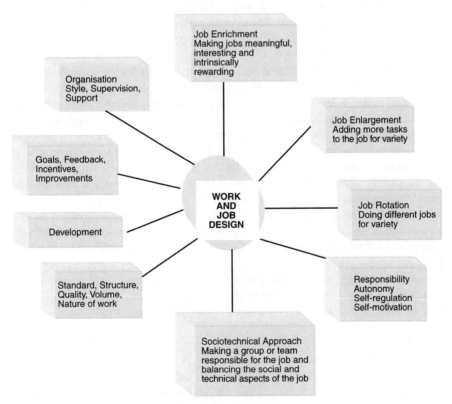

Figure 5.5   Job design

It is within this context that job enrichment, job rotation, job enlargement and empowerment activities are to be considered. If carried out effectively, motivation and commitment can be generated in any staff or occupational group, whatever the working situation and provided that the behavioural satisfaction aspect is also addressed. It should be noted that the converse is also true: where jobs and occupations are not effective, productive and satisfying, demotivation and demoralisation occurs whatever the interests inherent in the particular profession may be.

The other prerequisite for effective job and work design is the existence of effective channels of communication, and the presence of constant feedback giving absolute knowledge of results. The outcome of this is a clarity of purpose both of the occupation in question, and also of the context in which it is carried out.

■ Rewards

Rewards are a major means by which organisations set and maintain their standards of activity attitude and behaviour. It is important to establish what they are given for. This covers the area of achievement, success, loyalty and conformity, and relates both to individual and team performance.

Each organisation sets its own reward mix within these broad boundaries. The relationship between motivation, effort and reward from the organisation's point of view is thus clearly indicated. Those working there are shown the pathways to achievement in the particular situation. The opportunity is afforded either to accept or reject these pathways.

Demotivation and disaffection occur when the pathways are not clearly indicated or if the achievements at their end are not then duly rewarded. This also happens in individual cases where people have been taken on by the organisation or given tasks to do within it on the basis of misunderstandings of what was expected or what the rewards were to be. It is essential to be clear about this. There is no point, for example, in recruiting or retaining task-oriented staff in situations where rewards are for loyalty and time service (or vice versa). Where specific achievements are required, these must be stated in clear and unambiguous terms and rewarded accordingly.

The converse of this is the requirement for a clear understanding of the aspirations of the particular staff employed. It is no use offering rewards for achievement if the staff concerned value continuity and longevity with rewards based on loyalty, and vice versa.

A reward must be issued if the person or team concerned has fulfilled all the requirements necessary to achieve it. The reward should be issued promptly and with gladness and satisfaction on the part of the organisation to its staff.

❒ Financial rewards

Money – in the form of wage and salary – is the reward for performance, especially (and ideally) effective and successful performance. Wages and salaries are paid by organisations to individuals to reward them for bringing their expertise into the situation and for their efforts. The payment made must therefore reflect:

- the level of expertise brought by the individual and the ways in which he has been required to apply it;
- the quality and intensity of effort;
- the effectiveness of individual performance, and the effectiveness of overall performance;
- the value that the organisation places on the presence of the particular expertise;
- the value placed by the individual on his expertise;
- the expectations of the individual for particular levels of reward;
- the anticipation of continuity and improvement in reward levels.

These must then be set in a wider context.

Herzberg makes the point that money is of limited value as a motivator even where pay levels are good, but that it is very demotivating when pay levels are bad and do not meet expectations.

■ Perceptions

There is a strongly perceived relationship between pay and job importance. A Chief Executive who takes an annual salary of £20 000 will be widely considered not to have a great deal of responsibility or authority. A marketing officer on £80 000 a year will be generally perceived to have a responsible and high-powered job. This also extends to the individual: if people perceive themselves to be on 'only £x' it affects their self-esteem and self-worth because it is a statement of limited value. The converse is also true: where people can state that they are on 'good money' this underlines feelings of high value.

■ Continuity

In conditions of relative stability and permanence, people are more disposed to accept or trade off between current levels of reward and the certainty of continuity. In the UK, over the period from 1945 until the late 1970s, this was virtually explicit in many organisations; while at no stage would reward levels be particularly high, they would be steady, would gradually improve, and would last an entire working life and beyond by paying a retirement pension.

In times of turbulence and uncertainty the drive is for higher immediate rewards, part of which is a hedge against the vagaries of the long-term future.

■ Economic rent

This is the term used to describe the necessity to pay particular rates (usually high) for scarce skills, knowledge and expertise. It is further enhanced where the particular expertise is required at short notice, possibly involving a consultancy or subcontract arrangement.

■ Value

Given that people are employed on the basis that there is work required of them, and that they are therefore of value, pay levels and methods should reflect this.

These levels should be as high as possible as a part of maximising the long-term confidence and quality of relationship. Organisations may also legitimately take the view of 'high wages for high levels of commitment and hard work' when pay levels are raised.

The levels of pay and value also quite legitimately indicate expectation levels. The higher the level of pay, the greater the levels of expectation placed on the employee, and the more disposed the employee is to accept these raised levels of expectation.

■ Comparisons

Ultimately pay comparisons between different jobs in different organisations are spurious. However, they have a very strong psychological drive. If one person is receiving a particular salary for carrying out a given job, and then finds out that 'the same job' in the neighbouring firm carries a salary of double what she receives, she will become dissatisfied and frustrated.

■ The going rate

This occurs where the problem of comparison is overcome by setting local, regional and national rates for the same (or very similar) generic occupations. It applies especially to public professions (for example, teaching, nursing and social work); while the job content and application of expertise may vary widely between establishments, the job output and expertise required are very much the same.

This also applies to pay rises. If one sector or occupation gets a rise of 5 per cent, for example, then those in others that get only 4 per cent will tend to feel slighted, while those who get 6 per cent will tend to feel that they have done rather well. Percentage rises in general also underline the value – or lack of value – placed on categories of staff. A low percentage therefore tends to give feelings of being under-valued or unvalued, even where the percentage may be known to reflect a low rise in the cost of living and seek only to compensate for this.

■ Equity and equality

The converse of comparisons is the application of principles of equity and equality within and across organisations. The term 'equal pay, for equal work, of equal value' is widely used and is a legal (as well as moral) obligation in the UK.

Problems arise when a particular expertise is only available on terms that will break the principle. Some organisations, including some that are very successful and effective, will break their salary and reward structures if they find their need for the individual and his qualities over-rides other considerations.

More generally, the presence or absence of equality and equity in rewards is indicative of the general relationship between the organisation and its employees. Where there is little or no equality, this always means that different levels of value are placed on categories of employees for whatever reason.

■ Expectations and obligations

Problems are greatly reduced in the money area where expectations and obligations are clearly set out, understood and accepted by both organisation and individual at the outset (see Figure 5.6). Problems occur where the individual has not understood the nature of effort required to achieve rewards; and where the organisation has not made clear (either through ignorance, accident or deliberately) the levels of effort and commitment that it requires.

People in particular organisations have expectations of payment methods. For example, the salesperson may expect all or part of her reward to be in the form of bonus or commission because this has worked well for her in the past. She therefore perceives herself to be able to earn much more through this means than through a simple salary and to control her own earnings level. Operative and clerical staff may expect part of their work to be paid as overtime; this is again perceived to enhance the ability to earn and also underlines the intrinsic feeling of value based on 'You are so important to us, you must stay and work, we cannot possibly allow you to go home yet – and we will pay you extra.' Problems occur in these areas when the facility is introduced, institutionalised, becomes expected and is then withdrawn.

■ Frustration

Frustration occurs when the relationship between expectation, effort and reward is skewed for reasons outside the individual's control. It is caused by a range of factors.

1 The removal of anticipated rewards during the effort phase. For example, an individual may pursue qualifications in the expectation, anticipation – even near certainty – that he will receive job promotion, enhancement and opportunities when he has finished his course. Towards the end of the course, if the organisation is taken over, or moves into new fields, or if the individual's superior changes jobs, the reward disappears.
2 The cancellation of anticipated rewards through arbitrary (or even rational) action by the organisation. To take a similar example, the achievement of qualifications may have led in the past to pay rises, but then there is a change of policy during the course of the individual's studies and the rewards are now no longer available.
3 When promised or indicated opportunities for training and development do not materialise for whatever reason.
4 When the intrinsic satisfactions afforded by the job do not meet the wider needs (especially esteem and economic) of the individual. This has occurred in recent years in the UK with public services and occupations, such as teaching, nursing and social work.

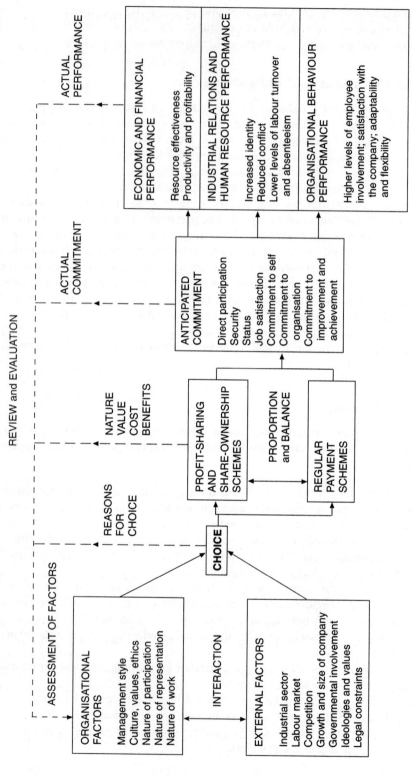

REVIEW and EVALUATION

ASSESSMENT OF FACTORS

REASONS FOR CHOICE

NATURE VALUE COST BENEFITS

ACTUAL COMMITMENT

ACTUAL PERFORMANCE

ORGANISATIONAL FACTORS

Management style
Culture, values, ethics
Nature of participation
Nature of representation
Nature of work

INTERACTION

EXTERNAL FACTORS

Industrial sector
Labour market
Competition
Growth and size of company
Governmental involvement
Ideologies and values
Legal constraints

CHOICE

PROFIT-SHARING AND SHARE-OWNERSHIP SCHEMES

PROPORTION and BALANCE

REGULAR PAYMENT SCHEMES

ANTICIPATED COMMITMENT

Direct participation
Security
Status
Job satisfaction
Commitment to self
Commitment to organisation
Commitment to improvement and achievement

ECONOMIC AND FINANCIAL PERFORMANCE

Resource effectiveness
Productivity and profitability

INDUSTRIAL RELATIONS AND HUMAN RESOURCE PERFORMANCE

Increased identity
Reduced conflict
Lower levels of labour turnover and absenteeism

ORGANISATIONAL BEHAVIOUR PERFORMANCE

Higher levels of employee involvement; satisfaction with the company; adaptability and flexibility

Figure 5.6 The relationship between pay and performance

5 When the nature of opportunities afforded and anticipated do not match up, based on misperceptions on either part.
6 When the individual knows or strongly believes that she is not being offered the opportunities that her talents and qualities merit; this occurs especially when the individual feels that this is as the result of the perceptions of her superior.
7 Where opportunities are simply not available, causing individuals to have to look elsewhere for their future prospects.
8 Restriction of the capability to act by rules, regulations and procedures.

5.3 Pay and motivation as a process

Each element and factor indicated contributes to the pay and reward process. By the very nature of the continuity of the wage work bargain, this in itself is a continuous process, and as such it requires constant attention and maintenance. If this is not done, people perceive that they are being taken for granted and, if this persists, it leads to feelings of being neglected. The process is therefore maintained in ways equivalent to anything else.

1 With regularity, consisting of regular and frequent reviews; stated occasions for rises; stated levels or criteria for rises and improvements; and ensuring that these are paid in full on the required dates.
2 Rewarding enhanced performance, either because people have developed and enhanced their skills, knowledge and expertise and therefore their value to the organisation; or because the organisation has had a successful, effective and profitable year. In the latter case especially, there is a current consensus that the staff of organisations should receive their fair share of the rewards that have been generated by their efforts. This applies equally to the best public services and not-for-profit activities, rewarding staff from the proceeds of enhanced effectiveness of performance (for example, the enlargement of jobs or workload that enables the organisation to reduce staff levels), or from other efficiencies and savings (for example, in premises charges or through the simplification of procedures).
3 Issuing regular symbols of value. Part of this includes praise and recognition. Genuine recognition is enhanced through the use of small, creative, varied and frequent rewards issued to everyone regardless of rank, status or occupation, and based on the total contribution of everyone to organisational performance.
4 Ensuring that pay levels are kept up to the organisation's own absolute standards and taking remedial action where this has been allowed to slip as soon as possible. Further, it may have been necessary in the past to reduce or depress pay levels for reasons of organisation performance; when things get back on track, the staff should be rewarded for their loyalty and commitment over the difficult period.
5 Never losing sight of the absolute value of the staff to the organisation and their need to be valued, of which one of the main manifestations is the nature and level of financial reward over the long-term.

This constitutes a basis of the relationship between motivation and money (see also Table 5.1). Some general points should now be made. Monetary reward does not make a job more satisfying or interesting except in the very short term though it may, and does, lead to high levels of commitment (again, especially over the short term) if the individual has an over-riding need to earn. Moreover, lack of adequate financial reward for a job that is otherwise very satisfying leads to frustration and stress and the individual struggles to reconcile the conflicting pressures of loving the job but not being able to afford to stay in it.

■ Attendance and other bonuses and allowances

These have been used in many forms and in a variety of situations over the years. At their best, they reward (or give the perception of rewarding) special efforts and commitments such as working at night, at weekends and over bank and public holidays and away from home.

In many cases, however, they simply demonstrate the limitations of this approach, and the consequent limitation of money as a motivator if other types of reward and achievement are not present.

1 The bank room wiring operations group at the Hawthorne Works actively conspired against their organisation's bonus system because they perceived that it would be changed to their disadvantage if they demonstrated the full capacity to which they could work.

Table 5.1 Payment methods, incentives and motivation

Method	Aspects of motivation
Weekly cash wages	Meets traditions and expectations of industrial and also commercial sectors and other parts of society.
Monthly salary into bank account	May be status attached to being 'salaried'.
Time rate	Encourages attendance for particular periods; over-time may be desired and available outside set times.
Piece rates	Encourages production volume (and possibly also quality and deadline achievement).
Flexitime	Encourages attendance, especially where there is the opportunity for over-time or time off once sufficient time has been accrued.
Commission, bonuses	Relates performance output to payment level.
Profit-related pay	Relates to organisation performance and payment levels; difficulties lie where profit levels are outside the control of the staff.
Performance-related pay and merit pay	Relates own performance with payment levels; difficulties lie with setting, assessing and validating performance objectives and targets, especially in unquantifiable areas.

2   In the 1970s, the UK National Coal Board went through a phase of offering 50 per cent of attendance pay to the miners if they turned up for four days. The other 50 per cent would be payable only if the staff attended on the fifth day. It had no effect on attendance patterns. This approach was copied by the Rootes/Chrysler and British Leyland car manufacturing companies, and also had no effect.

3   In the 1980s and 1990s, the Allied Irish Bank gave an additional week's holiday to every member of staff who took no time off for sickness during the previous year. Once people had had a day's sickness, they therefore would tend to take at least another five working days to ensure that they did not miss out anyway.

4   In the 1970s and 1980s, the Batchelor's Food Company undertook a policy which stated that anyone who was more than 10 minutes late for work would lose half a day's pay. The result was that anyone who was more than 10 minutes late – whether at the start of the day or returning after lunch – would simply take the rest of the period off.

■ Profit-related pay

The purpose of relating pay to profit is part of the process of targeting the reward package and also the motivation and commitment effort. By combining the two elements, the line of reasoning is that all staff are both focused on the purposes for which they are supposed to be working and assume a positive stake in its commercial success.

Profit-related elements come in two main forms. The simplest of these is to allocate a percentage, or proportion, or amount from the surplus generated by the organisation, and to share this out. For maximum equality, this will be as a percentage of salary to everyone. The other approach is to offer shares and equity in the organisation; the employees therefore become investors in their own future.

The relationship between profit, ownership, commitment and pay is a constant theme of the Excellence Studies. In the UK, the Bell–Hanson Report of 1989, researching 113 publicly quoted companies, found that profit-share companies out-performed others by an average of 27 per cent on returns on capital, earnings per share and profit and sales growth.

For best results, the scheme must be believed in, valued and understood by all concerned. The overall purpose of profit-related pay is to reward effort and achievement on the part of the staff. Staff must also clearly understand that this payment will be forthcoming if the organisation has a good year; and that it will not be forthcoming if for any reason the organisation has difficulties or does not make profits.

Above all, profit-related pay is never to be used as a means of cutting wage and salary bills. Its purpose is to target these and to reward efforts and not to penalise them. Its general effect is to put up wage and salary bills and, as stated in the text above, this both raises the expectations of the individuals concerned and is a quite legitimate means by which the organisation can raise its expectations of the individuals.

5.4 Conclusions

The standpoint taken is that people work better when highly motivated and when there is a direct relationship between quality of performance and levels of motivation, and that volume and quality of work declines when the motivation is lower or when demotivation is present. The need to motivate and be motivated is continuous and constant. Some specific conclusions may be drawn.

1 Motivation comes partly from within the individual and partly from the particular situation. It is therefore both constant and also subject to continuous adaptation.
2 Value, esteem and respect are basic human requirements extending to all places of work and all occupations (and indeed, to every walk of life). The key features of this are the integrity of relationships, levels of knowledge and understanding, general prevailing attitudes (whether positive or negative) and the nature of rewards, including pay.
3 All people have expectations based on their understanding of particular situations, and they will be drawn to, or driven from, these in anticipation of rewards and outcomes.
4 People respond positively to equality and fairness of treatment, and negatively when these are not present.
5 People respond positively to variety, development and opportunities when they know or perceive it to be in their interests to do so. They are less likely to respond to genuine opportunities if they do not understand or perceive them as such.
6 People respond positively when they know the attitudes, behaviour, values and ways of work required; and negatively or less favourably when these are not apparent or not strong.
7 People need constant attention to their individual wants and needs and will seek this from many sources, including work. If the work is demotivating, they will seek it elsewhere.
8 The key to positive motivation is the establishment of a high level of mutual trust, commitment and responsibility. The main obligation here lies with the organisation. Individuals may be expected to respond positively when these are present. They may not be expected from individuals when the organisation is itself uncommitted to this, or where it takes an expedient, confrontational and adversarial view of its staff.

⬛ M̌ 6 Personality and roles

6.1 Introduction

Individual personality may be defined as 'the total pattern of traits and characteristics, of thoughts, emotions, attitudes, values, behaviour and beliefs, and attributes and qualities, and their interactions'. Since the strength, presence and interaction of these varies between individuals, each individual is unique. The concept of personality also embraces perception, motivation, aspiration, learning and development. It is therefore necessary to recognise at the outset that human personality is highly complex and that steps must be taken by organisations to understand these characteristics, interactions and complexities exhibited by their people (and those who are potentially their people) if an effective working relationship is to be produced. Some useful distinctions may be made at the outset.

6.2 Personality

■ Traits and characteristics

From an organisational behaviour point of view, the purpose is to identify those necessary to produce effective activity and harmony of relationship and to seek these among the individuals who come (or who would like to come) and work. The important traits are therefore those that are:

- strong, dominant and frequently exhibited;
- weak and less frequently exhibited;
- over-riding, often based on emotional response to particular situations (for example, aggression, shyness, anger, temperament);
- positive/negative, often related to general disposition, attitude to work, approach to problems.

■ Qualities, talents and attributes

These are the physical and mental capabilities of the individual. All people bring some of their capabilities into all situations. It is the relationship between those that are demanded in the given situation in relation to the range offered by the individual that is important here. For example, a qualified airline pilot who can also cook and make tea and coffee is clearly qualified to be a catering assistant, but whether he would want to be would need careful consideration on the part of both the individual and also any organisation which might be thinking of offering him a job as a catering assistant.

❒ Identification of qualities, talents and attributes by organisation

This is the basis on which personal specifications are drawn up. It is the identification of qualities, talents and attributes that are deemed necessary to carry out particular sets of activities effectively. This then becomes the basis on which job selection is based.

The process is most likely to be successful when those qualities, talents and attributes are easily observable and identifiable, and can proven or tested. It is less likely to be successful if they have to be inferred or based on a short conversation or part of an interview.

■ The desire for achievement

Desire for achievement is a basic human drive in most societies. The problem lies in the definition of achievement which means something different to each individual: for example, money, status, power, helping others, a large house, invention and creativity, excellence in a chosen field (social or occupational). For organisations, the problem lies in what they mean by achievement, where the contribution of individuals to that lies and in attracting the right types of individual to ensure that this happens.

Individual desire for achievement is based on:

- economic pressures, the need to support a continuity and quality of life;
- social pressures, exerted by peers, friends, family and relations;
- esteem and value, what the individual regards as important, and what   as important by others;
- status afforded by both self and others to particular achievements;
- association with particular organisations, groups, expertise and activities;
- individual pressures, and the need to live up to (or down to) particular expectations from different parts of society.

The desire for achievement in work situations is based on:

- the nature of the work itself, variety, routines, technical expertise;
- the value of the work to self, the organisation, peers, customers, clients and the community;
- the relative need for development, new opportunities and horizons;
- the need of the individual to demonstrate a range of abilities and qualities;
- the need to be seen as excellent, to be highly thought of in a range of areas;
- the need to complete that which has been commenced (dislike of leaving things unfinished);
- the need for working relationships to be operationally productive and effective as well as friendly;
- time, the need to get things done as quickly as possible, to avoid things being dragged out.

In general, the higher the desire for work achievement, the more likely it is that the individual will use those items in the second list to meet the pressures indicated in the first.

The lower the desire for achievement at work, the greater the likelihood that the individual is concerned with security, status, the regard and esteem in which she is held by others, social pressures and the pressures of association. Her desire for achievement is based on her own preoccupations and feelings and the presentation of herself to the rest of the world.

6.3 Roles

In simple terms roles are combinations of behaviour and activities that are undertaken by individuals in given situations (see Figure 6.1). This is, in turn, set against a backcloth of the variety of expectations that go with each role. The source of these expectations is overwhelmingly a product of the particular community and society in which the individual lives and works.

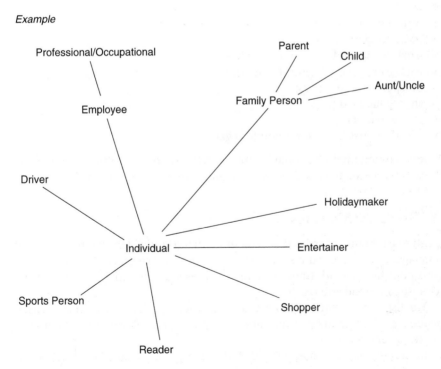

Example

Each role has expectations, pressures, rewards and consequences. There are overlaps between each and measures of honesty, discord and conflict.

Figure 6.1   Individual roles

■ Role sets

People have a great range and variety of roles. Some of these are dominant, some subordinate. Some of these are constant; some are continuous; some are intermittent; some are short term, others long term. The total number of roles adopted by the individual constitutes the role set.

It is useful to compartmentalise roles in this way in order to establish a basis for the understanding of the ways in which people behave in the different situations indicated. Often this behaviour is contradictory – the bullying manager, for example, may also be a loving parent – and it is necessary to be able to understand and explain the reasons (or a set of reasons) for this.

The role is therefore a combination of:

- who you are;
- what you know; what you don't know
- what you can do; what you can't do
- what you want to do; what you don't want to do
- what is important and of value to you;
- economic factors;
- social factors;
- who you work for;
- who works for you;
- who you associate with;
- who associates with you;
- what is expected of you and by whom;
- what you expect of yourself and why;
- prospects and progress;
- situational factors;
- ethical factors;
- specific constraints (for example, legal).

Roles differentiate between people, activities, social segments and sectors. Roles vary between work, family, social and community situations.

■ Roles within roles

Each role identified carries the elements with it. Handy identifies the roles of the manager as being executive, planner, policy maker, expert, controller of rewards and punishments, arbitrator, exemplar, representative of the group, scapegoat, counsellor, friend and teacher.

The list may be extended to include: guardian, teacher, disciplinarian, friend, leader, cook, first-aider, arbitrator, exemplar, general resource, fountain of authority and wisdom.

In some case this may also include: energiser, personality, teacher, idol, advertisement, star, friend and fashion-setter.

The same breakdown can be carried out on all main roles.

■ Role clarification

Roles may usefully be clarified under the following headings.

❑ General categories

There can be broken down into the following type:

- **family:** mother, father, son, daughter, uncle, aunt, grandparent, niece, nephew, cousin, taxi, cook, teenager, child, consumer, customer, servant, adult;
- **work:** defined by job title, profession, training, location, hours of work, freedom or otherwise to operate (autonomy/direction, creativity/regimentation);
- **social:** neighbour, friend, sportsman/sportswoman, gardener, dog walker, taxi (again), organiser, servant, consumer;
- **community:** American, Japanese, school governor, customer, pillar of community, councillor, elder, organiser;
- **formal:** by any of the titles indicated above;
- **informal:** on an *ad hoc* basis and normally behavioural in orientation.

❑ Behavioural aspects

Workplace examples of these are as follows.

1 **The bully:** either physical or psychological; with particular categories of staff (especially junior); threatening and menacing; abusive and harassing.
2 **The braggart:** normally a self-publicist; if boasting on the organisation's behalf braggarts normally put themselves in the spotlight also.
3 **The barrack room lawyer:** leader of the informal organisation and sometimes also an influential figure in the formal, especially if the management involved is weak or insecure.
4 **The clown or comedian:** a useful safety valve for the group in which they exist. Clowns attract attention and stories about themselves. The role may be hard to shake off. Clowns are often regarded both as irritant by the organisation and with measures of envy and jealousy.
5 **The devil's advocate:** questions and queries everything and is constantly looking for flaws; it is a useful, valuable, even essential role; it is also a major irritant to top managers and those trying to get pet schemes and projects off the ground.
6 **The film star:** looks, acts, sounds, plays the part; is always immaculately dressed; has all the relevant trappings; problems arise only when asked to be the part.
7 **The eccentric:** eccentrics are accommodated because of qualities and expertise that they also bring; eccentricity is also the means by which a reputation or distinction may be achieved (provided that it is at least perceived to be attached also to results); it is rationalised as being colourful or larger than life.

8 **Scoutmaster/scoutmistress:** develops the next generation of talent for the organisation; is accommodated as long as this does not threaten the current equilibrium, *modus operandi* or vested interest.

9 **The advocate/lobbyist:** a chaser of causes, some lost and others not; may also be a whiner and whinger; has strong moral and ethical principles, often at variance with those of the organisation.

10 **The peacemaker:** has a rich supply of oil to pour on troubled waters and consequently often adds pollution to the problems that already exist. The worst form of this is the person who sees no evil, hears no evil and speaks no evil.

11 **The scapegoat:** attracts blame for everything that goes wrong in the given situation; may go out of his way to do this in order to gain identity (however corrupted or toxic this may be).

❐ Trappings and signs

1 **Dress:** designer labels; colour coordinates; prestige labels (for example, Armani and Gucci); fashion labels (for example, Rebok, Nike); dress imitation (of the top management, for example); cheap and expensive, special clothing (for example, tuxedo).

2 **Possessions:** make, model and year of car; domestic hardware and technology; may also include spouse, children, mistress, lover, friends and associates.

3 **Fashions and fads:** appearance; self-presentation; job title; also includes dress and possessions and may also include spouse, children, mistress, lover; belonging to the right clubs and associations and groups; taking part in the right activities.

4 **Technology:** car again; hobbies and interests, make and model of kitchen appliances, television, audio and video, home computer.

5 **Titles:** Mr, Mrs, Doctor, Reverend; specific titles such as Your Excellency, Your Grace, Mr President; organisational/functional titles such as Chief Executive, Assistant Manager, Sales Person; professional titles such as Doctor, Surgeon, Actor, Musician.

The elements of title, behaviour and trappings thus combine to indicate the particular role set. They also give off particular perceptions and expectations to those with whom they interact. This is also a part of the wider perceptual process.

Above all, however, it indicates the complexities, issues, inconsistencies and uncertainties that are key and continuous features of human behaviour (and therefore clearly of organisation behaviour).

■ Role uncertainties and ambiguities

These arise when there is a lack of clarity as to the precise nature of the role or roles at any given point. They relate to:

• uncertainty about aims and objectives, resulting in uncertainty/lack of clarity as to what constitutes successful and effective performance;

• uncertainty about job/task/occupational boundaries in terms of extent, range and depth of coverage, quality of performance (especially where this is not easily or precisely measured);

- uncertainty about the nature of commitment expected/anticipated/required, including areas of responsibility, authority and accountability;
- uncertainty of expectations arising from misconceptions at the outset; expectations placed on the role by the individual which are not met in the ways anticipated; expectations of others;
- uncertainty concerning relationships within the group, between groups and across the whole organisation;
- uncertainty as regards prospects, development, enhancement and advancement;
- uncertainty about stability, continuity and confidence.

Each contributes to a lack of clarity of relationship and expectations, and is a source of potential stress and conflict. They may also give rise to clashes, anger, lack of confidence and respect.

■ Incompatibility

Incompatibility arises when an individual is unable to carry out the role. This is normally either because she lacks the capability or because she is unable to perform it in the ways required.

The first is exemplified by the 'Peter Principle' – promotion to the level of incompetence – whereby someone is given a job or task for which he has no aptitude or capability.

The second is to be found, for example, where a supervisor is required by her superior to run a highly structured operation and where the staff prefer (and are used to) a more relaxed and less formal style.

Incompatibility is also to be found where values and beliefs are called into question. A supervisor may be required to discipline or dismiss a member of staff and find himself unable to do so because he believes it to be wrong. If the rest of the group also believe that it is wrong, this will adversely (possibly fatally) affect the supervisor's future relationships with the other group members.

■ Overload

This occurs where the individual is required to take on:

- too much work, too many tasks;
- too much responsibility, authority and accountability;
- too much pressure, stress and strain;
- incompatibility, as above.

The result is that all of the work is unsatisfactory; or that some of the work is effective at the expense of the rest; or that some aspects are not covered at all.

Overload can only be sustained in the short to medium term (while the organisation is getting through a crisis, for example). Continued overload normally leads to loss of performance, loss of achievement, and damage to the health of the individual.

■ Underload

Underload occurs where there is not enough in the role to keep the individual happy and satisfied. This is normally related to feelings of:

- under-value, including where the individual feels that she is being under-paid and under-rewarded, and also where her contribution is not being fully recognised;
- under-performance, where the individual feels that could be going on to better and higher things;
- not being needed, a lack of confidence in the quality, worth and contribution of the work itself;
- lack of feeling on the part of the organisation for the well-being of the staff, or on the part of superiors for subordinates;
- loss of self-respect, self-esteem and the esteem and regard of others;
- external and internal pressure, a consciousness on the part of the individual that she is capable of doing far better and of achieving much more (this is compounded when peers, friends, family and acquaintances all believe the same thing).

This may clearly have nothing to do with absolute volumes of work. Indeed, it is most likely to hinge on the individual's perceptions of their own capabilities and potential. People are much more likely to put up with something that does not meet their expectations if they feel that it is a means to an end, a stepping stone on the path of progress. Frustration sets in where these prospects are not present or not apparent.

■ Stresses and strains

Stresses and strains become apparent where the problems caused by ambiguity, uncertainty, overload and underload become irreconcilable (see Figure 6.2). The symptoms are:

- poor communications, in terms of both volume and quality, lack of accessibility and visibility;
- over-attention to trivia and detail at the expense of the broader picture, aims and objectives;
- over-attention to and over-use of procedures and rules at the expense of issue resolution and problem solving;
- polarisation of approach (everything is either very good or very bad);
- poor interpersonal relationships, the presence of tension, friction and irritability;
- withdrawal, including absenteeism and sickness;
- the presence of blame, the search for scapegoats;
- loss of volume and quality of performance.

If allowed to go unchecked, the effects of stress and strain invariably include loss of general performance, motivation and morale, and the decline of general working relationships. Individuals within the department withdraw themselves,

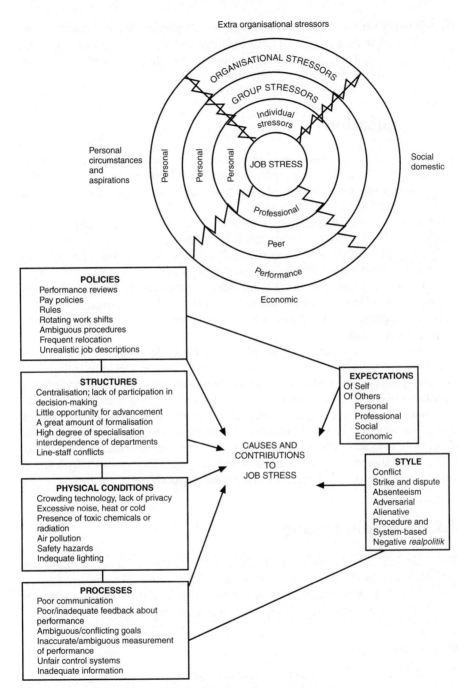

Figure 6.2 Stress: sources, causes, symptoms

seeking to ensure that they carry out their tasks satisfactorily; at the same time, they will tend to seek opportunities elsewhere to remove themselves from the current situation. They pursue their own objectives at the expense of, rather than in harmony with, those of the organisation.

6.4 Application

Interaction with and between individuals is a continuous feature of all organisations. The main lesson, therefore, lies in understanding the complexities of the perception, personality and roles that individuals bring with them to all situations and the pressures that arise.

Recognition of this means that organisations can then establish the key characteristics and traits that are required, rather than trying and invariably failing to cope with the whole individual. For this to be successful, information must be gathered systematically to ensure that as wide and complete a picture is built up about and around the individual in relation to the organisation's requirements of them. This is also the context for effective work design and division; creation of structures and cultures; and organisational progress, development and change.

In turn, the effectiveness of all of this is dependent upon the nature of individuals brought into the organisation in the first place. The onus is therefore on making the recruitment and selection activities as accurate and informative as possible. This is to ensure as effective and harmonious a match as possible between individual and organisation. This is the context in which all recruitment and selection activities should be seen. The purpose is to find someone who can do the job, who will fit into the organisation (both the particular niche and the wider internal environment) and who brings potential for the future. This is the basis of an effective, continuous and harmonious working relationship.

6.5 Selection testing

The main purpose of selection is therefore to be as clear as possible about the individual's main characteristics, aptitudes and capabilities. The best way to do this is to isolate those required by the organisation and then set up a series of tests that indicate the extent of their presence in the particular individuals.

■ Forms of test

These each have their place in particular situations.

1 **Physical:** to indicate strength, fitness, physical durability, robustness, ability to stand extremes of heat and cold.
2 **Intelligence:** to indicate mental agility, mental dexterity and mental awareness.

3 **Verbal reasoning:** to indicate how arguments are presented and developed, how an individual may present or develop a case, sales pitch, negotiating position and so on.
4 **Presentation:** to indicate self-presentation, awareness of audience, use of time, structure and a logical order of material, aims and objectives of a situation.
5 **Numeracy:** to indicate level of understanding and application or numerical forms, skills in adding, subtracting, multiplying and dividing, use of numeracy technology.
6 **Literacy:** to indicate levels of language usage and application, and also particular skills such as spelling and articulation.
7 **Skills:** to indicate levels and quality of skills in, for example, typing, shorthand, engineering, presentation.
8 **Aptitude:** to indicate the relationship between what the individual can do now as a prediction of what she may be able to achieve in the future.
9 **Attainment:** to indicate the depth of knowledge or skill achieved to date in terms of the organisation's current and future requirements.
10 **Pressure:** to indicate how the individual copes, prioritises and carries out work when put under some form of pressure (for example, time, interruptions); these tests may also be developed to indicate how the individual might cope with stress.
11 **Work sampling:** to indicate the range and quality of past activities as an indication of current level of competence.
12 **Personality:** to indicate the personality traits of the individual (such tests are normally carried out through the use of multiple choice questionnaires).

None of these should be seen in isolation from other selection activities (see Table 6.1).

For each of these the word 'indicate' is used. None proves a certainty of performance. A typing test that the individual completes successfully proves that he *can* do it; but it does not prove that he *will* do it in the work situation, and this applies to each form of testing indicated. Those that are less precise in output – intelligence, aptitude, personality – have to be structured further to provide a correlation between:

- the traits and levels identified;
- those that are required;
- why they are required;
- the extent to which past successful holders of the particular job exhibited these;
- the extent to which these were key elements of that success.

They also do not predict or guarantee performance.

Tests are therefore used in combination with other forms of assessment for best effect (see Table 6.1). A small part of the personality and other properties of the individual is opened up by each. The greater the number of openings found, the greater the likelihood of effective assessment.

Table 6.1 Selection methods: summary

Method	Advantages	Disadvantages
Interview	• Opens up human relationships and contact • Enables discussion and questioning • May indicate key strengths/weaknesses	• Halo effects • Stereotyping • Self-fulfilling prophecy • Time constraints • Personal bias
Panel interview	• As above • Brings the views of several to bear	• As above • Different perceptions by panel members • Lack of cohesion • Defending preferred candidates
Handwriting	• None	• Unscientific
References	• A view and perception from independent sources	• May be corrupted • Personal bias • Incomplete • Dwells on past • Useless as predictor of future performance
Supervisory evaluation	• A view and perception from an interested and related party	• Personal bias • Dwells on past
Work sample	• First-hand indication of the achievements and output of the individual to date	• Based on past and current performance
Personal history, CV, application form	• Gives standard and standardised data	• Subject to perception and bias • Dwells on past achievements rather than shortcomings
Testing	• Indicates skills, knowledge, attitude, behaviour and traits • Meets precise aims and objectives	• Needs to be related to future required performance • Aims and objectives of the tests need to be precisely drawn up
Use of agencies	• Cuts down on time spent • Use of agencies' access to candidate fields	• Needs clear understanding of brief
Use of specialist agencies (head hunters)	• Cut down on time spent • Use of specialist knowledge and agencies' access to specialist candidates	• Needs clear understanding of brief

Note: There are time and resource implications (and expense) in pursuing each and all of these effectively. This has to be weighed against the fact that making wrong or ineffective appointments is extremely expensive. Again, none of these predicts performance.

■ Job descriptions

Job descriptions are collections of activities and tasks parcelled up into forms suitable for being carried out by individuals, either in isolation or else in cooperation with others. The best job descriptions indicate the nature and range of work to be carried out while leaving a degree of flexibility to enable organisations to maximise/optimise staff usage and individuals to progress and develop.

■ Person specifications

These are statements of the skills, knowledge, attitudes, behaviour and experience required by the organisation of its staff and potential staff. In general, the fitting the job to the person/fitting the person to the job process indicated in Figure 6.3 matches these qualities with job requirements. The best use of the personnel specification also includes wider indications of qualities and attributes, potential for development, and professional and related interests so that there is an awareness of the general pool of talent which may become valuable at a later date.

■ Measuring attitudes and values

The problem of measuring and assessing the intangible aspects – attitudes, values, commitment and enthusiasm – have never been fully resolved. Each may be observed or inferred over periods of time and in certain situations. Conclusions may be drawn from demeanour, expression and the amount of energy shown.

■ Interviewing

The best approach to interviewing lies in preparing a structure based on the qualities and attributes demanded by the job description and around which the specification has been drawn up. Each individual is interviewed to the same format so that a form of comparison can be made.

A proper framework such as this goes a long way to ensuring that matters of equality of opportunity and other legal constraints are addressed. It also allows for a certain amount of flexibility. It enables the interviewer to ensure that everything of relevance is covered. It also enables time and space to pursue points of contention, points that have not been covered to their satisfaction and to probe on particular matters.

■ Work and aptitude sampling

This is where a candidate is asked to submit a portfolio of work carried out in the recent past or on which they are currently working. This enables the selector to make a first-hand judgement of the standard and quality of work, areas of interest (and possibly also breadth of expertise), and the type of approach taken.

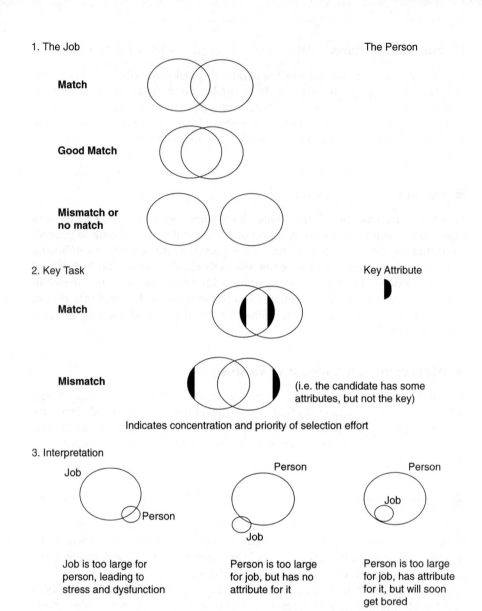

1. The Job   The Person

Match

Good Match

**Mismatch or
no match**

2. Key Task   Key Attribute

Match

Mismatch   (i.e. the candidate has some
                                       attributes, but not the key)

Indicates concentration and priority of selection effort

3. Interpretation

Job   Person   Person   Person
       Person   Job   Job

Job is too large for   Person is too large   Person is too large
person, leading to   for job, but has no   for job, has attribute
stress and dysfunction   attribute for it   for it, but will soon
                                                    get bored

Purpose: indicates requirement to define personal attributes in relation to the job. In all organisations, the process must be **validated:** that is, the relationship between key tasks and key attributes must be related to effective job performance. It must also be **reliable:** that is, any test used to predict performance from the process must demonstrate the quality concerned, and relate it to job performance, in all circumstances and this is very difficult to achieve.

Figure 6.3   Fitting the job to the person: fitting the person to the job

Where required skills are easily tested, a work simulation can also be set up: for example, school teachers may be required to conduct a class under the eye of the assessors, or sales persons may be asked to make a presentation to a customer (either real or simulated).

■ References

References are virtually entirely useless for predicting future attitudes, behaviour and performance. They normally take the form of a short note or telephone conversation centred on impressions, aptitudes and qualities of the candidate. The usual participants are the current and future employer. The current employer will normally not have a full understanding of the future job; the future employer will not normally have a full knowledge of the current job. The result is that any impression formed is then left to the perception of the potential new employer who has only the selection information available on which to match up the reference and to make an informed judgement. References given are nearly always couched in bland tones in order to avoid giving false and misleading impressions. Any negative element must, in any case, be supported by specific information. The whole is limited, either to a single sheet of paper or brief conversation.

Some useful general points should also be made:

- excellence of past performance does not prove excellence of future performance;
- excellence of past relationships does not prove excellence of future relationships;
- unsatisfactory past performance does not prove unsatisfactory future performance;
- unsatisfactory current relationships do not prove unsatisfactory future relationships;
- personal dislike of the candidate by the current supervisor does not prove personal dislike of the candidate by the future supervisor;
- personal liking of the candidate by the current supervisor does not prove personal liking of the candidate by the future supervisor;
- current strengths and weaknesses of attitude and commitment do not prove future strengths and weaknesses of attitude and commitment;
- current position in an organisation does not prove adequacy for a future position in a future organisation;

When viewed in this way, most references are little more than a convention. In the UK the only legal requirement is to confirm the dates on which an employee commenced and left employment with a particular organisation. In particular, references taken up about middle-aged employees concerning occupations in the dim and distant past are normally completely worthless.

■ Assessment centres

Effective selection and the basis for the successful role and occupational development is likely to be based on a combination of each of these needs. Tests, questionnaires, interviews and activities are structured:

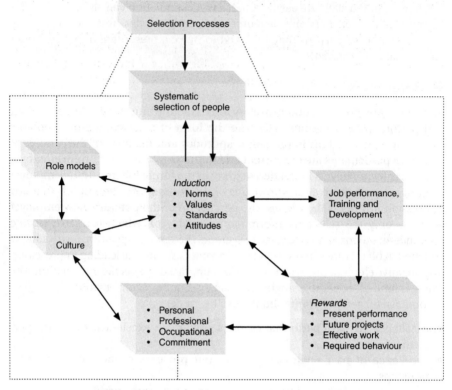

Figure 6.4 Effective individual and role development

- to bring out the skills and qualities required, indicating their presence or absence;
- to identify the required traits and characteristics;
- to provide consistency of assessment.

Initially expensive and time-consuming, the returns are found in the selection of successful and effective staff. Assessment centres are based on sound personnel specifications and the establishment and use of the best means of pinpointing, identifying and, where necessary, observing and inferring the required characteristics.

6.6 Conclusions

The importance for organisations lies in understanding and recognising the concepts of the whole person. This includes the complexities and contradictions of perceptions, roles, attitudes, values, drives and motivations. It includes the pressures of the environment, society, profession and occupation; and also the need to conform and cooperate. It requires attention to specific achievements and learning, development, variety and opportunity. The individual also needs to be valued and to be treated with respect and esteem.

Organisations therefore need to design and structure work, jobs and roles that meet and satisfy as much of this as possible. They must recognise that this is the basis of productive, effective and successful work, of individual and mutual satisfaction in both occupational and personal terms. They must also recognise the fact that problems are likely to arise, and the nature of these when insufficient attention is paid and where there is a lack of full understanding.

Especially, much more attention needs to be paid to selection processes, both for those coming into organisations and for movements within. This means targeting as much as developing the selection process; and this is based on the understanding indicated above, establishing the true nature of the qualities required for successful performance and assessing the extent of these in individuals. Where necessary or desirable, this includes attention to particular attitudes, values and beliefs and to the pressures of the wider environment, as well as distinctive capability and expertise.

▮ ✓ 7 Communication

7.1 Introduction

Effective communication is based on information:

- the volume that is available;
- its quality;
- the means and media by which it is transmitted and received;
- the use to which it is put;
- its integrity;
- the level of integrity of the wider situation.

Communications and information feed the quality of all human relations in organisations. Good communications underline good relations and enhance the general quality of working life, motivation and morale. Bad and inadequate communications lead to frustration, and enhance feelings of alienation and lack of identity and unity.

It is therefore necessary to consider each aspect of the communication process in turn. This is followed by a discussion of the elements that contribute to their quality and effective usage.

7.2 One-way communication

This is where edicts are issued by organisations to their employees, usually without any regard for their effect. This is invariably due to ignorance, and the effect is always dysfunctional. It occurs only in the worst organisations with the most alienated workforce and the most insular management and directorates.

7.3 Two-way communication

This is the dialogue process, the engaging in a communication-and-response process, the results of which are understanding, enlightenment, effective action and progress. It takes place in written and non-verbal, as well as oral, formats and constitutes the relationship between any sender and recipient of a communication.

7.4 Upward and downward communication

■ Upward

The nature, content and volume of upward communication arises from management style. At the extreme, where management is absent or inaccessible, this is limited to formalised channels such as joint consultative committees and joint negotiating committees, and the raising of disputes and grievances. At the opposite end of the scale, where managers and supervisors walk the job and have regular continuous contact with their staff, a greater, more regular and more accurate use for volume and quality of information is gained.

■ Downward

This is the use of communication hierarchies and structures for communication purposes. Information is cascaded down from directors to senior managers, from senior managers to junior managers and then to supervisors and their staff. This is also the means of promulgation of policies and directives, instructions, employee handbooks, rules and regulations, reports, memoranda, newsletters; and the focus of electronic information systems. Use is made of committees, structures and methods.

7.5 Channels of communication

These are as follows.

■ Formal

These are the hierarchies, systems, procedures and committee structures referred to above. This also includes the use and operation of written procedures and policies and the use of electronic systems.

■ Informal

These are the *ad hoc* gatherings that take place between people all the time at every place of work. This includes scribbled notes, post-its, canteen and tea room gatherings. Above all, it includes the organisational grapevine: the things that people gossip and chat about and other general discussion sessions.

■ Consultation

Consultative means of communication are used in the implementation of decisions and policies. The purpose is to ensure that those being consulted understand what is required of them and why, and the opportunities and threats of a particular situation (see Figure 7.1). It is also a reflection of the requirement

MODEL

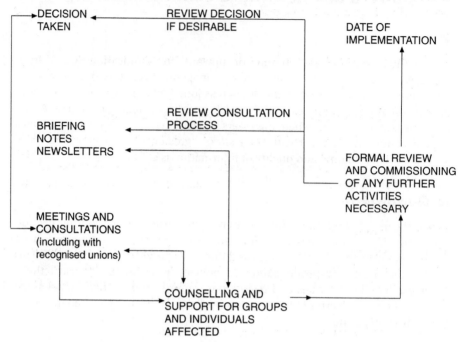

Figure 7.1 Consultation process following a decision

that people have for confidence in those in charge and in the directions that they propose. Effective consultation and the associated processes normally reflect the fact that what is proposed has been well thought out and tested.

Genuine consultation is also the means by which any flaws in decision-making processes or the implementation of particular proposals may nevertheless be raised. However well or thoroughly an issue has been thought through, it must be capable of wide general scrutiny and examination.

Genuine consultation and participation require effective and clear decision-making processes that have both to satisfy the openness and cooperation indicated, but without discussing, stifling and analysing everything to the point of inertia. Effective participation must meet the criteria of both effective communication and effective decision-making.

■ Committees

Committees are constituted for a variety of reasons. From the point of view of communication, the important point is that they should enhance both the quality and value rather than act as a blockage. If this is to happen, the purpose, scheduling of meetings, size, composition, agenda, control and recording must be managed. The ultimate test of the value of any committee is in its output. If this is either not forthcoming or not effective, then alternative means should be found of tackling the issues that the committee or committee system of the organisation is supposed to be facing.

■ Elements necessary for effective communication

These are as follows.

❐ Clarity of purpose on the part of the sender or initiator

This means addressing the questions of what the message is and why it is being sent; the receivers and their likely reactions and responses; the possible range of reactions and responses; what is to be achieved as a result and what the barriers to this achievement might be. This is the basis of 'saying what is meant and meaning what is said'.

❐ Integrity of purpose

This is the relationship between what is said and what is meant. This means using clear, concise and unambiguous terms so that there is no doubt about the impact on the receiver. The message is honest and straightforward, subject to as little interpretation and uncertainty as can be achieved by the sender.

❐ Integrity of parties and relationships involved

The basis of this is the mutual trust and honesty of the particular relationship, as well as the roles, personalities, work relations and context of communication involved.

❐ Use of language and media

The language and media should be those most suited to the receivers. The simpler and more direct the language used, the greater the likelihood that the message will be understood on the part of the receiver. The basic rule is: say what needs to be said; write what needs to be written; reinforce what is spoken with simple and direct written documentation.

❐ Visibility

People respond much more positively if they know who is issuing things. This is better still if they have a general and continuous face-to-face relationship based on mutual respect and understanding. This is much more likely where the particular manager or supervisor manages by walking around and demonstrates an active and positive interest in staff and activities.

❐ Clarity and unity of overall purpose and direction

Clear communications, therefore, tend to reinforce clarity of both overall purposes and subsidiary aims and objectives, and also to concentrate the minds of those responsible for the ordering and direction of the organisation on the fact that overall purposes and secondary aims and objectives should be clear at the outset.

❐ Being positive

A positive approach to communications reinforces general positive attitudes, values and feelings on the part of all concerned. Language and messages should reflect all the associated elements of encouragement, enhancement, enrichment, satisfaction, achievement, fulfilment, potential, creativity, innovation, progress and improvement.

❐ General factors

These are matters of common courtesy, manners, the extent of genuine and general friendliness of approach between members of an organisation. The degree to which these prevail is a reflection of the prevailing mutuality of interest and common purpose. They also contribute to the avoidance of problems and disputes and, when these do arise, to their early settlement to the satisfaction of all involved. They also help to engender positive attitudes and values and mutual concern and respect.

■ Non-verbal communication

Non-verbal communication gives an impression of people to others without saying or writing anything. It also reinforces what is being said or written, and tends to give the real message: the non-verbal message is usually much stronger. The main components that must be understood are as follows.

1 **Appearance:** this includes age, gender, hair, face, body shape and size, height, bearing, national and racial characteristics, clothing and accessories. Each of these items and their combined effect has great implications for: interviewing, public images, creating impressions, advertising, public relations, salesmanship, presentation, design, brand, marque, layout, comfort and familiarity.
2 **Manner:** indicating behaviour, emotion, stress, comfort formality/informality, acceptability/unacceptability, respect/disrespect.
3 **Expression:** expression, especially facial expression, becomes the focus of attention and that is where people concentrate most of their attention.
4 **Eye contact:** regular eye contact demonstrates interest, trust concern, affection and sympathy. The depth of expression in the eyes generates deeper perception of feelings, such as anger, sorrow, love, hatred, or joy.
5 **Pose:** this is either static or active, relaxed, calm, agitated, nervous or stressful. It reinforces the overall impression conveyed. Different parts of the body (especially arms and legs) are used for expression, emphasis, protection and shield.
6 **Clothing:** especially in work situations, clothing provides an instant summary of people. A technician is instantly recognised by her overalls, police and traffic wardens by their distinctive uniforms; and so on. Many organisations whose staff deal regularly and consistently with the public insist either on a dress code or the wearing of a uniform as it helps to reinforce organisational image and the trust and confidence of the public.

7 **Touch:** this reinforces a wide range of perceptions. Consider the difference between different people's handshakes and the impressions that these convey. Touching also reinforces role and sex stereotypes, such as the chairman banging his fist on the desk; or the woman meticulously arranging her clothes.

8 **Body movement:** this may be purely functional and fulfilling certain requirements (for example, cleaning the car). Movements may be exaggerated, conveying anger or high emotions; languid, conveying comfort, ease or indolence; or sharp and staccato, conveying forcefulness and emphasis.

9 **Position:** this reinforces formality/informality; dominance/dependency; superiority/subordination. People use position to enhance feelings of control and influence. For example, people may face each other across a large desk which conveys a sense of security and defence to the person whose desk it is and provides a barrier to be crossed by the other. Chat show hosts sit without tables and ensure that their guests do not have recourse to this prop either. This puts the professional at an advantage and ensures that the guest is sufficiently alien to the environment to be subservient to the host.

10 **Props and settings:** props and settings are used to reinforce impressions of luxury and formality. They are designed to ensure that whatever happens does so to the greatest possible advantage of the instigator. They either reinforce or complement perceptions and expectations; or else they contrast perceptions and expectations, so that the person coming into the situation is impressed for whatever reason.

11 **Discrepancy:** this occurs where the body conveys one message while the spoken or written convey others.

12 **Social factors:** people are conditioned into have preconceived ideas and general expectations of particular situations. For example, people do not generally attend promotion panels or job interviews unshaven or dressed informally. There is no rational for this other than the expectations of society and the general requirement to conform.

13 **The other senses:** other aspects of non-verbal communication include: the use of scent and fragrance; the use of colour and coordination of colours; matters of social and ethical importance and expectation; design and use of materials.

14 **Listening:** listening is both active and passive. Passive listening may be no more than awareness of background noise; it may also be limited to a general awareness of what is going on. Active listening requires taking a dynamic interest in what is being received. While the message is received through the ears, it is reinforced through eye contact, body movement, pose and through the reception of any non-verbal signals that are given by the speaker.

15 **Reinforcement:** non-verbal communication tends to reinforce: relative and absolute measures of status, value, importance and achievement; relative and absolute measures of authority, power and influence; confidence and well-being; and psychological barriers.

7.6 Barriers and blockages

Barriers and blockages arise either by accident, negligence, design or distance.

■ Accident

This is where the choice of language, timing or method of communication is wrong with the best of intentions. In such cases, those involved will simply step back from the situation and rectify it as quickly as possible. This is the only sure remedy. The worst thing that can and does happen is that the organisation rather takes on a defensive position and that a simple misunderstanding quickly becomes a major dispute or dysfunction.

■ Negligence

This is where barriers and blockages are allowed to arise by default. The organisation and its managers perceive that things are at least 'not too bad' or 'going along pretty well'. In such cases communication dysfunctions are seen as 'one of those things'. Specific problems are ignored or treated with a corporate shrug of the shoulders. From the staff point of view, however, these are the first signs of corporate mêlées and neglect. If allowed to develop, the overwhelming perception on the part of the staff is that the organisation does not care for them or what happens to them.

■ Design

This is where the barriers and blockages are both created and also used by those within the organisation to further their own ends. They are used to bar the progress of others. In these cases, above all, information becomes a commodity to be bought and sold, to be corrupted, skewed and filtered in the pursuit of the sectoral interest in question. This is endemic throughout the middle to upper echelons of the military, civil and public service institutions, multinational companies and other multi-site organisations with large and complex head office institutions where an active and negative form of realpolitik exists.

■ Distance

Distance in this context is both physical and psychological. The physical barrier also carries psychological overtones. For example, when one is operating at a physical distance from the organisational headquarters, there is a psychological feeling of autonomy as well. This is compounded by the presence of over-mighty subjects. The institution therefore generates its own identity. All of this acts as a barrier to effective cross-organisation communications.

At a more localised level, the psychological distance is compounded or reduced by the presence (or absence) of trappings such as offices, secretaries, forms of address and titles.

Visibility – especially a lack of visibility – compounds any psychological barriers that may also exist. In particular, a lack of visibility on the part of those issuing communications reinforces any feelings of one-wayness in communications that may already exist.

■ Channels of communication

The more filters through which a message must pass, the longer the channel of communication (Figure 7.2).

7.7 Communication agenda

This is the frame of reference for the communication in question. This is either direct and precise with the result that the message is clearly and unambiguously understood and received by those concerned or, conversely, it is indirect and imprecise with exactly the same result, except that in this case those involved assess the other negative and dishonest features of the communication in coming to their conclusions and understanding of it.

■ Stated or primary agenda

This is the way in which the communication in question is presented. The extent to which this is the real message depends upon the nature and clarity of the message and of the language used in support of it; and the extent to which the organisation then gives life and substance to it through the use of resources, the placing of it in the system of priorities, and the behavioural encouragements and sanctions with which it is under-pinned.

The reverse also exists. If the words used are empty and if there is no support for what is stated, the primary agenda will be disregarded and those concerned will look for the secondary and hidden agenda that always exists in such cases.

The problem also arises if the organisation changes and the initiative in question requires resurrection or rejuvenation. New forms of presentation and language must invariably be found when this occurs.

■ Secondary agendas

Secondary (and indeed multiple) agendas exist where the primary has no substance. There are many forms to look for and of which to be aware. Individuals put particular items out for a variety of purposes (for example, self-aggrandisement, to be seen to be doing something, to prove that they have done something, or because they know that the subject is close to the heart of the patron). Organisations put out messages that appear frothy and insubstantial, but which will contain something, somewhere, which is the item or concept that has the genuine purpose. While most of the offering gets ignored, the one item does therefore gain a foothold and familiarity.

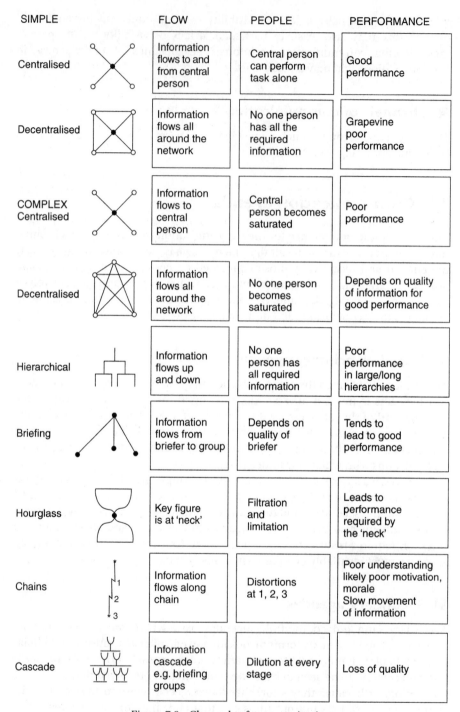

SIMPLE		FLOW	PEOPLE	PERFORMANCE
Centralised		Information flows to and from central person	Central person can perform task alone	Good performance
Decentralised		Information flows all around the network	No one person has all the required information	Grapevine poor performance
COMPLEX Centralised		Information flows to central person	Central person becomes saturated	Poor performance
Decentralised		Information flows all around the network	No one person becomes saturated	Depends on quality of information for good performance
Hierarchical		Information flows up and down	No one person has all required information	Poor performance in large/long hierarchies
Briefing		Information flows from briefer to group	Depends on quality of briefer	Tends to lead to good performance
Hourglass		Key figure is at 'neck'	Filtration and limitation	Leads to performance required by the 'neck'
Chains		Information flows along chain	Distortions at 1, 2, 3	Poor understanding likely poor motivation, morale Slow movement of information
Cascade		Information cascade e.g. briefing groups	Dilution at every stage	Loss of quality

Figure 7.2 Channels of communication

■ Hidden agenda

This is the extreme form of the above. It usually takes on some form of intra-organisational collusion or conspiracy. It is often a cause-and-effect type approach: for example, a low pay rise is offered in the knowledge that the staff will strike, and can therefore be dismissed. This form also occurs in the field of new technology and new market introduction. New technology is introduced so that the old (and those working on it) can be divested. New markets are proposed in the knowledge that the sales team will not be able to cope, and that they too can be dismissed.

A variation occurs when a department takes on a highly prestigious or critical project. Once this is up and running and cannot be cancelled without great losses (including prestige), the particular department pleads for more resources.

This also occurs where a department or individual is given a particular task that it/he cannot possibly complete in the full knowledge and for the purpose of exposing it/him as a failure. The victim again becomes a target for corporate cuts.

Illustrated in this way, the phrase 'hidden agenda' is a contradiction in terms. Watchers of organisational realpolitik felt those directly involved and also (where appropriate) organisational analysts had all recognised the hidden agendas at an early stage. Hidden agendas are key indicators of organisational and managerial mêlée and of organisational toxicity.

7.8 Organisational toxicity

Organisational toxicity and toxic communications exist in organisations that have acquired malady or disease. Symptoms of toxicity are as follows.

1 **Blame and scapegoat:** the organisation finds individuals to carry the can for its corporate failings. Sales departments get the blame for falling profits, while personnel departments get the blame for disputes and grievances. Individuals are blamed for specific failures (for example, the failure of a particular promotion campaign; the failure of work restructuring). They are often also named in this respect and their failure publicised around the organisation.

2 **Accusation and back-stabbing:** this is a development of blame and scapegoat. It exists where it is allowed to exist: that is, where the organisation either actively encourages, or at least acquiesces in, departments and individuals making accusations and allegations about each other. This is an integral feature of any blame culture.

3 **Departmental feuding:** this is where forms of internecine warfare exist between individuals, departments and functions. This is a derivation of both blame and accusation, where both become institutionalised. Again, some organisations either actively encourage this or at least acquiesce.

4 **Meddling:** this is where persons meddle outside their legitimate areas of activity. One of the most extreme forms of this is where top and powerful individuals promise favoured customers that special activities and deals can be done on their behalf and where, as the result, production, sales, marketing, finance and human resource functions are seriously disrupted.

5 **Patronage:** meddling also includes the promotion and appointment of family and friends on the basis of kinship and friendship rather than capability. It includes other forms of favouritism and opportunism, and concerns both departments and individuals.

6 **Secrets:** this is where information becomes a commodity to be used as a source of influence. Information becomes graded and classified. There emerges a culture of information bartering and exchange at an institutional level, and an over-active and destructive grapevine at an informal level.

7 **Corporate self-deception:** this usually occurs in two ways. The first is where an elite is created (or where a group is encouraged or comes to see itself as such). Securing its unassailable excellence, it produces plans, proposals, outputs that must necessarily also be correct and excellent. The second is that, rather than addressing present decline, it lives on past glories, retreating into itself and creating its own view of the world. This has come to be known as the 'bunker mentality'. The expression comes from the last days of the Third Reich in 1944–5, when the Nazi leadership created its own triumphal view of the world within its operations bunker in Berlin rather than face the reality of defeat and invasion that was going on outside.

7.9 Assertiveness

The 'assertive' approach to communications adopts the point of view that any communication can only be effective if it is well thought out, its effect is understood in advance, and the message is delivered clearly and directly to the recipient. Used universally throughout organisations, the approach is the most effective counter to barriers and blockages, misunderstandings, and any toxic elements that may be present.

It is necessary to understand the following forms of behaviour and demeanour, and their effects on communications, as a prerequisite to understanding the basis on which the assertive approach is effective.

1 **Aggressive:** characterised by shouting, swearing, table thumping, arguments (cross-transaction). The matter in hand is lost as the aggressor strives to impose her point of view. Winning the argument becomes everything.

2 **Hostile:** where the main emphasis is on the personalisation of the matters in hand. Often also characterised by shouting and table thumping, the outcome is normally a personal attack (sometimes in public on an individual or group).

3 **Submissive:** characterised by saying or doing anything that the other party wants so that he will finish the argument or transaction and remove himself.

4 **Inconsistent:** characterised by according people different levels of quality and value, using different standards for individuals and groups. This also extends to treating the same individual or group in different ways according to mood or the environment, for example.

5 **Non-assertive:** characterised by the inability of the individual to put her message across. This is either because she is not sure what to put across, or else she has not used the correct words or media.

In order to resolve the problems caused by these forms of approach, an absolute standard of behaviour demeanour and language is used. This is called assertiveness.

Assertive behaviour, demeanour and communications consist of the following.

1 **Language:** clear, simple and direct; easy to understand and respond to on the part of the hearer or receiver; the words used are unambiguous and straightforward; request and demands are made in a clear and precise manner and with sound reasons.
2 **Aims and objectives:** precise and clear; considered in advance, recognising the effect that the message is likely to have on the recipient.
3 **Delivery:** in a clear and steady tone of voice, or (where written) in a well presented and easy to read format. The use of voice is always even, neither too loud nor too soft, and does not involve shouting, threatening or abuse.
4 **Persistence and determination:** where problems or issues are raised by the recipient, the sender sticks to his message, aims and objectives; he does not become side-tracked; he answers any problems that are raised without diverting from the main purpose.
5 **Positive and negative:** the general thrust of the message is always clear and apparent; this does not vary, whether the overall tone is positive or negative. This approach is especially important in handling general staff problems, especially matters concerning grievances and discipline.
6 **Face and eyes:** the head is held up. There is plenty of eye contact and steadiness of gaze. The delivery is reinforced with positive movements that relate to what is being said (for example, smiles, laughter, nodding, encouragement; or a straight face when something has gone wrong).
7 **Other non-verbal aspects:** the body is upright; hands and arms are open (in order to encourage positive response and productive transaction); there is no fidgeting or shuffling; there are no threatening gestures or table thumping, or displays of other forms of behaviour.

■ Situational factors

Assertive delivery is based on an inherent confidence, belief and knowledge of the situation, and confidence in the people. Openness, clarity, credibility and personal and professional confidence all spring from this.

Any clarity of purpose or delivery is always spoilt through having to operate from a weak position or one which is not fully known or understood. This weakness or lack of clarity leads to other forms of behaviour and communications, as indicated above.

7.10 Conclusions

This chapter has concentrated on:

● the importance of communications as a critical factors of effective organisations;

- the extent and prevalence of barriers to effective communication;
- means by which the processes of communication may be understood.

The result of this is the ability to produce effective communications capable of being received, accepted and acted upon or responded to. This is an organisational group and individual issue requiring recognition at all levels and remedial action where communications are poor or ineffective. It reinforces the need for clarity of purpose and language, to which constant reference has been made. As many channels as possible or necessary should be used, giving the same message through each so that the message received is complete and not subject to editing, interpretation or distortion. Where communications are not direct, they are indirect and people will search for hidden agendas and meanings.

Organisations are therefore responsible for creating the conditions in which effective communications can exist. Managers and supervisors must be trained in both the content and processes. All staff must be made to understand the importance and value of their contribution and how this is best achieved. This only happens when there is a high quality working environment and a suitable general management style is adopted. Effective communications are an integral part of this. More generally, this is the foundation of all effective interpersonal, professional and occupational relationships and relations between departments, divisions, functions and levels in hierarchies and throughout organisations.

☒ 8 Influence, power and authority

8.1 Introduction

Influence, power and authority are present in all organisations and these stem from a variety of sources. It is first necessary to distinguish between them.

1 **Influence** is where a person, group or organisation changes the attitudes, values, behaviour, priorities and activities of others.
2 **Power** is the capability to exercise influence in these ways.
3 **Authority** is the legitimisation of the capability to exercise influence and the relationship by which this is exercised.

Authority is based on recognition and acceptance of the right and ability to restrict the freedom to act, to set boundaries and to encourage or order sets of activities for given reasons. Responsibility and accountability normally come with authority, especially in relation to the results achieved by the given activities and the ways in which these are ordered and conducted. Authority also refers to the establishment and enforcement of rules, regulations and norms.

Authority therefore legitimises the use of power and influence in organisations. If subordinates believe and accept that they are in junior positions, they legitimise the power and authority of the superiors. Chains of command, reporting relationships, spans of control and organisation structures all tend to reinforce the existence and legitimisation of authority and hierarchy. Legitimate power is a feature of many organisation roles. This may be supported and reinforced through the use of other power sources.

Authority is therefore a relationship that is recognised by those concerned, involving both exertion on the part of the superior and acceptance by the subordinate.

8.2 Sources of power and influence

These are as follows.

1 **Physical power:** the power exerted by individuals by reason of their bodily shape, size and strength in relation to others; and by organisations in relation to their financial market or operational size.
2 **Traditional power** is the ability to command influence derives from accepted customs and norms. For example, traditional power is present in

the hereditary principle whereby the office or position is handed down from parent to child.

3 **'Divine Right'** and **'The Natural Order'** should also be considered here. Both have been used in the past to reinforce the position and influence of those in power. Divine right was ascribed to European Monarchs over the Middle Ages and beyond; it attributed their position to the will of God so that anybody who rebelled against them was also attacking God.

4 **Expert power:** based on the expertise held by an individual or group and the demand for this from other parts of society. The power and influence that stems from highly prized expertise is dependent upon the volume and nature of demand, the location of the expert and her willingness to use her skill. Expertise comes as professional and technical skills, knowledge, aptitudes, attributes and behaviour. It also includes situational and social knowledge, and normally carries an economic value. This is dependent upon the nature of the expertise, on the value placed on it by those requiring it, and overall levels of demand. All expertise may be offered for sale, rent or hire.

5 **Referent power:** this is based on the degree of attractiveness of the person in the position of power. For example, someone with a high level of desired expertise may not be hired because of other undesired characteristics (he may be scruffy, a bad time keeper or hold extreme political views) while, on the other hand, someone with a lower level of expertise may be hired because her wider characteristics or points of reference are considered more suitable. Referent power is also based on the personal relationships and friendships that are found in working situations.

6 **Charismatic power:** charisma is the effect of one personality on others, the ability to exert influence based on force of personality. It is also the ability to inspire high levels of confidence and identity among other people.

7 **Resource power:** this is the ability to influence others both positively and negatively, based on the command of resources.

8 **Reward power:** this is the ability to influence behaviour and activities by holding out and offering rewards for compliance and acceptance. The extent of influence exerted in this way is dependent upon the nature and volume of rewards and the extent to which these meet the needs of those over whom influence is sought.

9 **Punishment power:** again, the extent of the influence exerted depends upon the nature of the punishment being threatened and whether this is felt to be important by those affected.

10 **Reputation and confidence:** organisations and individuals are able in some circumstances to exert influence based on their achievements to date and the respect and esteem in which these are held. Past reputation and influence, past triumphs and successes are used as the basis for securing future work, for example.

11 **Coercive power:** this is the ability to bribe, bully or threaten someone into doing something that he would not otherwise do. It is usually based on physical or economic strength and reinforced by negative and threatening attitudes and behaviour. It also normally carries dire consequences if the focus of effort does not achieve the required goals.

12 **Conformity:** this is where organisations and leaders set distinctive norms, attitudes, values and behaviour standards which those who wish to be a part of the situation are required to accept. This may be imposed formally by the organisation in the setting of rules and standards of behaviour and activity, or informally by groups exerting their own autonomous and informal pressures and norms.

13 **Position power:** this is where someone is given power and influence according to the position or role held. Military and organisational ranks carry different forms and extents of this depending upon their position in relation to others.

14 **Legal/rational power:** this is the limitation, ordering and direction of power and influence in the name of organisations. It is based on the setting of rules, procedures, regulations and norms for each job, role, department, division and sector.

■ Centres of power in organisations

Each department, division, function and group always has its own power base to a greater or lesser extent (see Figure 8.1).

Each group's position is further influenced by the following.

1 The nature of its own function in relation to all the others present, and the nature and extent of the influence that it is able to exert.

2 The nature and volume of resources that it commands and uses, the ways in which resources are allocated, and the wider question of availability of resources.

3 The nature of inter-group and inter-departmental relations; the extent to which these are positive and cooperative or negative, dysfunctional and divisive.

4 The physical size of certain groups and departments, the numbers of people involved and the scale and nature of resources and technology commanded.

5 Relations between operating departments and functions, and the organisation's top management (invariably the supreme centre of power).

6 Elements of group hierarchies. These are often found in sophisticated and diverse decentralised organisations where, for example, the head office and its functions have greater proximity to senior managers and directors, and therefore the physical capability and location to bid for resources, establish priorities, establish personal relationships and get ahead of the more distant activities.

7 The extent and nature of the authority vested in given officials; ranks, departments, divisions, groups and individuals; and the extent of autonomy and devolution that goes with this.

8 The capabilities of managers and group leaders both in absolute terms (the extent of their managerial expertise) and also in relation to each other.

9 Critical factors, such as the ability to command, limit, edit and filter information; the command of critical technology or expertise; and the influence of this upon the ways of working of other functions and groups, and of the organisation as a whole.

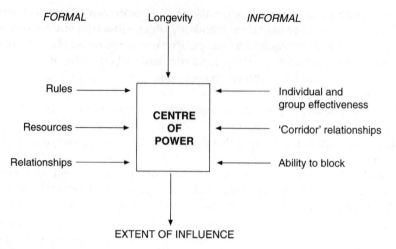

Longevity: people, groups and institutions become behaviourally both strong and influential when they have been in place for a long while. This has implications for needs and demands for change, reorganisation and restructuring.

Blocking: this is the power to prevent things from being done. It exists in most situations and is a combination of resource and reward restriction and work prioritisation. It is also the ability to call upon other resources and influences to ensure that the blocking process is effective.

Corridor diplomacy: this occurs as a route to be considered around problems when the formal procedures of the organisation have been exhausted. Power and influence are used between the parties concerned on an informal basis to try to explore other means of resolving the issue.

Success and failure: a run of successes may lead to an individual or group becoming acknowledged as expert, enabling their influence to grow. Conversely, a series of failure is likely to lead to loss of influence, whatever the absolute standard of the expertise present.

Group energy: this is the ability of the group as a whole to influence things, both positively and negatively. As regards the negative, groups can become very effective in dissipating the energies of those who come to them. For example, those dealing with bureaucracies and who are constantly handed on from one person to the next expend a great deal of energy in this and may well give up altogether if the goal is not important or if some other way of achieving it can be found.

Figure 8.1 Factors relating to the centres of power

10 The structure of the organisation and the extent to which certain functions are accorded higher status, importance, influence and authority than others in the formal structuring.

11 The priorities of the organisation in its dealings with its customers, clients and markets, and also internally in terms of its operational ways of working.

12 The culture of the organisation as a whole, and of its different functions and groups (if a distinction can be drawn between the two). This includes reference to prevailing shared values, attitudes and beliefs, and to general levels of motivation, morale, mutual trust and respect; ethical considerations; and any absolute standards of integrity and activity.

13 The extent and prevalence of pressure groups and lobbies, and the extent to which organisations feel that it is in their own best interests to extend forms of influence and representation to them.

14 Over-mighty subjects and over-mighty departments wield great levels of influence and autonomy in certain conditions, especially in multi-site and multinational organisations where a large measure of local independence of operation is granted.

8.3 Power and influence relationships

These exist within and between all groups, divisions, departments and functions; and also between the individuals involved. The main features are as follows.

■ Orders of priority

This refers to the position of each individual group or department in relation to all the others involved. This is often called the pecking order. It is established as a result of a combination of factors: the respect and regard held for the group or individuals by the organisation's top management; demands for resources and ability to command these; the extent of its influence on organisation output; the extent of its influence on internal ways of working; the size of the group and the nature of the expertise that it wields; its physical location; and the nature and quality of its leadership, output and results, both in absolute terms and also in those required and valued by the organisation.

■ Dominance–dependency

This is the extent to which some groups are able to influence, direct and dominate the courses of action of others, and the benefits and consequences that arise as a result (see Figure 8.2).

Ultimately, all those who work in an organisation are dependent upon it for rewards and continuity of employment. This involves at least acquiescence, and normally also acceptance and compliance with its given ways of working. Dominance and dependency are features of all organisational and interpersonal relationships. Dominance–dependency may be entirely one-way (though this happens very rarely in practice). It is much more likely to be complex: even a slave owner is dependent upon the slaves actually carrying out the work.

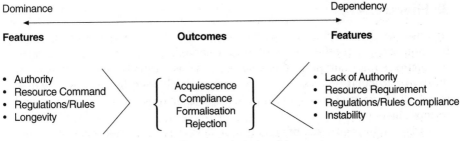

Figure 8.2 The power/relationship spectrum

It is much more useful therefore to see dominance–dependency as a process in which mutual responsibilities exist. Where groups are dependent upon the continued confidence of top managers for continuity and allocation of resources, the top managers are dependent upon the groups to produce results.

Another way of looking at this is as follows.

1 **Acquiescence:** where the people have no particular respect or liking for the organisation and its norms, rules, customs and practices, but go along with them because it is in their current interest to do so or where there are no alternatives apparent.

2 **Compliance:** a more positive approach than acquiescence, but where the fundamental basis of the relationship remains the same. This normally involves, however, at least adopting the required patterns of behaviour.

3 **Acceptance:** where people adopt the norms, values and standards positively and with some degree of enthusiasm and interest; but again are likely to see that at least part of this is dependent upon their current interest.

4 **Formalisation:** where conditions are placed on the particular relationships between the organisation and its staff, for example, the need to use particular processes, channels of communication and approaches.

5 **Institutionalisation:** where people adopt the norms, values and standards absolutely and use them as key factors in their life and work patterns. Such an approach is often very effective in both progression through the organisation, and also in giving a structure to wider aspects of life. Institutionalisation is also a key feature in the lives of school children; those in the full-time care of health and social services (and prisons); and those who work for long periods of time in large, sophisticated and highly structured organisations.

6 **Internalisation:** where people adopt the organisation's beliefs and where these affect their personal beliefs and value systems; eventually such people come to 'believe in' the organisation and all its works.

7 **Rejection:** where people reject the organisation and everything concerning it. This normally leads at the very least to those concerned having stresses, strains, disputes and grievances. People who reject in this way are ofter neutralised: for example, by being given project work that removes both them, and their negative feelings, from the mainstream activities. This may drive them to change their feelings from negative to positive. If this does not happen, the organisation normally rejects them.

■ Hierarchy

Organisational hierarchies are normally based on a combination of rank and function and this is reflected in job titles (marketing director; quality manager; production supervisor; personnel assistant). This is normally well understood by those in particular organisations. The process is clouded by job titles such as secretary, officer, executive and controller, and again these have to be understood by those involved.

The hierarchy is a feature of organisation design and is composed of structure, job and work allocation, and rules and procedures. It indicates where power and

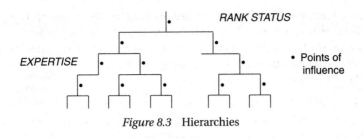

Figure 8.3   Hierarchies

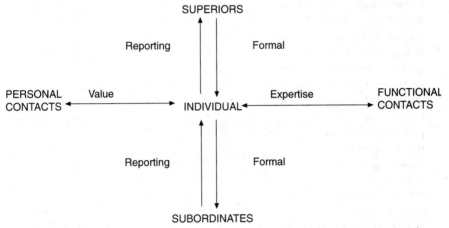

Figure 8.4   Influence relationships: the individual's position in the hierarchy

influence lie and its extent and nature. It indicates spans of control, areas of responsibility and accountability, chains of command (the scalar chain) and reporting relationships. As well as a functional and divisional map of the organisation, the hierarchy is a representation of the nature and limits of power and influence (see Figures 8.3 and 8.4).

■ Status

Status influences the perceptions of power relationships in organisations. It is also a reflection of general perceptions of influence. Status is a reflection of the rank or position of someone (or something) in a particular group. Relative status is based on the inter-relationship of each position. Status is based on the importance and value ascribed to the rank by the organisation and individuals concerned and by the esteem and respect that accrue as the result of holding the given rank. Status is also based on the ambition, self-esteem and self-worth of the rank holder: the ability to say with pride 'I hold job X' or 'I work for organisation Y.'

Status is therefore both given and taken. It is a feature of both individual and group perception. It is formalised largely by rank and capability, but has informal features based on personality and integrity. Other individual capabilities,

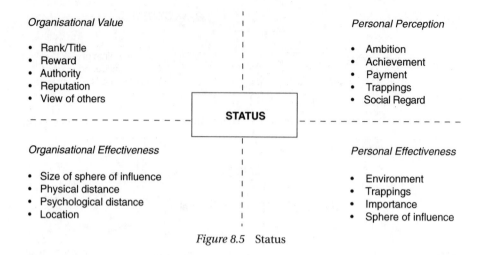

Organisational Value	STATUS	Personal Perception
• Rank/Title • Reward • Authority • Reputation • View of others		• Ambition • Achievement • Payment • Trappings • Social Regard
Organisational Effectiveness		Personal Effectiveness
• Size of sphere of influence • Physical distance • Psychological distance • Location		• Environment • Trappings • Importance • Sphere of influence

Figure 8.5   Status

whether critical to group functioning and effectiveness or not, also influence status (see Figure 8.5).

Status is reinforced by the trappings that go with the rank held (personal office, expensive furniture, car, mobile phone, expense account), and by the volume and quality of items such as these.

It is also reinforced by the responsibilities of the rank held: size of budget, numbers of staff, performance requirements. It may also be reinforced by the physical location of those concerned: for example, whether their offices are in the 'corridors of power' (that is, the same as that of the top managers). In wider social circles it may also be reinforced by perceptions of glamour or excitement that are assumed to exist in certain occupations, such as show business, publishing, travel.

■ Friendships

Friendship influences power relationships in organisations, where people who have positive feelings for each other also work together. A part of the way of working then becomes the desire to support the friend to ensure that she derives some of the benefits that are to accrue from particular courses of action. The use of friendships, of personal contacts to resolve problems and address issues, is a general feature of the informal organisation. It represents the ability to use personal influence (referent power) to the organisation's advantage.

■ Dislike

The converse is where antagonism exists between people. This is nearly always a barrier to effective organisational activities. It is used to block or hinder the progress of the other individual or group, and is compounded where operational reasons are given for the purpose of satisfying a personal grudge or grievance.

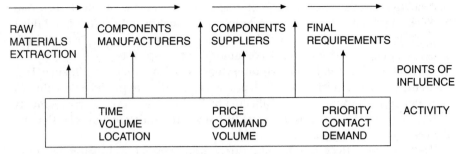

Figure 8.6 The supply chain and points of influence

This is influenced by other personal emotions, possibly including envy, jealousy, hatred and resentment. It is also influenced by organisational and operational matters of expediency, especially where there is the need to find a scapegoat for a failure.

■ Organisational features

Some organisational features are easily seen as power relationships: for example, the supply chain, which is the process by which materials are drawn and combined together to produce finished goods and services. Influence can be exerted by groups that have key tasks to perform in this. By regulating their own output in pursuit of some other course, influence can be brought to bear for the stated purpose. Pressure is exerted to help ensure that the other purpose is satisfied (see Figure 8.6).

For example, a workforce unloading supplies from lorries may deliberately regulate its efforts in order to take a particular length of time. This may be: to prove or indicate that the reason that it took so long was because of a shortage of staff; to lobby for extra equipment (cranes, forklift trucks); to seek more money ('We will work faster if you pay us more'); to act in support of another group further down the chain that it knows to be under pressure.

8.4 Control mechanisms

The main control mechanisms are as follows.
1. **Financial controls**: in which influence resides in the demands for financial information and the ways in which this is presented. It is also present in budgeting and resource allocation activities, and in checks on resource utilisation, time scales, progress chasing and checking, and the pressures exerted by those responsible.
2. **Staff controls**: discipline, grievance and disputes mechanisms, the ways in

which these are constituted, and the approaches taken by those responsible for their handling.

3. **Quality controls**: the standards of quality set, the means by which these are achieved, and the means by which problems of quality are identified and dealt with. This is likely also to include attention to customer satisfaction (both internal and external) and systems of inquiry and complaints.

4. **Work allocation and job descriptions**: these are also sources of influence. This takes the form of requiring people to attend at set times, to produce set volumes (and quality) of output. It is also affected by flexibility of working arrangements and lines on job descriptions that state (usually at the end) 'Anything else that the organisation may require you to do.'

5. **Factors that affect the health, safety and general well-being** of those concerned, the means by which these are controlled and the extent and influence of health and safety committees, welfare offices and occupational health professionals. This also influences the design of work environments and workstations. Further, there are legal constraints affecting many aspects of work (for example, extremes of heat and cold, length of time worked without breaks, or length of time in front of computer screens) with which organisations must comply. Influence therefore resides in the hands of those who must enforce each of these features.

6. **Ethical controls**: related to general standards of best practice and also to particular features such as equality of treatment. The driving force here (for good or ill) is likely to derive from the organisation's stated policy or point of view. Clear direction is given in the best cases. A form of direction emerges in the worst cases, or where standards are not set, by the approaches taken by individuals and groups to these matters, and the extent to which they are condoned and supported by the organisation.

7. **Sanctions**: taken against individuals and groups, and the ways in which these are applied. The power lies in those who carry out the sanctions and is also found in the relative ability of those affected to resist or combat them. This is, in turn, influenced by the general standpoint that is adopted by the organisation. It affects all aspects of organisational performance, either directly or indirectly: general, individual and group behaviour, relationships between superiors and

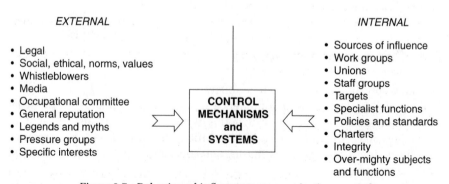

Figure 8.7 Behavioural influences on organisation control

subordinates and the collective attitude and state of morale. It also affects perceptions of fairness and equality (or otherwise) of treatment.

8.5 Delegation

Delegation is the allocation of work to subordinates accompanied by the handing down of:

- authority in a given area to carry out the work and to make requests for equipment, materials and information, or to act in the name of a department, group or superior in a given area;
- control over the process by which the work is to be carried out. This normally involves, in turn, relaxing a part of the process of work supervision. Activities taken in pursuit of the task are normally left entirely to the subordinate.

There is an effect on the wider issues of responsibility and accountability. Overall responsibility, especially to the wider organisation, normally remains with the superior. Any problems arising, especially questions of failure or ineffectiveness, therefore remain a matter between the superior and the rest of the organisation. However, this is invariably accompanied by discussions between the superior and subordinate. Where such problems do arise, to apportion blame to the subordinate in dealings with the wider organisation leads to loss of morale and accusations of scapegoating.

8.6 Misuses of power and influence

In organisations the most commonly found misuses of power and influence are as follows.

1 **Favouritism:** the ability to influence an individual's career, prospects and advancement by virtue of a personal liking and at the expense of others.
2 **Victimisation:** the converse of favouritism; the blocking or reduction of career prospects and advancement.
3 **Lack of manners:** calling out rudely to people, abusing and humiliating subordinates in public.
4 **Lack of respect:** treating subordinates with contempt, giving individuals dressing downs in public; conducting discipline in public.
5 **Bullying and harassment:** overwhelmingly by superiors of subordinates. This is usually found in the following forms:

   (a) racial prejudice;
   (b) sexual harassment (especially of female staff by males);
   (c) bullying of the disabled by the able-bodied;
   (d) religious manias and persecutions (for example, where a Catholic company bullies the elements of its workforce that are of other religions);
   (e) personal likes and dislikes, especially where the dislike is based on a perceived threat to the security of the senior's position.

6 **Scapegoating:** the need to find someone to blame for the superior's errors.

7 **Inequality of opportunity:** the setting of a priority order for the advancement of staff based on gender, race or disability elements

The extent and prevalence of each of these misuses is always fully understood by the staff, at least at an informal level. The presence of each is always extremely damaging to both individual and overall motivation and morale.

■ Relationship structures and spheres of influence

The main factors to be understood are as follows.

1 The nature of the relationship between all the parties, and whether this is cooperative, competitive or conflicting; based on mutual trust or antagonism; if more than two groups, whether there are alliances or other areas of mutuality between some of them; the personalities involved; whether the groups are permanent or *ad hoc*; the rules and boundaries within which the relationships take place.

2 The nature of the matters in hand and the extent of their importance to each individual and party concerned: for example, the organisation's tea person wields great influence over the Chief Executive if her desire for tea is overwhelming and if she cannot easily go elsewhere to get it.

3 The relationship between the overt, primary or stated agenda and any parallel, secondary or other hidden agenda, either on the part of the groups involved or some of the individual players. For example, trade union officials will often fight cases which they know that they cannot win because it shows their concern and care for every member whatever their difficulties. Further, the trade union officials involved have their own career paths to follow and concern for all members is likely to be a key feature and requirement. The official therefore gains a reputation for being prepared to fight any corner, and this, in turn, leads to both his own advancement and also increased membership brought on by feelings of confidence and goodwill generated by the approach.

4 Management style of the organisation and its tolerance of parallel, secondary and hidden agenda; the recognition of any dominance or dependency exerted in the steps that it takes to minimise and control this; the extent and presence of physical and psychological remoteness and distance.

5 The conduct of the relationships. This is likely to be based on:

   (a) conflict, a power struggle, the need for ascendancy in a particular situation;
   (b) cooperation – the establishment of areas of mutual interest; harmony – recognition of the need to resolve any issues for the greater good of all; openness – the extent to which each party involved is able (or feels able) to declare its own position completely; expediency – the need to gain a result quickly for some reason;
   (c) publicity (what others are to make of the outcome of the matter in hand once this is known).

6 Isolation is a power relationship as follows.

   (a) Physical isolation brought on because of the remoteness of a group from the rest of the organisation (for example, an overseas subsidiary) leads on the one hand to feelings of loss of control and involvement on the part of the main organisation and, on the other, to feelings of autonomy and independence on the part of the subsidiary.

(b) Psychological isolation is brought on by matters such as resource starvation, denigration and general lack of respect and regard for the work of the group or for its members. This leads to the adoption of a siege mentality on the part of the group affected as it defends itself from the pressures of the rest of the organisation; and also on the part of the organisation as it seeks to make fresh inroads into the already beleaguered group.

(c) Group-think is also a form of isolation. For example, top managers and directors may create their own view of the organisation in its environment without reference to reality or based on a historic perception and reputation. Project groups and think tanks may also find themselves in this form of isolation if their relationship with the rest of the organisation is not carefully nurtured and managed.

❑ Spheres of influence

These are created by a combination of formal and informal authority and power. They relate to the nature of activities and operations. They overlap and interact with each other (see Figure 8.8). Spheres of influence are less easy to define than areas of legitimate, expert and role/office power. They encompass, especially, areas of coercive/conformist referent and charismatic power. They also include specific areas of functional and legitimate power: for example, trade union officials have legitimate positions in any areas where they have members and the union is recognised; the human resource function has legitimate areas in any other function that requires their services, such as in recruitment selection and handling disciplinaries and grievances.

Spheres of influence may be defined as 'the psychological territory of the individual or group'. Individuals and groups may have many spheres of influence in an organisation. Handy developed the idea as follows.

Ownership of territory is conferred partly by deeds and partly by precedent, squatting or staking a claim. The boundaries of the territory are set out in various ways; physically with screens, offices, separate buildings; procedurally, through committee memberships and circulation lists; socially, through dining groups, informal groupings, carpets and other status signs. Some conclusions may be drawn:

- territory is prized by its inhabitants; they will not willingly relinquish it, or allow it to get overcrowded;
- some territories are more prized than others;
- trespassing is discouraged (you enter another territory by invitation only);
- one can seek to increase or improve one's own property even to the detriment of the neighbourhood as a whole;
- territory is not to be violated; if so, there will be retaliation and conflict;
- territory is jealously guarded, especially in relationship to its own trappings and status, including office sizes, dining rooms, cars, personal assistants and secretaries;

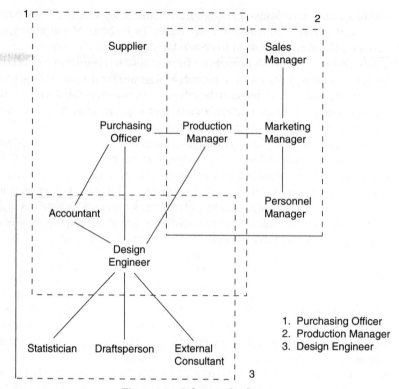

Figure 8.8 Spheres of influence
Source: from Luthans (1986).

- territory is always to be improved and enhanced, both in the interests of maintaining the current position and also in order that this may be improved.

Pressures to maintain and increase the sphere of influence depend on a variety of factors.

1 The confidence, respect and regard in which an individual or group is held. If it is high, those concerned seek to enhance and build on this. If it is low, those concerned are likely to seek other means of gaining influence (for example, through the control of information and functional triumphs).
2 Functional expertise, and the extent to which this is prized and valued by the organisation. Again, especially if this is low, other sources of influences will tend to be sought.
3 The rewards of influence. These are normally better work, increased resources, enhanced reputation, moves up the pecking order. They also include (in some organisations) the ability to influence the direction, activities and operations of the organisation, and therefore transform (rather than merely enhance) the prospects of a particular department or individual.
4 Attaching oneself to an over-mighty subject or department in the expectation of favours and enhancement.

5 Increased status and prestige for those involved. This often leads to increased benefits and pay and increased prospects (especially from within the organisation) for those concerned.
6 Favouritism on the part of the organisation's top managers, driven by real or perceived operational necessity, the top manager's own expertise and familiarity (for example, the director who came up through the ranks of the marketing department is likely to continue to favour marketing), personal friendships, expediency, the availability of a triumph.

8.7 Conclusions

The acquisition and use of power is a basic human as well as organisational need. The need and ability to control and influence the environment, and to make it comfortable and supportive, is a factor in all behaviour. It is necessary to understand the ways in which people seek to do this in organisations, and the effects of this on aims and objectives, performance, behaviour and resource utilisation.

How power is used and what type of power is used affects all aspects of performance, as does the means of dividing and allocating responsibility and authority. From this point of view, a key part of the creation, design and structuring of organisations consists of creating patterns of control and influence. This is formalised in hierarchies, reporting relationships, functional and expert activities and results areas. Space is also created for the operation of communication and information systems, and group and inter-group relationships (both formal and informal).

It is also necessary to pay constant attention to the ways in which power, influence and authority are used and wielded within organisations to ensure that this continues to be legitimate, and to ensure that issues of conflict and organisational politics, which might otherwise arise, are kept under control.

▽ 9 Leadership

9.1 Introduction

The need to study and understand leadership arises from the need for successful and effective direction of organisations together with the need to identify those characteristics required to be a successful and effective director, manager, supervisor: that is, leader (whether of a total organisation or of a particular organisational sphere, function, department or division).

The following definitions are useful.

1 A leader is 'someone who exercises influence over other people' (Huczynski and Buchanan 1993).
2 Leadership is the 'lifting of people's vision to a higher sight, the raising of their performance to a higher standard, the building of their personality beyond its normal limitations' (P. F. Drucker 1986a).
3 A leader is: 'cheerleader, enthusiast, nurturer of champions, hero finder, wanderer, dramatist, coach, facilitator and builder' (Peters and Austin 1986).
4 The leader 'must have infective optimism. The final test of a leader is the feeling you have when you leave their presence after a conference. Have you a feeling of uplift and confidence?' (Field Marshal Bernard Montgomery)
5 Leadership is 'creating a vision to which others can aspire and energising them to work towards this vision' (Anita Roddick).
6 There is a need in all organisations for 'individual linking pins who will bind groups together and, as members of other groups, represent their groups elsewhere in organisations. Leadership concerns the leader themselves, the subordinates, and the task in hand' (C. B. Handy 1993).
7 Leadership can be described as a 'dynamic process in a group whereby one individual influences others to contribute voluntarily to the achievement of group tasks in a given situation' (G. A. Cole 1994).

From this range of definitions, certain initial key elements may be established:

- getting things done through people and all that entails (the organisation of people into productive teams, groups, departments and functions);
- the creation of effective means of communication;
- the resolution of conflicts, both behavioural and operational;
- creating direction for the organisation, department, division or function;
- organising resources in support of all this;
- taking informed, effective and successful decisions.

Some general priorities may also be established:

- getting optimum performance from those carrying out the work in whatever terms that is defined;
- ensuring continuity, development and improvement in those carrying out the work; monitoring and evaluating both the work and those involved; taking remedial action where necessary;
- relating the skills and capacities of those involved in the work to the work itself;
- seeking continuous improvement in all aspects of the work environment, and providing opportunities for continuous development and advancement for those in the organisation, department, division or function;
- motivating and encouraging the staff, and promoting positive, harmonious and productive working relations.

Leadership is therefore studied as an aspect of organisational behaviour for two major reasons. It is a critical function in itself; and it is critical to organisation success.

9.2 Leadership and management

From this, certain features begin to emerge.

1 **Results.** These are measured in terms of what leaders set out to achieve and what they actually achieved; how and why these were achieved; how they were viewed at the time and subsequently by posterity; and whether this represented a good, bad or indifferent return on the resources and energy expended in their pursuit.

2 **Inspiration.** In order to achieve success, leaders must have their own clear understanding of what this is, at least in their own terms. In order that people follow, and resources are attracted to their cause, this is normally translated into a simple, direct and positive statement of where the leader is going and how and why this is to be achieved and the benefits that this is to bring to others as a result. They must be capable of inspiring others; it is no use having a good idea if people do not recognise it as such.

3 **Hard Work.** For all this to occur, leaders must have great stores of energy, enthusiasm, dedication, zeal and commitment. They have to inspire and energise people and resources in pursuit of the desired ends. They also set the standards for their followers: in normal circumstances, hard work cannot be expected of others if the leader is not also prepared to put this in.

4 **Honesty.** People follow leaders, either because they believe in them or because it is in their interest to do so (or a combination of the two). Leaders who fail to deliver are normally rejected or supplanted. Leaders who say one thing and mean another will not be trusted and people continue to work for them only until they can find something else.

5 **Responsibility.** Leaders accept their own part in both triumphs and successes, and also disasters and failures. This extends to rewards and consequences.

■ Leadership factors

Peters and Austin (1986) identified a long and comprehensive list of factors present in a 'leader', and they contrasted this with the mirror attributes of the 'non-leader' (see Table 9.1).

■ Traits and characteristics

Attempts to identify the traits and characteristics present in successful leaders are largely inconclusive, in that none identify all the attributes necessary to lead, direct or manage in all situations. However, the following characteristics are found to be applicable to most situations.

1 **Communication:** the ability to communicate with all people with whom the leader comes into contact regularly, continuously and in ways and language in which those on the receiving end will be able to understand and respond to.
2 **Decision-making:** the ability to take the right decisions in given situations, to take responsibility and be accountable for them, and to understand the consequences of particular courses of action. Part of this involves being able to take an over-view or strategic view of particular situations, to see the longer term and to take a wider general perspective. This is sometimes called 'the helicopter view'.
3 **Commitment:** to both matters in hand and also the wider aspects of the organisation as a whole. This includes an inherent willingness to draw on personal, as well as professional, energies and to bring qualities of enthusiasm, drive and ambition to the particular situation.
4 **Concern for staff:** respecting, trusting and committing oneself to them; developing them, understanding them and their aspirations and reconciling these with the matters in hand. Staff should be treated on a basis of equality and confidence.
5 **Quality:** a commitment to the quality of product or service such that, whatever the matter in hand, customers receive high value and high satisfaction, and the staff involved receive recognition for their effort.
6 A given **set of values** with which others will identify, and to which they will commit themselves. There are few examples of leaders, directors or managers who succeed by being all things to all people in all situations.
7 **Personal integrity:** this includes vision, enthusiasm, strength of character, commitment, energy and interest; it also includes the setting and establishment of high absolute standards of moral and ethical probity.
8 **Positive attitudes:** held by the leader and transmitted to staff and customers.
9 **Mutuality and dependency** of leaders with their staff; successful leaders know their own weaknesses, the importance and value of the people that go with them; above all, they know what they cannot do and where and when to go for help and support in these areas.

Rosemary Stewart quotes from an American study in which organisation executives were asked to identify what they thought were the main desirable qualities of managers. They came up with the following list.

Table 9.1 Leadership

Leader	Non-leader
• Carries water for people	• Presides over the mess
• Open door problem solver, advice giver, cheerleader	• Invisible, gives orders to staff, expects them to be carried out
• Comfortable with people in their workplaces	• Uncomfortable with people
• No reserved parking place, dining room or lift	• Reserved parking place and dining table
• Manages by Walking About	• Invisible
• Arrives early, stays late	• In late, usually leaves on time
• Common touch	• Strained with 'inferior' groups of staff
• Good listener	• Good talker
• Available	• Hard to reach
• Fair	• Unfair
• Decisive	• Uses committees
• Humble	• Arrogant
• Tough, confronts nasty problems	• Elusive, the 'artful dodger'
• Persistent	• Vacillates
• Simplifies	• Complicates
• Tolerant	• Intolerant
• Knows people's names	• Doesn't know people's names
• Has strong convictions	• Sways with the wind
• Trusts people	• Trusts only words and numbers on paper
• Delegates whole important jobs	• Keeps all final decisions
• Spends as little time as possible with outside directors	• Spends a lot of time massaging outside directors
• Wants anonymity for himself, publicity for the company	• Wants publicity for himself
• Often takes the blame	• Looks for scapegoats
• Gives credit to others	• Takes credit
• Gives honest, frequent feedback	• Amasses information
• Knows when and how to discipline people	• Ducks unpleasant tasks
• Has respect for all people	• Has contempt for all people
• Knows the business and the kind of people who make it tick	• Knows the business only in terms of what it can do for him/her
• Honest under pressure	• Equivocation
• Looks for controls to abolish	• Looks for new controls and procedures
• Prefers discussion rather than written reports	• Prefers long reports
• Straightforward	• Tricky, manipulative
• Openness	• Secrecy
• As little paperwork as possible	• As much paperwork as possible
• Promotes from within	• Looks outside the organisation
• Keeps his promises	• Doesn't keep his promises
• Plain office and facilities furnishings	• Lavish office, expensive facilities and
• Organisation is top of the agenda	• Self is top of the agenda
• Sees mistakes as learning opportunities and the opportunity to develop	• Sees mistakes as punishable offences and the means of scapegoating

Note: Peters and Austin add the following two riders to their version of these columns.

'You now know more about leaders and leadership than all the combined graduate business schools in America.
You also know whether you have a leader or a non-leader in your manager's office'.

Source: from Peters and Austin (1985).

judgement	dependability	initiative	emotional stability
integrity	fairness	foresight	ambition
human relations	dedication	drive	objectivity
skill	cooperation	decisiveness	

The problem with this approach is that it is very difficult to pin down those qualities and to measure the true extent of their prevalence. They are simply widely perceived to be held or to have been held by those characters who were studied. It also takes little account of the negative attributes that may be present, such as stubbornness, vanity, self-centredness, arrogance and conceit. In the particular context of situations where conflict existed – for example, those centred around kings and queens or around military operations – the nature and extent of technology owned by each side must be taken into account. In general, it is quite possible for a bad leader in those situations to succeed at the expense of someone who was better but who simply did not have access to, or command of, sufficient levels of resource technology or equipment.

■ The leadership functions model

This model was developed by John Adair, working at the University of Surrey during the 1960s and 1970s. It recognises that certain traits, qualities, capabilities and aptitudes must be present in leaders, and that these must be translated into action. It then reconciles this with emphasis on the work and the group that are the main features of this style of approach to leadership (see Figure 9.1).

The leader addresses the key tasks of achieving the task, building the team and paying attention to the individual members. Again, a balance between the three is required. The leader who concentrates only on the task by going all out for production schedules, while neglecting the training, encouragement and motivation of the group, will always have problems of dissonance and dysfunction.

The leader who concentrates only on creating team spirit, while neglecting the job or individuals, will not get maximum involvement and commitment which

Figure 9.1 Leadership functions model

only comes from an environment that is both harmonious and genuinely productive. Staff members would therefore lack any true feelings of achievement or success.

The key leadership functions required are:

direction	planning	communication
communication	appraisal	decision-making
coordination	control	creativity
assessment	development	resourcefulness

Having identified these functions, Adair used them as the basis for developing leadership and management training and development courses, relating each to the stated essentials of achieving the task, building the team and maintaining concern for the individual.

■ Types of leader

The following different types of leader may be distinguished.

1 The traditional leader, whose position is assured by birth and heredity. Examples of this are the kings and queens of England (and of other places in the world). It may also be found in family businesses, whereby child succeeds father as the CE or Chair when the latter retires.
2 The known leader, whose position is secured by the fact that everyone understands this, at least in general. Kings and queens are examples again. Priests are known to be leaders of their congregations. Aristocrats are known to be masters and mistresses of their own domains. It is known also that they will be succeeded by one from their own estate when they die or move on.
3 The appointed leader, whose position is legitimised by virtue of the fact that she has gone through a selection, assessment and appointment process in accordance with the wishes and demands of the organisation and the expectations of those who will now be working for her. This invariably carries a defined and formalised managerial role in organisations.
4 The bureaucratic leader, whose position is legitimised by the rank that he holds. This is especially true of military structures and is reinforced by the job titles used and his known position in the hierarchy (corporal, captain, major, general). It is also to be found in more complex and sophisticated, commercial and public organisation structures. This also normally implies managerial responsibilities.
5 The functional or expert leader, whose position is secured by virtue of her expertise. This form of leadership is likely to be related to particular issues: for example, the industrial relations officer may be a junior functionary who, however, becomes the acknowledged leader, director and problem-solver wherever industrial relations problems arise, and whatever the rank or status of other people involved.
6 The charismatic leader, whose position is secured by the sheer force of his personality. Many great world leaders (good or evil) have (or had) this:

Napoleon, Adolf Hitler, Winston Churchill, Margaret Thatcher, John F. Kennedy.

7 The informal leader, whose position is carried out by virtue of her personality, charisma, expertise, command of resources, but is not formally legitimised by rank, appointment or tradition. This position may also be arrived at by virtue of some other activity for which she is particularly responsible (for example, local trade union representative).

■ Charisma and personality in leadership

Charisma may be defined as the 'distinctive element (or elements) of personality with which others identify'. It is enhanced by other aspects: job title, the organisation worked for, numbers of persons and other resources controlled, successes and failures, media image, stories, myths and legends. It is also a reflection of the degree of personal influence that is brought to bear on the situation (often in spite of the position held). This is the degree and the extent to which the individual remains influential when removed from the high office in question.

Charisma and the force of strength and personality both attracts and repels (this gives full meaning to the phrase 'magical personality'). Strong personalities are not 'all things to all people'. Charisma is also very brittle. Once the personality is breached, once illusions of strength, confidence and capability are shattered, strong negative feelings invariably come to the fore. The leader who fails to deliver what was promised or who fails to save the organisation that he was brought into lead is thus rejected in this way.

■ Trait theories

This approach is taken to identify the traits, attributes and characteristics that are present in effective and successful leaders. The problem with this is immediate: identifying those attributes present in all leaders.

Handy identifies three only: above-average intelligence; a good measure of initiative; and a high level of self-assurance. He is also the first to point out that possession of these three do not in themselves make one a good leader.

On the other hand, to try to identify all those qualities necessary to carry out the complex and sophisticated range of tasks and activities indicated above (and emphasised in the note on CEs) is so broad as to be meaningless also.

Other studies bring different angles to bear on this. Peters and Austin entitled their book *A Passion for Excellence; The Leadership Difference*. They identify a long list of attributes present in leaders which they compare and contrast with converses that are not to be found in genuine leaders but which may well be found in administrative and bureaucratic functionaries who have acted as substitutes for genuine leadership over the post-war period.

P. F. Drucker identified high principles of conduct and responsibility; high standards of performance (in whatever sphere and in whatever ways that was measured); and respect for staff, both as people and as workers.

Glass identified confidence; appreciation of people (again in both personal and operational terms); personal and professional tenacity; excellence in communication and listening; approachability; and resilience.

The great value in identifying such characteristics and attributes is that if it can be done successfully the following great benefits accrue:

- if they are attitudes, values, beliefs and personality traits then potential leaders and managers can be tested for these at the selection stage;
- if they are skill, knowledge and behaviour related they can be taught to those who exhibit 'potential' and who have other organisational and operational attributes that may be required by the organisation in question.

More generally, it is plainly essential to have some means of identification of the attributes required by those who are to direct organisations.

Trait approaches provide a useful starting point. This is their great strength and attraction. The weakness is where these attributes become cast in stone and become immovable or an organisational nostrum ('all our leaders/managers/ supervisors have quality x'). Organisations that take such an approach at least acknowledge that there is a fundamental difference between carrying out a job and organising, leading and directing others in the carrying out of it.

■ Style theories

The rationale for studying management styles is that employees will work better for managers who use particular styles of leadership than they will for others who employ different styles.

It is usual to classify leadership styles on an authoritarian–democratic continuum (see Table 9.2). There is a body of evidence that also relates high levels of success in business and work, job satisfaction and employees and fewer disputes and grievances to the participative and consultative end of the continuum (see Figure 9.2).

Much of the basis for this is to be found in the Theory Y concept of McGregor. Other studies that tend towards this view include those of Blake and Mouton (the managerial grid), and Likert (System 4). From a different standpoint this is also supported by the view that effective working methods and participative styles of management feed off each other, so that each improves the other. There is also a measure of support for this view in the Excellence Studies (both in the UK and USA).

There are caveats, however. Any management style must be supported

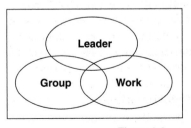

Figure 9.2

Table 9.2   Leadership and management styles

Autocratic (benevolent or tyrannical)	Consultative/participative	Democratic/participative
1. Leader makes all final decision for the group.	1. Leader makes decisions after consultation with group.	1. Decisions made by the group, by consultation or vote. Voting based on the principles of one person, one vote; majority rules.
2. Close supervision.	2. Total communication between leader and members.	2. All members bound by the group decision and support it.
3. Individual members' interests subordinate to those of the organisation.	3. Leader is supportive and developmental.	3. All members may contribute to discussion.
4. Subordinates treated without regard for their views.	4. Leader is accessible and discursive.	4. Development of coalitions and cliques.
5. Great demands placed on staff.	5. Questioning approach encouraged.	5. Leadership role is assumed by Chair.
6. Questioning discouraged.	6. Ways of working largely unspecified.	
7. Conformist/coercive environment.	7. Leader retains responsibility and accountability for results.	

by mutual trust, respect and confidence existing between manager and subordinates. If these qualities are not present then no style is effective. There must be a clarity of purpose and direction in the first place, and this must come from the organisation. Participation can only genuinely exist if this clarity exists also; it cannot exist in a void.

The factors are inter-related. Account must also be taken of the fact that where leadership style is to be truly democratic, the decisions and wishes of the group must be accommodated, whatever is decided and whether this is 'right' or 'wrong' in terms of the demands of the work and the pressures of the wider environment.

The relationship between the leader, the work, the group and the environment may also be represented as shown in Figures 9.3 and 9.4.

The factors also conflict with each other. The end result is the identification and adoption of a leadership style that is considered suitable for the matters in hand and taking into account the range of elements that each factor brings with it to the given situation.

❑ Blake and Mouton: the managerial grid

The managerial grid is a configuration of management styles based on the matching of two dimensions of managerial concern: 'concern for people' and

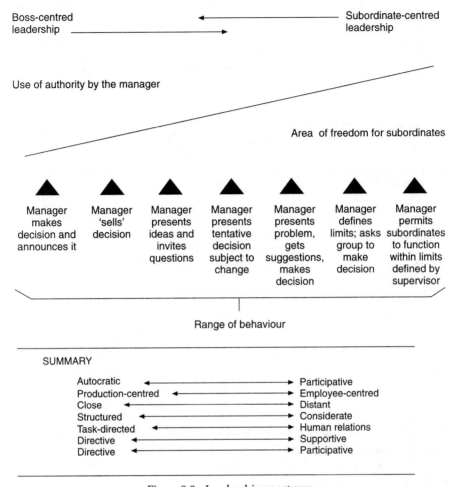

(a) LEADERSHIP CONTINUUM

Boss-centred leadership ← Subordinate-centred leadership →

Use of authority by the manager

Area of freedom for subordinates

| Manager makes decision and announces it | Manager 'sells' decision | Manager presents ideas and invites questions | Manager presents tentative decision subject to change | Manager presents problem, gets suggestions, makes decision | Manager defines limits; asks group to make decision | Manager permits subordinates to function within limits defined by supervisor |

Range of behaviour

SUMMARY

Autocratic	← →	Participative
Production-centred	← →	Employee-centred
Close	← →	Distant
Structured	← →	Considerate
Task-directed	← →	Human relations
Directive	← →	Supportive
Directive	← →	Participative

Figure 9.3 Leadership spectrum

'concern for production/output'. Each of these dimensions is plotted on a 9-point graph scale and an assessment is made of the managerial style according to where they come out on each (Figure 9.4). Thus, a low score (1-1) on each axis reflects poverty in managerial style; a high score (9-9) on each reflects a high degree of balance, concern and commitment in each area. The implication from this is that an adequate, effective and successful managerial style is in place.

The 9-9 score is indicated as the best by Blake and Mouton. This illustrates the targets to be striven for and the organisation's current position in relation to each axis.

It also implies that the best fit is along the diagonal line: concern for the task and concern for the people should be grown alongside each other rather than the one emphasised at the expense of the other.

The information on which the position on the grid is based is drawn from

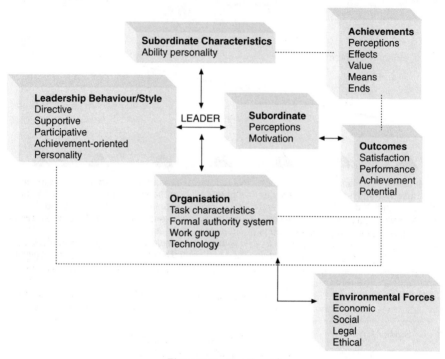

Figure 9.3   Continued

structured questionnaires that are issued to all managers and supervisors in the organisation section, unit or department to be assessed, and also to all their staff.

■ Contingency approaches

Contingency theories of leadership take account of the interaction and inter-relation between the organisation and its environment. This includes the recognition, and accommodation of, those elements that cannot be controlled. It also includes recognising that those elements which can be controlled and influenced must be addressed in ways that vary in different situations: the correct approach in one case is not a prescription to be applied to others. In each case, therefore, there is a constant interaction between the leader's job and the work to be done, and between this and the general operations of the organisation in question.

The concept of contingency approaches to leadership was first developed by F. E. Fiedler in the 1960s. Above all, Fielder's work identified situations where both directive and participative styles of management worked effectively. The directive style was found to work well at the extremes, where the situation was either very favourable to the leader or very unfavourable.

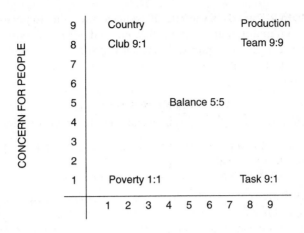

Other styles that Blake and Mouton identified are:

- **9-1:** the country club – production is incidental; concern for the staff and people is everything the group exists largely to support itself.
- **1-9:** task orientation – production is everything; concern for the staff is subordinated to production and effectiveness. Staff management mainly takes the form of planning and control activities in support of production and output. Organisational activity and priority is concerned only with output.
- **5-5:** balance – a medium degree of expertise, commitment and concern in both areas; this is likely to produce adequate or satisfactory performance from groups that are reasonably well satisfied with working relations.

Figure 9.4   The Managerial Grid
Source: Blake and Mouton (1986).

Favourable was defined as a combination of circumstances where: the leader was liked and trusted by the group; the task was clearly understood, easy to follow and well defined; the leader had a high degree of respect within the group; the leader had a high degree of influence over the group members in terms of reward and punishment; the leader enjoyed unqualified backing from the organisation.

Unfavourable was defined as the converse of this; where the task was not clearly defined; and where the work was to be carried out in an extreme environment (discomfort, working away from home).

At either extreme the structured, prescriptive or directive approach was found to work well. In the former, the group would accept it because of the high general level of regard; in the latter, it brought at least a measure of order and clarity. Indeed, to be too participative in the latter extreme may be regarded as compounding the uncertainty and therefore as a sign of weakness and ineffectiveness on the part of the leader.

Adair identified three variables in any working situation. These are: the task; the team or group; and the individuals that make up the team. They are defined as unique; as having dual relationships; and as being fully interactive. The job of the manager is to harmonise the three in productive activity. This therefore is concerned with the reconciliation of differences, attending to personal goals and ambitions, team maintenance and production and output scheduling. This must all be carried out in an organisational setting that is infinitely variable and developing and, above all, unique.

Each may be:

Effective ⎫ dependent upon their application and
Ineffective ⎬ appropriateness to given situations

This is developed into a three-dimensional (3D) model (Figure 9.5).

❐ Appropriate, effective

1 **Bureaucrat:** low concern for both task and relationships; appropriate in situations where rules and procedures are important.
2 **Benevolent autocrat:** high concern for task, low concern for relationships; appropriate in task cultures.
3 **Developer:** high concern for relationships and low concern for tasks; appropriate where the acquiescence, cooperation and commitment of the people is paramount.
4 **Executive:** high concern for task, high concern for relationships; appropriate where the achievement of high standards is dependent on high levels of motivation and commitment.

❐ Inappropriate, ineffective

1 **Deserter:** low concern for both task and relationships; the manager lacks involvement and is either passive or negative.

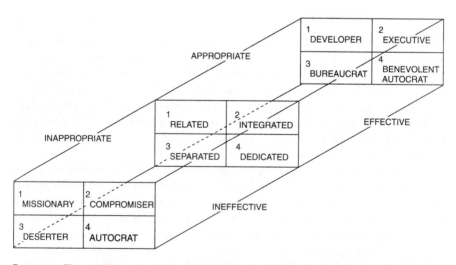

Purpose: The middle set of boxes identifies the four archetype leaders of Reddin's theory These archetypes may then be translated into APPROPRIATE EFFECTIVE or INAPPROPRIATE INEFFECTIVE personal types.

Figure 9.5 W. Reddin: leadership and management behaviour

2 **Autocrat:** high concern for task, low concern for relationships; the manager is coercive, confrontational, adversarial, lacking confidence in others.
3 **Missionary:** high concern for relationships, low concern for task; the manager's position is dependent on preserving harmony and there is often a high potential for conflict.
4 **Compromiser:** high concern for both tasks and relationships; manager is a poor decision-maker, expedient, concerned only with the short term.

■ C.B. Handy: The best fit

This is a summary view: that is, all leadership theories have a contribution to make, but none by itself is the right or complete answer.

The Handy model of best fit relates the leader, the subordinates, the task in hand and the environment. These elements are both interactive and mobile.

This must be developed further. For example, if the group is ineffective it becomes easy to state 'best fit was not achieved' without necessarily carrying out any further investigation, which is very superficial.

Handy describes this as consisting of:

- support – behaviour that enhances group members' feelings of personal worth;
- interaction/facilitation – encouraging members to develop mutually satisfying and supportive relationships;
- goal emphasis – behaviour that stimulates desire and drives for excellent operational performance;
- work facilitation – classical management activities of scheduling, coordination and planning.

Peters states that to this may be added the need to nurture qualities of flexibility, commitment, responsiveness and drive. This is achieved by a combination of direction and support on the part of the leader, and is a responsibility of anybody who conducts any form of leadership or supervision.

Furthermore, in many parts of the Western world there has emerged a consensus culture. In its widest terms this means that people need, want and are entitled to know where they stand, both so that they may consent to work and so that they may understand the basis on which this consent is requested or demanded.

Best fit is therefore a form of 'the organisation in its environment' approach to leadership: a super-contingency approach. It recognises the need to translate qualities and attributes into situational applications, and that each approach to leadership has a contribution to make.

9.3 The complexities of leadership

When the position of leader/manager/supervisor is taken on, certain assumptions are made and certain roles are adopted.

■ Assumptions

The leader acts in the name of the particular organisation, department or function. She must therefore have a degree of power, influence, authority, responsibility and accountability, which should be used in the pursuit of effective leadership performance. This may be enhanced, diminished or withdrawn by the organisation at any time (in Western organisations, this is usually, but not always, as the result of some form of consultation or appraisal of performance).

The leader must be acceptable to all those with whom she comes into contact. This applies both inside and outside the organisation. The range and complexity of relationships that she must develop are dependent on this.

The leader has certain clearly defined tasks, activities and directions. The leader also has a sphere in which her personal judgement and initiative are to be exercised. This includes the qualities of flexibility, dynamism and responsiveness, and also includes characteristics of honesty, trustworthiness and integrity.

Leaders must have a working knowledge and understanding of the tasks being carried out by those in their sphere of influence. This does not mean being a technical expert. For example, managers who have secretaries cannot always type, but they must understand what typing is, how long typing takes, what is an acceptable level of performance, what is an acceptable level of presentation, what is the best and most suitable machinery on which typing is to take place, and so on; this extends to all spheres of activity. Where there is no such understanding dysfunction always occurs.

9.4 Functions of leaders in organisations

This is a general list of these functions. They may be found in all directorial, managerial and supervisory positions to a greater or lesser extent.

- setting, agreeing and communicating objectives;
- providing suitable equipment, resources and environment to enable people to meet their objectives;
- monitoring, evaluating and reviewing performance, appraisal of groups and individuals;
- giving feedback;
- setting standards of attitude, behaviour and performance;
- solving problems, both operational and human; administering rewards and punishments wherever necessary; dealing with grievances and discipline;
- organising and harmonising resources;
- ensuring inward flows of materials;
- ensuring that deadlines for outputs are met;
- taking effective decisions;
- developing the capabilities and performance of the group and its members;
- development efficiency and effectiveness of the group and its output;
- figurehead and representative roles inside and outside the department;
- parenting role.

It is clear from such a list that much of the leadership function of managers and supervisors is behavioural. Those aspects that are not overtly so still require attention to the behavioural aspects. For example, creation of an effective working environment requires consideration of such matters as personal proximity; organising work requires an understanding of the best ways to organise people to ensure that output is as good and as high as possible over long periods of time. From this, a further range of leadership qualities required in managers may be developed.

1 **Empathy:** understanding the reactions of people to particular requests, situations and problems; understanding and sympathising with their point of view; the ability to identify with the likes, dislikes, aspirations, hopes and fears of the group and its members.
2 **Communication:** in clear and straightforward terms, and in the language of the receivers.
3 **Equality, evenness and fairness:** arising especially from the performance, monitoring, problem-solving, rewarding and punishment elements.
4 **Creativity and resourcefulness:** in developing the work and the staff involved; and in developing effective and positive relations with those from outside the group or department.
5 **Attention:** the active participation and involvement of all aspects of the direction of the work, of the functioning and interest of those carrying it out and to those external factors that affect it.

9.5 Conclusions

When studied in this way it becomes clear that, for all its dependence upon quality, styles, roles and assumptions there is much in the concept and content of leadership that can be pinned down fairly precisely. We have said little about appearance, manner or bearing: that is, the extent to which individuals look the part, sound the part, act the part (anything, in fact, rather than being the part). Rather, it is clear that there is a substantial body of knowledge and expertise upon which to draw both in the assessment of what leadership is and also in the identification of who will make a good leader (and who will not). There are lessons here for those in charge of organisations and personnel and human resource professionals. It is possible to take positive, informed and enlightened steps towards the successful and effective identification, development and appointment of the right people for these positions.

It is also clear that leaders are made and not born. People can be trained in each of the qualities and elements indicated so that (as with anything else) they may first understand, then apply, then reinforce and finally become expert in the activities indicated. This is understood to be on the same basis as aptitude for anything else, however. Not everyone has the qualities or potential necessary in the first place. There is nothing contentious in this: not everyone has the qualities or potential to be a great chef, racing driver, nurse or labourer, and in this respect leadership is no different.

10 Teams and groups

10.1 Introduction

Teams and groups are gatherings of two or more people that either exist or are drawn together and constituted for a purpose. This purpose is understood and accepted by all those involved. This purpose may be:

- largely social – sports and leisure clubs;
- work or task-oriented – workplace groups, committees, task and project groups, other *ad hoc* but organised gatherings;
- based on the norms and expectations of society, above all the family (nuclear and extended);
- based on the beliefs and values of the members – churches and religious groups;
- based on the expertise of members – professional bodies, legalised associations;
- mutual interest – trade unions; also hobbies and interests.

Joining organisations and their departments, divisions, functions, locations and activities also constitutes team and group membership.

In society, people become members of groups and teams from an early age and move into and out of these throughout their lives. Very young children often go to play groups. A child may belong to the cubs or brownies and move on to the guides and scouts because there is an age barrier to membership of each. More generally, belonging to a school class or school sports team constitutes group membership. The process of belonging to, and joining and changing groups, is established at an early age and is part of the wider and general socialisation process. By the time of joining a workplace this is well understood.

Additionally, groups may usefully be defined in the following ways.

1 **Formal:** constituted for a precise purpose. Formal groups normally have rules, regulations and norms that support the pursuit of that purpose. Formal groups also normally have means and methods of preserving and enhancing their expertise. There are also likely to be means and methods that enable people to move in, contribute and move out of a given group.
2 **Informal:** where the purpose is less precise but still clearly understood and accepted by all involved. A card school falls into this category, as does a Friday night gathering of friends and colleagues at the bar.
3 **Psychological:** viewed from the point of view that membership is dependent

upon people interacting with each other, being aware of each other, and perceiving themselves to belong.

Groups may be distinguished in these ways from gatherings of people drawn together for a more general purpose: for example, queuing to pay at the supermarket or waiting for a bus or train. Even in these circumstances a group identity may start to form. If the queue takes a long while to clear or if the bus or train is late, people start to form an identity (at least for the moment) based around the particular set of circumstances. This may lead to the constitution of a more enduring group for the future (a travelling group on the train, for example).

From this, an initial general set of group characteristics may begin to be identified.

1 The ability of each member to communicate with every other member of the group.
2 A collective identity based on a combination of the circumstances and environment in which members find themselves.
3 Shared aims and objectives – in the examples indicated above, these are the ability to travel and arrive at the required destination; the expectation (hope) that eventually those present will be served by the cashier at the supermarket; and the need to pass the time involved productively and comfortably in the activities indicated (that is, waiting and travelling).
4 Roles and structure – again, in the examples indicated these may be: a joker; the finder of a compartment in which to sit; the provider of newspapers and magazines; and so on. The leadership structure may begin to be based around one who makes suggestions: 'Why don't we move to another queue/call the supervisor?'; 'Why don't we bring sandwiches/tea/ beer/cards?'; and so on.
5 Norms and rules – personal behaviour starts to become modified as the result of membership of the group. Smokers may resist or curtail their habit when in the presence of group members; patterns of dress may start to emerge. This is the general basis on which organisational groups are structured and developed.

10.2 Purpose

Organisational groups are constituted for a purpose, to meet a set of aims and objectives. These purposes generally fall into one of the following categories:

- distribution work, by department, division, function, location, skill, aptitude, expertise and quality;
- controlling work, through the placing of managers and supervisors at the head of teams and groups of people constituted for the purpose of conducting work;
- project work and problem-solving, often constituted on an *ad hoc* basis and for the life and duration of the specific matter in hand (though there are certain circumstances where this leads to future activities);
- creative activities, brainstorming, information pooling and gathering, the generation of bursts of energy and enlightenment in response to given issues;
- the conduct of inquiries into past activities, both successful and those which fail;

- the investigation and resolution of conflicts, grievances, disputes and arguments between individuals and groups;
- clustering: of persons of the same profession or occupation from different departments; of equivalent levels of expertise in different fields; of equivalent rank (for example, managers and supervisors); for the purposes of exchanging and gathering general information and knowledge; and a wider understanding of the total organisational and professional picture;
- taking responsibility for the direction and management of particular organisation's activities and services;
- coordinating and harmonising sets of activities, often from different sources, functions, departments, divisions and expertise;
- implementing initiatives, directions, policies, strategies and decisions;
- for other specific organisational matters, especially health and safety, staff relations and consultation.

Whatever the purpose, more precise characteristics and factors are required if the group is to be successful and effective.

■ Work groups and the individual

Work groups serve organisational purposes and provide a useful and effective means of dividing and allocating tasks. Individuals have a high propensity to work in this way. As stated in the introduction, movement into, around and out of groups is a pattern of general behaviour learned and instilled from a very early age. Belonging to work groups, therefore, is a means of satisfying social and affiliation needs long since learned while present within the organisation.

Through membership of work groups individuals also seek the following:

- distinctive work roles within which they can be comfortable and happy, and which satisfy their feelings of self esteem;
- establishing a self-summary and self-concept which can be presented both to others in the work group and also to the world at large;
- contribution to productive, positive, profitable and effective activities (this, in itself, leads to satisfaction and feelings of personal success and raised levels of self-esteem);
- the ability to fulfil personal aims and ambitions which normally have to harmonised and entwined with those of a particular organisation.

These reasons for belonging overlap and conflict. Group norms and processes may also create distinctive pressures on individuals to perform in given ways, at certain speeds and to adopt given patterns of behaviour. This creates conflict between the requirements of the organisation, the group and the individual.

■ Conformity

This also indicates the pressure to conform. In many cases the individual must either conform to the group norms or be expelled or rejected.

If individuals choose not to conform they may be ostracised. Others in the group may choose not to work with them, either out of choice or because of group pressure placed on them to conform. These individuals may themselves be ~~rejection~~ threatened with rejection or expulsion.

Conformity is therefore a very powerful pressure. It is a critical part of the norming process. It also impacts on both the nature and the effectiveness of the performance of the group. Conformity may also lead to group-think and the bunker mentality (strength and belief in the world according to the view held by group members).

10.3 The creation of effective groups

Tuckman (1965) identifies four elements as follows.

1. **Forming**. The coming together of the individuals concerned; beginning to learn about each other (personality, strengths, capabilities); assessment of the group purpose; introduction to the tasks, aims and objectives; initial thoughts about rules, norms, ways of working and achieving objectives; initial social and personal interaction; introduction to the group leader/leadership; acquiring and setting resources; constraints, drives and priorities.

2. **Storming**. The first creative burst of the group; energising the activities; gaining initial markers about its capabilities and capacities and those of its members; creating the first output and results; mutual appraisal and assessment of expertise and process. Initial conflicts tend to become apparent at this stage, together with the need for means for their resolution. Opportunities and diversions may also become apparent. Conflicts between group and personal agendas start to emerge. *— Conforming to grap norms*

3. **Norming**. The establishment of norms: the behavioural boundaries within which members are to act and operate; the establishment of rules and codes of conduct that underline and reinforce the standards set by the norms. By doing this, the group provides itself with means of control and the basis of acceptable and unacceptable conduct, performance and activities.

For rules and norms to be effective they must be clear, understood and accepted by all. They must be capable of doing what they set out to do. They must reinforce the mutuality, confidence and integrity necessary to effective group performance.

4. **Performing**. The addressing of matters in hand; attacking the tasks to be carried out; getting results; assessing performance. This includes attention to group effectiveness and cohesion, as well as absolute performance measures; the two are invariably entwined.

This has to be seen as a process rather than a linear progression, a series of steps and stages: for example, early successes in the life of the group may come strictly under 'performing' but are nevertheless essential to the gaining of mutual confidence, trust and reliance that are integral to effective 'forming'.

■ Issues facing work groups

The following are an indication of the main issues facing work groups:

- atmosphere and relationships;
- the nature of relationships (closeness, friendliness, formality and informality);
- participation (the nature and extent to which participation is to be allowed);
- understanding and acceptance of aims and objectives and the commitment required for this;
- availability, access and use of information;
- means for handling disagreements and conflict;
- means and methods of decision-making;
- evaluation and appraisal of member performance;
- evaluation and appraisal of group performance;
- expression of feelings – how this should be done, the consequences of this, whether penalties (formal or informal) are to be issued and, if so, by whom;
- leadership, relating both to the leadership of the total group and also to the individual tasks for which it has been constituted;
- maintenance activities, including the development of group members and the bringing in of new and fresh talents and expertise as and when required.

■ The final curtain

Owen (1985) finds that it is better for the future of the individuals concerned if a celebration of the group's achievements is held when it finishes. This gives everyone a point of reference for the work that has been done and the personal and professional commitment that was made. This is equivalent to a funeral or wake, both mourning and celebrating its passing. Those involved then go on into the future, knowing that the past is complete and behind them and that a successful job was done with good people.

■ Group size and characteristics

There is a range of factors to be taken into account here. There are some absolutes: the size of a tennis doubles team is two; of a football team, eleven. In work situations the technology used may determine that a group size is three, eight, thirty or whatever.

In general terms there is a balance involved between size, contribution and participation: the larger the group, the greater the range of expertise and quality is drawn in, but the lesser the chance of a full participation by individual members.

Larger groups also have a greater risk of splitting into subgroups (either formal, based on the work, or informal, based on workstation location, friendship, the establishment of common bonds and interests). Total group identity may then become diluted. The interaction between the subgroups becomes a barrier to the progress and achievement of the full group. The subgroups create their own barriers themselves, especially if these have become constituted around the

Table 10.1 Characteristics of effective and ineffective groups

Effective groups	Ineffective groups
• Informal relaxed atmosphere	• Bored or tense atmosphere
• Much discussion, high level of participation	• Discussion dominated by one or two people
• Tasks, aims and objectives clearly understood	• Discussion often irrelevant, unstructured and away from the point
• Commitment of members of the groups to each other	• No common aims, objectives and purposes
• Commitment of members of the group to the tasks, aims and objectives	• Members do not value each other's contribution or listen to each other
• Members respect each other's views and listen to each other	• Conflict is allowed to develop into open warfare; it may also be suppressed
• Conflict is brought out into the open and dealt with constructively when it arises	• Majority voting is the norm; pressure is put on minorities to accept this
• Decisions are reached by consensus; voting is only used as a matter of last resort	• Consensus is neither sought nor achieved
• Ideas are expressed freely and openly; rejection of ideas is not a stigma	• Criticism is embarrassing and personal
• Leadership is shared as appropriate; is divided according to the nature of the tasks; ultimate responsibility, authority and accountability rests with the designated group leader	• Leadership is by diktat and is issued by the group leader only
• The group examines its own progress and behaviour	• The group avoids any discussion about its behaviour

Source: from D. McGregor (1961).

distinctive expertise of members. If this is in high demand by the rest of the main group, the subgroup establishes its own filter and priority systems based on its preferences and criteria.

On the other hand, smaller groups tend to avoid the subgrouping effect; they may, however, develop a group identity so strong that it tends to lead to belief in its own infallibility and indispensability.

The size of any group therefore has clear implications, both for its management and leadership and also for participants if these pitfalls are to be avoided.

❒ Leadership

In group situations, leadership is especially concerned with:

- management of the task: setting work methods, time scales, resource gathering, problem-solving and maintenance functions;
- management of the process: the use of interpersonal skills and the interaction with the environment to gain the maximum contribution from everyone involved;
- managing communications: between different work groups and subgroups and the disciplines and professions involved to harmonise potential conflicts

and to ensure that inter-group relations are productive and not dysfunctionally competitive;

- managing the individual: making constructive use of individual differences and ensuring that individual contributions are both valued and of value;
- management style: the creation and adoption of a style that is appropriate and suitable to the situation;
- maintenance management: ensuring that both the effectiveness of the work and of the group itself are supported, appraised and developed;
- establishing common aims and objectives that are understood, valued and adopted by all group members;
- establishing shared values and absolute standards of honesty and integrity;
- creating an effective and positive group and team spirit;
- maintaining and developing the group so that its cohesion improves, and its output increases.

■ Group ideology

This is normally based around concepts of participation, involvement and recognition of the value of the contribution that each member makes, and it is under-pinned by norms and rules.

On the other hand, a measure of conformity is normally expected of individuals by the groups to which they belong. This works best where the individual aims and objectives are capable of being harmonised and integrated with those of the group.

Individuals may also choose to belong to a group (or seek to join it) because of the strong and distinctive ideology. Trade unions and religious institutions are clear examples of this. Some organisations – for example, Body Shop, Nissan – also attract people because of their strong commitment to the environment or product and service quality.

■ Power and influence

This is the position of the group in relation to others in the organisation. It is based on both behavioural and operational factors.

The behavioural factors mainly concern the matters of relative respect and regard with which the group in question is held by others within the organisation. There are questions of perception also related, for example, to the extent to which the given group is seen or believed to be high status, a stepping stone on the path to success, or a cul-de-sac from which no-one ever emerges with credit.

The operational concerns include the nature of the work carried out and the value that this adds to the organisation's activities. It also concerns the ability to command and wield resources and information.

There are also elements of realpolitik involved: for example, the ability to block progress, to filter resources and information, to determine the speed, volume and quality of work.

■ Group behaviour

The following forms of group behaviour may be identified.

❐ Conformity

Conformity is the outward manifestation of a combination of behavioural, professional, organisational and operational activities. Its purpose is to ensure series and sets of standards and outputs, and to give the organisation in question and its groups their own distinctive identity and consistency.

In pursuit of this, standards of behaviour, address, attitude and performance are required and established. The organisation establishes norms, customs, modes of dress, modes of behaviour, attendance patterns, work manners, work organisation, and performance measures of this work. The basis of all this is established at the induction stage and developed alongside other ways in which the organisation and its groups behave.

❐ Regimentation

This is the coercive approach to conformity. This is imposed by the organisation or by parts of it on the staff concerned. It consists of requirements to adhere strictly to codes of practice, conduct, dress and address. It is most useful in dangerous and other extreme conditions where sets or series of behaviour can be devised in order to control the danger as far as possible and to provide step-by-step approaches as and when emergencies do arise. It is also used to an extent in military forces, and emergency services.

Moreover, it is to be found in those forms of organisation designed along strictly hierarchical lines where there are strict orders of progression from position to the next, where promotion and advancement are based on loyalty and longevity of service and where there are highly structured and restricted jobs, tasks and practices.

❐ Internalisation

This is the receptive approach to conformity. In this, those working for the particular organisation adopt its attitudes, values and beliefs as their own. The interests of the organisation and its groups and those of the staff coincide exactly. There is an overwhelming responsibility placed on the organisation if this is what is required and/or if this is what happens in fact.

The attitudes, values and beliefs in question must be positive, beneficial, ethical, and have a universal long-term interest. All of this is itself subject to interpretation by the wider society in question, and by those in whose interest the attitudes, values and beliefs are engendered. The whole process is both subjective and highly corruptible. Examples of the extreme results of this include the Inquisition, Nazism, Pol Pot and the 'killing fields' of South-East Asia, and the ethnic cleansing of the new countries of the former Yugoslavia.

❐ Compliance and acceptance

This is the recognition of the validity of the organisation's claim upon the talents and expertise of the person in question and of the requirement to go along with this. It constitutes behavioural acceptance of the need to conform and a willingness to do this. It does not indicate anything deeper than this.

This is closely related to the discipline of the organisation. By accepting a job with the organisation, the individual accepts also any strictures and rule and regulations that may legitimately be devised and enforced in the pursuit of its purposes.

❒ Eccentricity

This type of behaviour organisations neither condone nor encourage, and but neither do they reject. Organisations are normally prepared and willing to accommodate eccentricity for its own purposes (for example, where particular individuals have rare or special skills that are required).

Forms of eccentric behaviour may be encouraged and nurtured by the organisation as part of its own creative processes. Research and development departments, for example, require creative and imaginative individuals who defy and question conventions.

The main organisational behavioural problem is the extent to which such organisations are both prepared and willing to accommodate this behaviour. This is less trite than may first appear. Eccentricity may be dysfunctional to the rest of the organisation. It may in itself create resentment among those in mainstream and steady-state mode departments and functions. It may create the perception (or indeed the reality) that eccentricity is tolerated in some parts of the organisation but not others.

■ Sources of stress and malfunction in groups

These are as follows.

1 The clarity of purpose of the group.
2 The nature of the working environment, including ergonomic factors, technology, location and design of workstations, the physical distance/proximity that exists between group members. This also includes extremes of temperature, climate, discomfort, danger and location.
3 Levels of performance. Stress and strain is more likely to occur when the particular group is going through a bad patch or one that has no tangible result for a long period of time. It also occurs during levels of very high performance when individuals start trying to take credit for the team's total achievement.
4 Matters outside the group's control. To minimise the effect of these it is necessary to recognise what they are and the extent and frequency of their occurrence. Worrying about them is both unproductive and debilitating.

❒ Team and group malfunction

Causes of group malfunction are as follows:

- lack of clarity of purpose, direction, aims and objectives; and conflicting directions, aims and objectives;
- lack of leadership and direction; inappropriate leadership style; extended and complex chains of command;

- lack of resources; inadequate and inappropriate resources, including finance, expertise, premises and technology;
- lack of mutual confidence, trust, respect and regard among group members;
- lack of responsibility and autonomy (within the broadest context); lack of control; lack of ability to shape and influence its own destiny;
- inappropriate, convoluted, complicated administration, reporting relationships and procedures;
- lack of balance of group maintenance and operational elements (What usually happens in this case is that the group spends all its time on its own development to the detriment and neglect of the work in hand);
- lack of wider regard and respect (on the part of the organisation and other groups) for what the group is trying to achieve, for its achievements, for its needs and wants.
- lack of recognition of progress and achievement; lack of measurement and assessment of progress and achievement;
- lack of ability to act as its own advocate, lobby, self-promoter;
- lack of interest in the work; lack of perceived respect and value of the work on the part of the wider organisation;
- lack of equality of treatment, value, regard and respect of group members; lack of equality of treatment of the group itself in regard to the rest of the organisation;
- lack of consultation, participation and involvement in the communication, decision-making and directorial processes;
- failure to play to the strengths and talents of group members; giving tasks to people who have no aptitude for them.

These elements may arise through neglect and indifference on the part of the organisation concerned. They may occur simply because the work of the group in question is a little way down the order of priorities (even though it is actually valued).

Dysfunction can also be engendered. This occurs in the worst forms of inter-departmental strife, and also happens where the organisation makes a point of moving its malcontents or failures to one particular location.

Symptoms of group malfunction are as follows.

1 Poor performance, in which deadlines are missed, output is substandard and customer complaints increase.
2 Decline: members decline or reject responsibility for their actions and for the group itself. They become involved in lobbying and seek to blame others for these shortcomings. The group breaks up into subgroups and elites are created within the wider group. Individuals claim rewards and bonuses for team efforts. Scapegoating occurs showing destructive criticism and dismissive behaviour towards others, both inside and outside the group.
3 Becoming involved in grievances with other group members; increases in the numbers of these; personality and personal clashes; over-spill of professional and expert argument into personal relationships.
4 Increases in general levels of grievances, absenteeism and accidents; moves to leave the group.

5 Lack of interest in results, activities, plans and proposals of the group.
6 General attitude and demeanour that exists between group members; the general attitude and demeanour of individuals within the group; lack of pride and joy in the group; moves to leave the group again; difficulties in attracting new members to the group.

❐ Rejection

Malfunction is caused when individuals are rejected by the rest of the group. This occurs in two main ways. The first is where the individual is rejected because of an error that he has made which is seen to be extremely costly or detrimental by the other members.

The other form occurs in relation to new members who are ostracised and given no chance to settle in and become effective. This happens, for example, where a much-valued and respected (possibly also long serving and popular) member has recently left and the replacement is forever being compared unfavourably with the previous incumbent.

❐ Favouritism

This always arises as the result of bad leadership and management. The leaders or managers in question identify individuals whom they treat more favourably than the rest. The rest of the group find ways of coping with this. The most common form again is ostracism. The favoured individual may also be manipulated as a channel of expediency by the others (as a lobby for extra resources, for example).

❐ Blame

This is where individuals blame the team or the group of which they are members for their own failure to progress.

❐ Pecking order

One of the strategies for the management of variety of conflicts is giving everyone concerned the opportunity to do particular things (normally the most favoured or prestigious activities). When an individual does not get her turn she feels slighted and aggrieved.

❐ Attitude and behaviour problems

This is where 'one bad apple affects the whole box'. The individual who takes no pride or joy in the work, no interest in the results and who is constantly critical or negative affects all the rest of the group. The manifestation of this is in absence, lateness, sloppiness of work, rudeness, negative criticism, grumbling and complaints.

10.4 Group development

The creation and formation of effective teams and groups is not an end in itself. To remain effective, cohesion, capabilities and potential must be maintained and developed, and this takes the following forms.

1 Infusions of talent from outside, bringing in people with distinctive qualities and expertise to give emphases and energy to particular priorities and directions.
2 Infusions of new skills, knowledge and qualities from within through the identification of potential from among existing members and giving them training and development, and targeted work that has the purpose of bringing out the required expertise.
3 Attention to group processes when it is apparent that these are getting in the way of effective task performance; and attention to task performance when it is apparent that this is ineffective
4 Attention to the relationship between team and task. This may involve using a good team to carry out a difficult or demanding task; or using the difficult and demanding task to build a good and effective team. From either standpoint, the results will only be fully effective if the task achievement is within the capabilities of the group. As long as this is so, the rewards of success are likely to contribute greatly to overall group performance, well-being and confidence among members.
5 Attention to team roles, both to build on strengths and also to eliminate weaknesses. This is likely to involve reassessing what the requirements and priorities are; reassessing the strengths and weaknesses of each individual; and possibly leading to reallocation or rotation of roles and infusions of new talent, either from within or without.
6 Attention to team roles and expertise from the point of view that different qualities, expertise and capability are likely to be more or less important at different phases of activity. This may lead to infusions again, or to the buying-in of expertise (for example, using consultants) on an 'as-required' basis. It may also involve the recognition that members of the group may need to be divested once they have made their particular contribution.
7 Recognising the concept of group life cycle. Akin to that of the product life cycle, it recognises points at which infusions and divestments may need to be made. It also recognises the more general requirements for re-energising, revitalising, rejuvenating, or even ending; again, along similar lines to products.

Other factors in group development include the following.

■ Starters

This refers to the extent to which new members are welcomed into the group and steps taken to ensure that they settle in as quickly as possible, become comfortable and start to make a positive contribution to the work.

Insufficient attention to this – whether by accident, ignorance or design – is likely to cause dysfunction. It is certain to make the critical contribution of a new starter less effective. This may, in turn, colour the perceptions of his capabilities by the rest of the group forever, making it certain that he will never be fully effective.

■ Leavers

This refers to the view taken of individuals when they leave the group. It includes the extent to which their contribution continues to be valued after they have left, and the prevailing attitudes towards both themselves as individuals, and their capabilities and achievements.

Some groups take a negative view of individuals who leave. This is likely to stem from feelings that the group itself is being rejected, sometimes leading to questioning its value and worth among those who remain. It may arise also from envy on the part of those remaining where the individual is going on to demonstrably better things.

This negative view may also occur as a form of self-protection for those who remain behind. In order to help preserve the cohesion of those remaining, the leaver becomes 'the common enemy'.

■ Rejuvenation

This stems from a combination of realising that the group is under-performing or under-achieving, and the determination to do something about this. Successful rejuvenation normally comes about as the result of:

- general acceptance on the part of everyone concerned that this state of affairs exists;
- identity between members and within the group, together with a strong desire for it to succeed;
- universal acceptance of the way forward, whatever that may be (this is much more effective where it is agreed among the members, than where it is imposed; if a particular course of action is clearly indicated, then effort must be spent in convincing everyone involved of its merits, as a lesser course of action which has full support is often more effective);
- infusion of resources, such as skills, knowledge, qualities, finance and equipment, time and communications.

■ Reprocessing

This involves going through a version of the group cohesion process but with those already present. This can be seen as:

- reforming; and then
- re-storming;
- re-norming;
- re-performing.

It is most likely to be effective where the need for the group and its work is strong but where insufficient attention has been paid to group processes, where identity is therefore not strong, and where current levels of output are suffering as the result.

■ Recognition

This involves attention to the ways in which the work of the group is received. It is likely to be more of a problem where the organisation's style sets great store on recognition of achievement (rather than the fact of it) and also where there is a need on the part of group members for recognition.

Group development activities have the greatest effect when everyone is involved and where real problems and issues are addressed. The environment in which these take place is less of a problem than the content. If the content is artificial, then the effect may be counter-productive. In these situations, members often feel that they are wasting their time. In the end, the binding element is the purpose for which the group has been created, and this will ultimately be the measure of its net value, worth and achievements.

10.5 High performing teams and groups

The characteristics of high performing teams and groups may be summarised as follows.

1 High levels of autonomy, the ability to self-manage and self-organise. This also includes team responsibility for self-regulation and self-discipline. It encourages the fast and effective resolution of problems and a commitment to dealing with issues before they become problems.
2 Clear and unambiguous performance targets, capable of achievement and related to overall organisation purpose; which should be understood, accepted and committed to by all concerned.
3 Full responsibility for all aspects of production and output process, quality assurance, customer relations and complaints. Issues and problems are identified and addressed to the particular team so that improvements can be made directly without going through subprocesses and procedures.
4 Job titles do not include references to status, differentials or trappings, or other elements of psychological distance.
5 Team-based reward systems available and payable to everyone who contributed, based on percentages of salary rather than occupational differentials.
6 The open approach – to environment layout (no individual offices, trappings, barriers or other factors of physical and psychological distance); self-commitment for the whole team; open communication systems and high quality communications; open approaches to problems and issues; open airing of grievances and concerns (these are usually very few in such circumstances, so that when they do arise full attention is paid).
7 Federal relationship with the core organisation with reporting relationships based on monitoring, review and evaluation of production and output targets and other task-based indicators. General management style must be supportive rather than directive, bureaucratic or administrative.
8 Fast and easy access to maintenance and support staff to ensure that

equipment breakdowns are repaired as soon as possible and that production levels can be kept as high as possible for as long as possible.

9 Full flexibility of work, multi-skilling and inter-changeability between task roles. Group roles are assigned to people's behavioural strengths.

10 Continuous development of skills, knowledge, qualities, capabilities and expertise; continuous attention to performance quality and output; continuous attention to production, quality, volume and time; continuous attention to high levels of service and satisfaction.

11 High levels of involvement, confidence, respect and enthusiasm among group members, both towards each other and the work.

12 Attention to equipment and technology to ensure that this is suitable and capable of producing that which is required to the stated and expected standards of volume, quality and time.

13 Simple, clear and supportive policies and procedures covering organisational rules and regulations, human resource management and discipline, grievance and disputes.

14 Continuous monitoring and review to ensure that the intended focus and direction is pursued and that group activities are in accordance with this.

10.6 Conclusions

The creation of effective work groups increases the burdens placed on organisations and their managers in terms of attention to behavioural as well as operational factors. Successful groups come about as the result of a combination of the effectiveness of both of these elements. Both group members and group managers require the ability to think things through, develop and present arguments, make judgements and influence others to their point of view. The rewards to be gained by organisations are to be found in consistent and high levels of output delivered by committed people with a real concern for satisfaction and success. This is the rationale for constituting effective work teams.

⚡ **11** Conflict

11.1 Introduction

Conflict exists in all situations where individuals and groups are in disagreement with each other for whatever reason. This potential therefore exists everywhere, where two or more people are gathered together; a world without differences and disagreements is inconceivable! Much of the conflict of the world stems from the basic lack of recognition of this, and the inability to address it in ways designed to alleviate its effect or, better still, to identify the positive and beneficial potential that is inherent in most situations.

Prima facie, therefore, the potential for conflict exists in all forms of organisation. It is essential that all those concerned with conception, direction and ordering of organisations understand its sources and causes, and are able to address these positively (see Figure 11.1).

11.2 Levels of conflict

The following levels of conflict may be distinguished: argument; competition; and warfare. Argument and competition may be either positive, healthy and creative or negative, unhealthy and destructive. Warfare is always destructive.

The nature, symptoms and causes must be understood and these then become a focus for management action in striving for productive and harmonious places of work.

It is useful at the outset to establish the presence of conflict in organisations (as in all human situations). Conflict may be seen as positive and beneficial, a force capable of being harnessed for the greater good and contributing to organisation effectiveness. It is also clearly negative in many forms. Three distinctive variations on the theme are also apparent.

■ Argument, discussion and debate

This takes place between groups of two or more people and brings about (whether by accident or design) a better quality, more informed and better balanced view of the matter in hand. Provided that it is positive, the process of argument and debate leads to a better understanding also of the hopes, fears and aspirations of other group members. It also identifies gaps in knowledge and

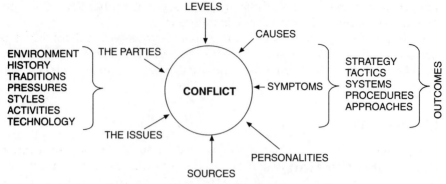

Figure 11.1   The nature of organisation conflict

expertise. This can then be remedied, either through training or the inclusion in the debate of persons with the required expertise. It helps in the process of building mutual confidence and respect. It also encourages individuals to dig into their own resources, expertise and experience and to use these for the benefit of all concerned. It helps to build group identity. It leads to a better quality of decision-making and understanding and acceptance of the reasons why particular directions are chosen.

Argument, discussion and debate become unproductive if not structured. People must be clear what they are debating, otherwise they will inevitably argue about different things. At the very least this leads to group dysfunction and disharmony in the particular situation. The essence is therefore to be able to set out the desired aims and objectives of the discussion and to have available as far as possible all necessary information.

❐ Rules for productive and positive argument, discussion and debate

These are as follows.

1 Mutual interest of all concerned in the resolution of the matter in hand.
2 Commitment to the debate itself and to the matters on the agenda.
3 Honesty and openness so that differing views may become public and be heard without prejudice or penalty to the holders.
4 A structure for the debate that addresses issues, facts, feelings and values and which has a clearly understood purpose. This is true of all good discussions. Creative acts (such as brainstorming) have the clear intent of producing a wide range of ideas in as short a time as possible. The best committees work to an agenda, remit and terms of reference.
5 Mutual trust and confidence in the personalities and expertise of those involved.

There are therefore both positive and negative aspects of the argument, debate and discussion process. It is likely to indicate where more serious differences may lie, especially if these indicate persistent clashes between particular individuals; where alliances start to form in the debating chamber and which carry on after the debate has finished; and where people adopt contrary positions based on countering the views of someone else in the group.

In these cases argument itself is not going to resolve the problems and it is necessary to look more closely into the situation. Invariably, there will be deeper, underlying conflicts that need to be addressed if the group is to be made effective again.

■ Competition

Competition exists between individuals and groups and within organisations. It also exists between organisations. It is either positive or negative, healthy or unhealthy. At its best, competition sets standards for all to follow, whether within the organisation or within the entire sphere within which it operates. On a global scale, the standards of production, quality and managerial practice of certain organisations are held up as models to which the rest of the world should aspire. Some sectors arrange their organisations into league tables, thus shining a competitive light on some aspects of the activities carried out.

The nature of competition may be:

- closed or distributive, where one party wins at the expense of others;
- open or integrative, where there is scope for everyone to succeed;
- collaborative, where the boundaries of operations of each party can be set to ensure that everyone has a fair share of 'the cake' (that is, whatever is being competed for). The competitive environment may be dominated by one party or a few large parties who each take what they want from the situation and whatever is left over is to be disputed among the remaining players.

In organisational behaviour terms, competition is more likely to be fruitful and productive if it is open, if the rewards for competing effectively are available to all. Competition is likely to degenerate into conflicts where, for example, competition for resources or accommodation is closed and one party succeeds at the expense of the others.

Competitive relationships exist best within organisations where attention is positively given to standards, creativity, the nature of the groups and the purpose of creating the situation. The aim is to bring out the best in everyone concerned, to improve performance and efficiency, to set absolute standards for activities and from this to form a base from which improvements can still be made. If these elements and rationale are not present, then organisations should consider alternative means of achieving their purpose. A negative competitive approach is likely to lead to inter-departmental strife, especially where the form of competition is closed.

■ Warfare

Warfare exists where inter-group relations have been allowed to get out of hand, where the main aims and objectives of activities have been lost and where great energies and resources are taken up with fighting one's corner, reserving one's position and denigrating other departments and functions.

❑ Causes

Resources

Internal organisation warfare is often centred around resource questions and issues. It emerges when departments and individuals perceive that those who have control over resources are susceptible to non-operational approaches. They are also perceived to have their own reasons for issuing resources to particular departments (for example, the availability or potential for triumphs), gaining favour and acceptance as a result.

Influence

Competition for power and influence is also apparent. A multiple agenda is normally pursued. Particular groups and individuals present their achievements in the best possible light. This takes various forms and aims to ensure that:

- real achievements are recognised;
- achievements are presented in ways acceptable to the sources of power and influence (for example, Chief Executive Officer (or CEO), top managers, particular shareholders and stakeholders, the community at large);
- the group is receptive to patronage and that there are rewards to be gained by both the patron and those who come within their ambit;
- they are presented as major achievements, the best possible return on resources and expertise put in;
- the department or individual is presented as having intrinsically high value and expertise, and is available for higher favours, better jobs; they can be relied upon to produce 'the right results';
- the results are attached (where possible or desirable) to questions of organisation success.

11.3 Sources of conflict in organisations

Most organisation conflict can be traced back to one or more of the following:

- competition for resources and the basis on which this is conducted;
- lack of absolute standards of openness, honesty, trustworthiness and integrity in general organisational behaviour and in dealings between staff, departments, divisions and functions between different grades of staff and between seniors and subordinates; lack of mutual respect;
- lack of shared values, commitment, enthusiasm, poor motivation and low morale;
- unfairness, unevenness and inequality of personal and professional treatment, often linked to perceptions (and realities) of favouritism and scapegoating;
- physical and psychological barriers, especially those between seniors and subordinates, and also those between departments, divisions and functions;
- inability to meet expectations and fulfil promises; this is always compounded by the use of bureaucratic (mealy-mouthed) words and phrases;
- expediency and short-termism that interferes with or dilutes the results that would otherwise be achieved;

- the nature of work and its professional, expert and technical context;
- the structure of work, the division and allocation of tasks and jobs;
- people involved, their hopes and fears, aspirations, ambitions, beliefs, attitudes and values;
- different perceptions of what is right and wrong; differences in attitudes, values and beliefs; different ethical standards;
- divergence of managerial, professional, technical and commercial objectives; divergence between service demands and budgetary pressures in public services.

11.4 Symptoms of conflict

These involve one or more of the following:

1 Poor communications between groups, individuals and the organisation and its components.
2 Poor inter-group relationships based on envy, jealousy and anger at the position of others, rather than mutual cooperation and respect. People turn inward to the members of their own group and away from others.
3 Deterioration of personal and professional relationships, increases in personality clashes.
4 Increases in absenteeism, sickness, labour turnover, time-keeping problems and accidents.
5 Proliferation of non-productive, ineffective and untargeted papers and reports, the purpose of which is publicity and promotion of the individuals and the departments that issue them.
6 Proliferation of rules and regulations, especially those covering the most minor of areas of activities.
7 Proliferation of changes in job title, especially 'upwards'. Thus, for example, a supervisor may become a 'section controller', or a financial manager the 'director of corporate resources'.
8 Escalation of disputes and grievances arising out of frustration and anger (rather than antagonism at the outset) and leading to personality clashes and antagonism as well as operational decline.
9 Proliferation of control functions at the expense of front-line functions.
10 Taking sides and ganging up so that when problems are identified, people join or support one side or the other. This happens with long-running disputes and grievances; in these cases the original cause has normally long since been forgotten.
11 Informal corridor and washroom gatherings that persistently discuss wrongs, situational and organisational decline.
12 The growth of myths and legends via the grapevine; minor events become major events, small problems become crises, a slight disagreement becomes a major row.
13 The growth of arbitration, such as the handing-up of organisational disagreements to higher (and sometimes external) authorities for

resolutions. The main cause of this is the need not to be seen to lose, especially as the result of personal efforts. At the point of decision, therefore, the matter is handed on to a different authority to remove the responsibility for the outcome from the parties in dispute.

14 The decline in organisational, departmental, group and individual performance. This is often mirrored by increases in customer complaints, relating either to particular individuals and departments or, more seriously, to the organisation as a whole.

15 Disregard and disrespect for persons in other parts of the organisation. This is mostly directed at management, supervision and upper levels by those lower down. It is also to be found among those at higher levels when they speak of employees in disparaging tones ('the workers' and 'these people', for example).

16 Over-attention to the activities of other departments, divisions and functions, together with spurious and pseudo-analysis of the particular situation.

17 Non-productive meetings between persons from different departments, divisions and functions based on the needs of individuals to defend their own corner and protect what they have.

These are the outward manifestations of organisational conflict. It is necessary, however, to look more deeply for the causes of conflict rather than treating the symptoms. Otherwise, for example, ever-greater volumes of communication reports and paperwork are fed into systems that are already overloaded, and to people who treat the content with disdain and eventually contempt. In personal relationships and disputes, the temptation is for organisations to take a firm, even hard, line with the warring parties. The normal effect of this is to escalate rather than dampen down the conflict.

11.5 Causes of conflict

The main causes of conflict in organisations are as follows.

1 Differences between corporate, group and individual aims and objectives, and the inability of the organisation to devise systems, practices and environments in which these can be reconciled and harmonised;

2 Inter-departmental and inter-group wrangles overwhelmingly concerned with:

   (a) **territory**, where one group feels that another is treading in an area that is legitimately theirs;

   (b) **prestige**, where one group feels that another is gaining recognition for efforts and successes that are legitimately theirs;

   (c) **agenda**, where one group feels that it is being marginalised by the activities of another;

   (d) **poaching and theft**, where one group attracts away the staff of another, and perhaps also their technology, equipment, information and prestige.

- The personalities involved
- The departments and functions involved
- The agenda of those involved
- The organisational point of view
- The interests of those involved
- Relative necessity and compulsion to win
- Wider perceptions of the dispute
- Wider perceptions of the outcome
- The presence and influence of third parties (for example, the CE, trade unions)
- Any absolute organisation standards, rules, regulations and practices involved
- Expediency
- Need for triumphs, scapegoats and favours
- Alliances: the ability to call on outside support

Figure 11.2   Sources of energy in conflict

3   The status awarded by the organisation to its different departments, divisions, functions, group and individuals. This should be seen as:

(a) formal relations, based on organisational structure and job definition;

(b) informal relations, based on corridor influence and possibly also personal relationships;

(c) favoured and unfavoured status, the means by which this is arrived at and what it means to those concerned;

(d) the organisational pecking order and any other means by which prestige and influence are determined.

4   Conflict arises also both from the status quo, where people seek to alter their own position, and from changes that the organisation seeks to make. For example, when an individual or group suddenly loses power, a void is left which all the others rush to fill. Conversely, an individual/group may suddenly find herself/itself in favour (for many reasons, such as operational necessity, expediency, the possibility of a triumph for the favour-giver) and the others rush to do her/it down.

5   Individual clashes – both professional and personal – lead to conflict if the basis of the relationship is not established and ordered. For example, one individual sees a point of debate as a personal attack or questioning of his professional judgement; or 'a lively discussion' may be regarded by one as the straightforward airing of a point of view, by the other as questioning her expertise and integrity. This is also often the cause of feelings of favouritism leading to clashes between the recipients (perceived or actual) of preferential treatment, and others around them. Bullying and scapegoating is also a form of individual clash, causing conflict between bully and bullied. This again may lead to conflict based either on support for the victim by others, or by others following the leader and setting upon the victim themselves.

6   Personality clashes also fall into this category. They become seriously disruptive if allowed to proceed unchecked and if steps are not taken to ensure that there is a professional or operational basis on which relationships can be based.

7   Groups may be drawn into conflict as the result of a clash between their leaders or between particular individuals.

8   Role relationships have the potential to cause conflict. This is based on the nature of the given roles. For example, trade union officials are certain to come into conflict with organisations in the course of their duties, often

Table 11.1 Operational and behavioural outputs of conflict

Operational	Behavioural
• Dysfunctional	• Loss of face
• Inefficiency	• Wounded pride
• Squandering of resources	• Triumphalism
• Loss of productive effort	• Scapegoating
• Customer complaints	• Humiliation
• Customer loss	• Loss of faith
• Loss of confidence	• Loss of integrity
• Loss of trust	• Loss of morale
• Loss of morale	• Loss of confidence
• Loss of performance	• Loss of trust

Several of these items occur in each column. The purpose is to draw the relationship in terms of business performance as well as organisation behaviour.

representing the interest of members who have some kind of trouble or dispute. Other role relationships that should be considered are:

(a) **senior/subordinates**: conflicts of judgement, conflicts based on work output, attitudes style;

(b) **appraiser/appraisee**: where there are differences (often fundamental) over the nature and quality of the appraisee's performance and the action that this may cause to be taken;

(c) **functional roles**: conflicts between production and sales over quality, volume and availability of output; between purchaser (concerned with cost and quality) and producer (concerned with output); between personnel (concerned with absolute legal and ethical standards) and the departments which call on their services (concerned with solving problems, speed, expediency); between finance (efficiency) and other functions (effectiveness);

(d) **internal/external**: the priorities and requirements of external roles (shareholder, stakeholder, bank manager, lobbyist, public interest group, community), and reconciling these with the organisation's aims and objectives and those of their staff and activities;

(e) **parallel roles**: clashes occur, for example, where two or more people are competing for one promotion place; or where two or more people ostensibly carrying out the same job have (or are perceived to have) work of varying degrees of interest, quality, status and prestige.

11.6 Strategies for the management of conflict

Thus far it has been established that the potential for conflict is present in every human situation, and organisations are no exception. Indeed, much of what has so far been discussed clearly applies to a variety of areas (for example, families; social groups, guides, scouts). Many of these issues present throughout society are emphasised and concentrated by the fact of their being in work organisations and compounded by the ways, structures, rules and regulations in which these are constituted.

The first lesson, therefore, lies in the understanding of this. The second lesson is to recognise that, if attention is paid only to the symptoms, overload is placed on the existing systems of the organisation, as indicated above.

From this, in turn, there derives the need to adopt strategic approaches (rather than operational) to the management and resolution of conflict. This is based on a framework designed at the outset that should:

- recognise the symptoms of the conflict;
- recognise the nature and level (or levels) of conflict;
- recognise and understand the sources of conflict;
- investigate the root causes of the conflict;
- establish the range of outcomes possible;
- establish the desired outcome.

On to this framework can then be built strategies designed to ensure that the desired outcome is to be achieved.

It is clear from this that the symptoms are nothing more than the outward manifestation that something is wrong, and that it is what has brought these to the surface that needs to be addressed. For example, it is no use sending sales and reception staff on customer care courses because of an increase in complaints if the causes of the problems lie within production functions. It is equally useless to train managers and supervisors in the use of disciplinary and grievance procedures without also having an understanding of what discipline and grievance handling means in terms of a particular organisation.

The desired outcome therefore removes the symptoms of the conflict by addressing the causes rather than vice versa.

This is the starting point for effective conflict management.

Effective strategies for the management of conflict clearly vary in content between organisations and situations. In this context, the main lines of approach are as follows.

1 Attention to standards of honesty and integrity to ensure that people have a sound understanding of the basis on which the relationship between themselves, their department, division or group and the organisation as a whole is established. This is brought about by absolute commitment by the organisation and those responsible for its direction and its top managers, and translated into the required management staff by those responsible for the direction and supervision of the rest of the staff.
2 Attention to communications to ensure that these meet the needs of receivers, and that what is said or written is simple and direct, capable of being understood, honest and straightforward.
3 Attention to the hopes, fears, aspirations and expectations of all those who work in the organisation. Much of this is based on empathy and mutual identity and commitment, and may be dissipated by compartmentalising and differentiating between staff groups.
4 Attention to the systems, procedures and practices of the organisation and the ways in which these are structured, drawn up and operated. This especially

means attention to equality and fairness of treatment and opportunity; the language and tone of the procedures themselves; and the training and briefing of managers and supervisors in their purposes, emphases and operation. This also normally means the presence of sanctions for those who do not operate these systems with integrity.

5 The establishment of organisational purposes common to all those present in the organisation, with which they can all identify and which transcend the inherent conflicts of objectives. This is the approach most favoured, for example, by Japanese companies in their operations in Western Europe and North America.

6 The establishment of a universal identity and commitment to purpose. In organisation behaviour terms, this involves attention to the outputs of the stated purpose and the benefits and advantages that are to accrue as the result of their achievement. This is the starting point for the establishment of:

(a) performance-related and profit-related pay schemes, and the generation of the identity, commitment and interest that are the key elements of the best of these;

(b) briefing groups, work improvement groups and quality circles that reinforce the mutual confidence, commitment and respect of those involved.

7 The removal of the barriers that exist between departments and divisions. This involves attention to matters of confidence and respect and to the level, quality and style of communications that impact on, and effect operational relationships.

8 The establishment of organisation conformism based on creation of desired means and methods of participation and consultation, and fused with absolute standards of honesty and integrity. Attention is required here to:

(a) the representation of employees and the means by which this is to be achieved;

(b) their scope and structure;

(c) the agenda to be followed;

(d) the rules of engagement (the means by which these are to be operated).

These are the main organisational behaviour approaches required to address and tackle the sources and causes of conflict. They are based on the recognition of its universal potential to exist; the approach in particular organisations clearly varies. They arise from an understanding of the nature of conflict and of the need to recognise rather than attack the symptoms. Energy devoted to dealing with conflict represents energy not spent on more productive activities; time and resources used in understanding and assessing the causes and dealing with these therefore bring their own pay back in terms of reduced time expended on, and stresses and strains caused by, the reality of problems and disputes.

■ Operational approaches to the management of conflict

The operational approaches used by organisations normally take the following forms.

1 Developing rules, procedures and precedents to minimise the emergence of conflict and then, when it does occur, to minimise its undesirable effects.
2 Ensuring that communications are effective in minimising conflict; bad communications may cause conflict or magnify minor disputes to dangerous proportions.
3 Separation of sources of potential conflict, which may be done geographically, structurally or psychologically (for example, through the creation of psychological distance between functions and ranks).
4 Arbitration machinery may be made available as a strategy of last resort. Confrontation may be used to try to bring all participants together in an attempt to face them with the consequences of their action.
5 Benign neglect: this is the application of the dictum that 'a problem deferred is a problem half solved'. This can normally only be used as a temporary measure while more information is being gathered, or a more structured approach is being formulated.
6 The use of industrial relations operations for the containment and management of conflict, including consultation, participation, collective bargaining and negotiating structures.

■ Other means of reconciling workplace conflict

❐ Conciliation
This is a means whereby employers and employees seek to reach mutually acceptable settlements of their disputes, usually by placing the matter in the hands of a neutral and independent third party. Conciliators examine all sides of the case. They analyse areas of agreement and areas of dispute, and present these back to the parties involved. They identify areas where agreement can be made in order to try and effect a reconciliation between the parties.

❐ Mediation
If, for example, conciliation fails, two sides may seek a third party to mediate in the dispute. The mediator will put forward his own positive proposals aimed at resolving the matter in hand. The mediator may produce this in the form of a report outlining recommendations for a satisfactory settlement.

The benefit of the mediation and conciliation approach lies in the ability of the third party involved to see the dispute from a detached point of view and to find ways around the behavioural and operational blockages that inevitably exist.

❐ Arbitration
Arbitration differs from conciliation and mediation in that the arbitrator determines the outcome of the dispute by proposing a settlement; in cases that go to arbitration it is normal for both parties to agree to be bound by the findings of the arbitrator at the outset. The usual form of arbitration is open arbitration in which the arbitrator has complete discretion to award whatever she sees fit within the given terms of reference and which will provide an effective solution to the problem. The arbitrator also has regard to behavioural matters and the

forms of words in which agreements are couched; this is to accommodate the perceptual and behavioural niceties required, as indicated above.

Pendulum arbitration is a closed form of arbitration. Again, the arbitrator hears both sides of the dispute. He will then, however, decide wholly in favour of one party or the other. Someone therefore always wins (and is seen to win); and someone always loses (and is seen to lose). The concept of pendulum arbitration is based on the idea that faced with the prospect or possibility of losing a dispute, each party will wish to resort to resolving the differences without getting into this situation. The approach is widely used by Japanese companies operating in the West. In these companies there are strong cultural pressure on managers not to get into disputes and not to lose them if they do. Again, therefore, there is a pressure to resolve problems rather than to institutionalise them.

Pendulum arbitration normally represents the final solution to any dispute in organisations that use it. There is normally no appeal against the arbitrator's findings. This is clearly stated in the staff handbooks and agreements of the organisations concerned. Those entering into pendulum arbitration agree to be bound by the outcome before the arbitrator hears the case.

11.7 Conclusions

Understanding the sources and causes of conflict draws away from the hitherto accepted view that organisational strife is caused by troublemakers, trade unions, whistle blowers and other prima donnas or over-mighty subjects or groups. Strategies and systems for the handling and management of conflict clearly institutionalise rather than resolve conflict. They also tend to reinforce (rather than dissolve) more deeply held negative attitudes of mistrust, dishonesty and duplicity.

The current view, therefore, is that conflict is inevitable and that it is potentially present in all human relations and activities, and this includes work. In organisations it is determined by physical layout, physical and psychological distance, inter-group relationships, hierarchies, technology, expertise and by the interaction of individual group and organisational aims and objectives.

Rather than use channels, procedures, institutions and forms, the desired approach is to give everyone a common set of values, goals and purposes for being in the organisation which both recognise and transcend the presence of conflict and reconcile the differing aims and objectives. Destructive conflict is minimised and resources which are otherwise used in the operation of staff management and industrial relations systems can be released to be put to more positive and productive effect.

⚡ 12 Realpolitik

12.1 Introduction

Realpolitik is the art of survival in the particular organisation and situation. This requires knowledge and understanding of the ways in which both organisation and situation operate, and the different pressures and influences that are brought to bear. It also requires knowledge and understanding of the likely outcome of particular approaches. It is further necessary to adopt particular forms of approach to different individuals based on an understanding of what they are receptive to and what they are likely to reject.

All organisations have their own internal politics: the means by which influence and rewards are gained or lost. An understanding of this is essential from the following points of view.

1 The organisation itself, and those responsible for its governance, direction and performance, need to recognise the nature and prevalence of the different forms of political activity. This includes the effects on operations, effectiveness and success. Much of the infighting and competition at different levels and among functions may not be apparent to those at the top. Further, they may not perceive that their activities, those achievements for which they issue rewards and punishments, or the basis on which resources are allocated create strife and dissension elsewhere. They may also hide behind 'the need to consider the wider picture' and the equivalent as reasons and excuses for encouraging and rewarding the activities of lobbies and pressure groups, or of being seen to favour particular departments at the expense of others.

2 Organisation politics are also often encouraged and used as forms of control by those at the top. They observe the effects of encouraging this form of behaviour in terms of giving some form of direction and focus to different groups and individuals. They may also observe this behaviour as some form of 'rite of passage' (the opportunity for individuals or groups to prove themselves). In absolute terms, however, this only has any form of validity where it is clearly linked to organisational purpose and effectiveness. Success and failure should never be seen merely in terms of the ability to operate and compete within the system.

3 Teams and groups that depend on particular forms and resources, and support for their continued well-being and existence, need to establish relationships with those who hand these out. As well as performance

effectiveness, the basis of this is likely to include other matters such as support for the backers in other initiatives, sharing of the profits and merits of success, distance from any apparent failure.

4 Individuals need to be able to create physical and psychological space in order to be able to pursue their own aims, and practise and develop their expertise. Ideally, this will all accord with the organisation's overall direction; even where this is so, a certain amount of politicking and lobbying is normally required (for example, for new and improved equipment, or the opportunity to attend training and development). Where this is less apparent, the individual will in any case seek to ensure that her own aims and objectives are met to a greater or lesser extent, whether or not these comply with those of the organisation. Where the situation is very bad, individuals will pursue their own goals to the exclusion of those of the organisation.

5 Departments, divisions and functions become involved in organisation politics, overwhelmingly because of the need to compete for resources and to maintain their own reputation and standing. Again, this is invariably present to some extent even in the best of organisations. In other cases, competition for both resources and reputation is often based on the distributive principle whereby one succeeds at the expense of others and this becomes the driving force behind departmental success.

6 Understanding, surviving and operating in the political systems of organisations stem from this. It is very short termist, and anyone who tries to take a more rational, long-term and operational view is likely to lose out at the expense of those who know how the political system works and how to succeed within it. Otherwise, the major output of these forms of activity is inter-departmental and inter-individual conflict, together with the prioritisation and use of resources in the pursuit of political advantage at the expense of operational effectiveness.

12.2 Survival

Individuals and groups have to survive long enough to become successful and effective operators. They have therefore to be able to make use of systems, procedures, practices and support mechanisms. With the best will in the world, there is no point in taking an enlightened or ethical view of this if the organisation's ways of working will not support it. People therefore develop their own format for the niches that they occupy and the roles and functions that they carry out, in order to maximise their chances of being effective and successful operators (as distinct from expert in the performance of their expertise or function). In each case this consists of the following.

1 Developing approaches based on a combination of role, function and personality, adding a personal strand to the professional and operational. This means developing measures of trust, warmth and liking as a part of the professional and operational dealings.

2 Developing approaches based on individual influence. This involves

recognising the nature of the influence of the individual and the ability to present it in ways useful to others within the organisation.

3   Developing networks of professional, personal and individual contacts and using these as means of gaining fresh insights and approaches to issues and problems (see Figure 12.1).

4   Developing funds of bargaining chips – equipment, information, resources, expertise – which can be used as trade offs and for mutual advantage and satisfaction when required.

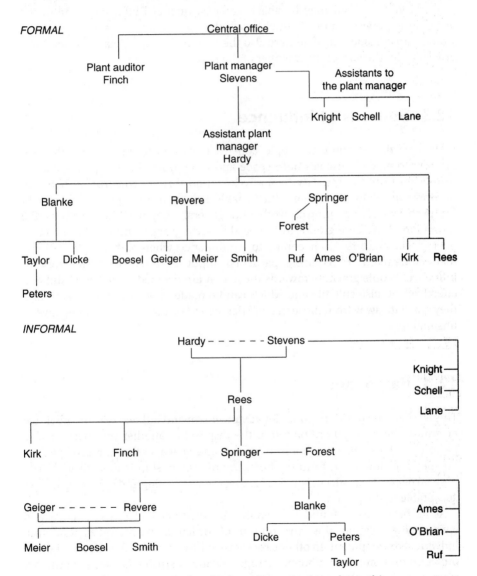

Figure 12.1   Formal and informal organisation relationships
Source: from Luthans (1990).

5 Developing a clarity of thought around the entire aspects of organisation operations and activities. This is based, on the one hand, on what is important, urgent and of value, and to whom; and on the other, on what facilitates progress, and what hinders or blocks it. This also involves recognition of where the true interests of the individual lie and how these can best be served in the situation.

Different forms of each approach are required for each role and function carried out. A different approach may also be required to the same individual or group where there is interaction on more than one basis. For example, a production supervisor may be able to request financial information from the accounts supervisor in one way, although the approach to the same supervisor would vary considerably if he were also the local union lay official representing a grievance on the part of the member of the production team.

12.3 Spheres of influence

In this particular context, people construct their own spheres of influence in order to give themselves both space and time to be able to operate a stage further on from the capacity to survive. Around this are constructed personal networks and support systems that enable help and assistance to be sought for problem-solving, project work and general support. This includes the formation of pressure groups and special interest groups, and professional and peer group clusters. Each comes to prominence when wider organisational matters demand it, requiring particular input or threaten its territory or influence. People gravitate towards those that are deemed to be successful and effective, and also suitable and which can be made to work to their advantage; they gravitate away from those that are deemed to be unsuccessful, ineffective or unsuitable.

12.4 Patronage

This is where the position, hopes for advancement and influence of an individual or group (the protégé) are placed at the disposal of another (the patron). The patron provides encouragement, resources and space so that the protégé may prosper and flourish. A form of effort-reward relationship is this engaged. The protégé depends for success on performing the task, acting and behaving in ways acceptable to the patron.

At its best, this is found in mentoring, nurturing and other positive and encouraging relationships, the output of which is both organisation and individual development. In other cases, it is at the core of organisation and intra-organisation power and influence struggles and consists of 'favours for favours': support and compliance in particular activities in return for rewards and favours when the struggle is over and successfully concluded.

12.5 Favouritism and victimisation

Favouritism is an extreme form of patronage. It occurs where the patron gives advancement or rewards to the protégé as the result of some personal quality or attribute.

The converse is victimisation and occurs when the patron takes a dislike to the subordinate, again for some personal reason. She is then used as a scapegoat or victim when required. If this is allowed to get out of hand, it is stressful and demoralising to the individual affected and also to those around her. The worst excesses of this are bullying, harassment, persistent personal attacks (physical and verbal), the blocking of opportunities and prospects for advancement.

12.6 The ability to influence

Both patronage and also general political relationships within organisations depend on the extent to which one party may exert influence over others. The key features of this are set out below.

■ Dependence

The greater the dependence of a protégé on a patron, the greater his susceptibility to being influenced to go in particular directions or to pursue particular projects.

■ Uncertainty

Where people are unclear or uncertain about the correctness or otherwise of an action, they will nevertheless tend to carry it out if requested or directed to do so by someone in authority because *their* responsibility for it is thus removed. Also, where people are unclear about current activities and behaviour, they are more likely to change to something that gives clear guidance or sets firm standards.

■ Expectations

Where the expectations of those in organisations and their groups are well understood, anything that is presented to them in ways that are perceived to meet and satisfy them is more likely to be accepted and complied with. Where expectations are not well understood or where there is a lack of attention to the presentation, acceptance is less certain.

■ Authority

The greater the authority behind a particular drive or initiative, the more likely it is that it will be accepted. This is true whatever the form of authority, whether rational, legal, expert or charismatic.

■ Confidence

This is the key element, the one which binds all the others together in patron–protégé relationships (indeed, in any superior–subordinate relationships). It is the confidence on the part of the patron that the protégé will deliver the matter in hand effectively and in ways beneficial to both; and the confidence on the part of the protégé that the patron is a reliable and adequate source of influence for her own purposes.

12.7 Refusals and blockages

The main reasons for refusing to deal with someone from elsewhere in the same organisation normally fall into one or more of the following categories.

1 Disdain – the people, department or activities are seen to have no value. This may be the result of general perceptions, but may also be the result of preconceived ideas and notions. It may have arisen as a matter of historic fact (for example, where previous results have been poor, or previous cooperation between those affected was disastrous).
2 Lack of clarity – where one or both parties views the activities of the others with suspicion based on a lack of knowledge and understanding.
3 Benefits of associations may not be clear – especially where one party perceives the benefits but the other does not.
4 The wider picture – whereby associating with one group may cause the feelings of other groups to be influenced in turn (for example, department X has a relationship with department Z; department X is approached by department Y to open up relationships. Department Y is the enemy of department Z. Department X therefore takes the whole picture into account before opening up relationships with department Y).
5 Dominance–dependence – the extent and nature of the need for the relationship, and the position of the two parties on the dominance–dependence spectrum.
6 The potential relationship – the perceptions of the extent to which it can and might be developed to mutual advantage and, above all, in the interests of the blockage. In this case, the onus is clearly on the approacher to indicate the likely benefits to the blocker.
7 Lack of trust – the extent to which those involved say what they mean, mean what they say; and the extent to which each can deliver what is promised.

12.8 Special relationships

The most important of these are those which exist between the CEO's Department and other functions; and between the head office and outlying functions of those organisations that are so designed. Invariably, there is a draw of resources, prestige, status and influence towards the head office (and very often this occurs at the expense of those both physically and psychologically remote from the centre).

Right or wrong, it is a key relationship and those who seek to operate successfully must recognise its extent. Where necessary, this relationship must be nurtured and developed and the interests of the CE or head office engaged. Conversely, it is a key part of the CE and head office function to recognise the presence and prevalence of this, and to ensure that the relationships between themselves and their more distant functions remain productive, effective and harmonious.

12.9 Confidence and trust

The key feature in the nature of organisation politics arises from the level of mutual confidence and trust held by those in particular relations. Where there is no confidence or trust the relationship is corrupted at the outset.

In terms of organisation politics, this may be a constraint within which the groups and individuals have to work. In the worst cases it tends to lead to blame, scapegoating and negative presentation (the denigration of the efforts of others as well as the promotion of self).

Confidence and trust are destroyed where one party gives these freely and they are not reciprocated; and where information or resources are given over and then used against the giver. They are affected by the balance of truth (the extent to which communications and interactions take place on an overt or covert basis) and, above all, the use of direct and indirect language, adherence to deadlines and orders of priority.

In organisations with highly developed political systems, confidence and trust start off at a low level, and both individuals and groups will make sure that they are very certain of the integrity of those with whom they are dealing before giving out hostages to fortune, departmental secrets and specific matters concerning their own expertise or trade.

12.10 Ideologies

From time to time individuals and groups are called upon to interact with those whose ideologies and values they find repugnant. While in absolute terms it is easy to encourage them not to have any association, in practice this is not always possible.

For example, it may be essential to deal with somebody who is known to be a bully to his staff (or his family) or with someone who is known to take all the glory and credit for success for herself and to find scapegoats and others to blame for failures.

12.11 Ambiguity

Problems arise when spheres of influence, roles and lines of activity are not clearly delineated. This especially occurs where everything else is overtly highly ordered and structured. It also occurs where aims and objectives are not clear and where people therefore tend to operate in a void. In such circumstances groups and individuals use this to extend their boundaries and to build their own empires and to pursue their own aims and objectives.

12.12 Realpolitik activities

These are normally based on one or more of the following.

1 **Alliances with powerful people and groups:** especially with those either in or close to the corridors of power and with others among the upper levels of the organisation. People may also seek out junior staff from the CE's Department and other highly influential functions – personal assistants and secretaries, for example – as informal friends, advocates and sources of information (secretaries and personal assistants at all levels have access to both volume and quality of information).
2 **Showing quick results:** this is in any case excellent for group morale. It is also often politically necessary to be able to prove to backers that their backing was not misplaced.
3 **IOUs:** this is where a favour given brings with it the expectation of something in return, whether instant or deferred; the debtor will be expected to pay up when asked.
4 **Information acquisition and manipulation:** as referred to elsewhere, information is a resource. When viewed from this standpoint, it may be filtered, edited, represented (even misrepresented and corrupted) to ensure that the given interest is best served. Information is also packaged in such headings as 'top secret', 'classified', 'restricted'; again, from the political point of view, this gives it exclusivity and desirability – and therefore value.
5 **Battlefields:** in political terms, people tend to avoid pitched battles because they may lose (and moreover be seen to have lost). The more usual approach adopted is the gradual or incremental: chipping away at the target, rather than setting out to destroy it in one fell swoop (apart from anything else, the victor of an overt and decisive engagement may be seen as a bully, and the defeated as a victim). The gradualist approach is generally much less noticeable and is therefore not regarded as a threat.

Guerrilla war is also engaged in where one department or group seeks to denigrate the efforts and achievements of others. It consists of sniping, gaining adverse coverage and identifying the weaknesses of others and spotlighting these (one of the most powerful positions of all is that of spotlighter, since the light is shone on the particular point desired and the spotlighter remains in the relative darkness and invisibility behind the light).

The language used here is that of military engagement and this reflects accurately the organisational behaviour equivalent. Battles and wars are fought both to preserve and maintain position, and also to enhance it. Those involved store up memories of victories and defeats so that they may build on successes and take steps to avoid future failures.

■ Lobbying and presentation

The key to all successful internal political activity lies in the effectiveness of lobbying and presentation. Much of this is implicit and even stated as part of the forms of political strategy indicated above. The rest lies in the ability to recognise those emphases of particular initiatives and activities that are likely to gain a sympathetic hearing and those that are not. The problem, then, is to find the right channels and media to be used to best advantage, and to combine these to form an effective case that can be well presented. As with all communications, therefore, success comes about as the result of understanding the requirements of the receivers and choosing the right media, format and language. In political activities, and especially when dealing with senior figures, this invariably includes attention to:

- flattery, vanity and triumphs;
- time scales (often the lobby has only a limited time in which to put across their case);
- the combination of substance and presentation (a fair case well presented invariably succeeds at the expense of a brilliant case poorly presented);
- to the merits and demerits of other lobbies and interests (part of any political process consists of denigrating opposing points of view as well as the sound delivery of one's own case).

Lobbying also involves, first, the engagement of other vested interests and special interest groups who may be persuaded to a particular point of view, whether because it is related to their interests, or because they may see an advantage accruing as the result of support, or in return for favours previously given; and second, use of statistics and other information supports and emphasises the case, especially when these can be related to direct and positive statements (for example, 90 per cent of people are in favour of this; by doing this we will double our market share in 12 weeks). These can also be used in less rational and even overtly spurious ways (for example, next door had a 12 per cent pay rise, you are offering us 3 per cent; what is the certain effect of this on our morale?) but which nevertheless may be effective. National politicians engaged in public and media debates are expert at this, as are trade union representatives.

12.13 Organisational health and well-being

Organisational politics are the barometer of its general state of health and well-being. The indicators of this are as set out below.

1 Levels of absenteeism, sickness and turnover, and the stated reasons why each of these occur and the attitude adopted towards them by the organisation at large as well as by individual managers and supervisors. The key features are: the nature and extent of procedures to deal with these and the ways in which these are used; the use to which any general and specific information thus

gained is put; the volume of time and resource expended on these, including the creation of departments and functions for their purpose. Particular figures can indicate both general and specific causes for concern (excess absence or departures from particular areas, for example). They are always a general indication of states of morale, confidence and motivation.

2 Levels, nature and purposes of meetings – the extent to which people are, in reality, employed to attend meetings (rather than for their substantive purpose) and the effects of this on the rest of the work. The purpose and agenda of meetings is a strong indication of this and is reinforced by the extent to which people need to be seen to be present as distinct from having any real contribution to make.

3 The nature of rewards and favours, and the reasons for which they are issued. Here the remedy lies directly in the hands of those in overall control. By simply offering rewards for achievement of aims and objectives rather than because of presentation, lobbying, visibility or sycophancy, a swathe of political battlegrounds may be removed.

4 The attitude to failures and mistakes: where this is negative and punitive it encourages those concerned to seek scapegoats and victims. It also develops fear and this, in turn, leads to the construction of barriers and protectors by which people can insulate themselves from failure. Where mistakes are viewed as a learning experience, again, much of this is removed. This should be seen from standpoint of both results and politics. Where the overall political system is positive and healthy, poor performance is likely to be seen as the starting point for learning and development. Where the overall system is unhealthy, this becomes more complicated. Excellent results may be unacceptable politically (for example, where somebody achieves something that nobody else had previously managed). The emphasis may be on presentation rather than achievement and so excellent results, poorly marketed or publicised, may not carry sufficient weight (see Figure 12.2).

5 The extent to which departments, divisions, functions and groups continue to serve the purpose for which they were created; the extent to which they are allowed to out-live their usefulness; and what happens to them after they have served their purpose (whether they are destroyed, reconstituted, rejuvenated, made redundant, re-deployed, given other projects, encouraged to seek work as the result of their own initiative and so on). The key factors are the extent to which the organisation assumes responsibility for this, and the extent to which

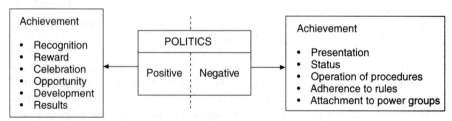

Figure 12.2   Politics and achievement

the group itself does so (for example, by making itself indispensable, and therefore indestructible); and the extent to which the skills, knowledge and qualities of those involved are transferable elsewhere. For more positive and enlightened organisations, the latter is much less likely to be a problem than the other two.

6 The balance of core and peripheral activities; primary and support functions; and the emphasis put on each. Special attention is required as regards the extent of checking and control functions; the extent of the influence of these; and the extent to which the interaction between these and other functions becomes a part of the ends (rather than the means or processes) of primary functions. Strong indicators of these are highly specialised job titles (for example, clock control supervisor, clock card clerk) or extremely vague job titles (for example, director of corporate affairs). They arise from the notion that 'something needs to be done' but without sufficient attention to what this might be, or why, or how. They may also arise as the result of having to find a niche (and therefore a job) for someone whose previous remit has expired; again, this often occurs without sufficient attention to the what, why or how.

7 The treatment, priority and attention given to vested interests, pressure groups, lobbies, special interests and other pressures, and the reasons why these either succeed or fail (and the reasons why they are perceived or seen to do so). This especially concerns whether they succeed or fail because of the particular merits of the case that they put forward, as distinct from their ability to energise powerful forces (for example, influential individuals and the media).

8 The extent to which information gathered for one purpose is used for others. For instance, at times of performance appraisal, individuals are often asked to state what their weaknesses are, wherein they think their performance could be improved and what needs for development they may have. In some cases such information may be used to block promotions, restrict openings and opportunities, and in the worst cases this may lead even to disciplinary action. This is also true of financial information: when a set of results are reported for one purpose, these may then be taken out of context and used to indicate particular levels of performance.

12.14 Conclusions

The main lesson is to recognise that politics exists in all organisations, and all organisations are political systems. Throughout the environment there are various agendas: departments and their managers have secondary and hidden agendas, promoting themselves and their advancement as well as undertaking particular courses of action.

Those responsible for the design and structure of organisations must therefore recognise these components and other vagaries of the work environment. In the medium to long term the negative aspects outlined have extremely demoralising and debilitating effects on everyone concerned, and this ultimately includes customers and clients. There is therefore a direct relationship between the state of organisational politics and performance success and effectiveness. Organisations must recognise these activities for what they are and take remedial steps wherever necessary and desirable.

⋮ 13 Ethics

13.1 Introduction

Ethics is that part of business that is related to absolute standards and moral principles. More generally, it is concerned with human character and conduct, the distinction between right and wrong and the absolute duties and obligations that exist in all situations.

Some views and perspectives on the relationship between ethics and business are now given:

'Business ethics applies ethical reasoning to business situations and activities. It is based on a combination of distributive justice – that is, the issuing of rewards for contribution to organisation goals and values; and ordinary common decency – an absolute judgement that is placed on all activities.' (Sternberg, 1995)

Ethical issues concerning business and public sector organisations exist at three levels.

At the macro level there are issues about the role of the business in the national and international organisation of society. These are largely concerned with addressing the relative virtues of different political/social systems. There are also important issues of international relationships and the role of business on an international scale.

At the corporate level the issue is often referred to as corporate social responsibility and is focused on the ethical issues facing individual and corporate entities (both private and public sector) when formulating and implementing strategies.

At the individual level the issue concerns the behaviour and actions of individuals within organisations. (Johnson and Scholes, 1994)

In their book *Changing Corporate Values*, Adams, Hamil and Carruthers (1989) identified a series of factors and elements as measures against which the performance of organisations could be measured in ethical terms. These factors are:

- the nature of business;
- the availability and use of information;
- participation, consultation, employment relationships, the recognition of trade unions, means and methods of representation;
- relationships with the Third World (where appropriate);

- the nature of particular products – especially where these included armaments, drugs, tobacco and alcohol – and the means by which these were produced, marketed and sold;
- connections with governments, especially where these were considered to be undesirable or where the regime in question was considered to be unethical itself;
- general approaches and attitudes to staff and customers;
- attitudes to the communities in which they operated;
- attitudes to environmental issues, especially waste disposal and recycling, replanting, and the ways and means by which scarce resources were consumed;
- business relationships with suppliers and markets;
- product testing (again, especially where this involved the use of animals or parts of the environment).

Peter F. Drucker (1955) wrote:

'The more successfully the manager does work, the greater will be the integrity required. For under new technology the impact on the business of decisions, time span and risks will be so serious as to require that each manager put the common good of the enterprise above self-interest. Their impact on the people in the enterprise will be so decisive as to demand that the manager put genuine principles above expediency. And the impact on the economy will be so far reaching that society itself will hold managers responsible. Indeed, the new tasks demand that the manager of tomorrow root every action and decision in the bedrock of principles so that they lead, not only through knowledge, competence and skill, but also through vision, courage, responsibility and integrity.'

Payne and Pugh (1990) identified the relationship between the absolute standards of the organisation and its 'climate'. They stated that 'Climate is a total concept applying to the organisation as a whole or some definable department or subsystem within it.' It is descriptive of the organisation. There are four main aspects of climate:

- the degree of autonomy given;
- the degree of structure imposed on work positions;
- the reward orientation, either in terms of individual satisfaction or organisational achievement;
- the degree of consideration, warmth and support.

There is clearly, therefore, a variety of points of view from which the wider question may be addressed. At the core, however, lies a combination of:

- the long-term view (rather than the short or medium);
- absolute standards relating to organisational policies, aims and objectives;
- common standards of equity, equality, honesty and integrity;
- relationships between organisation standards and absolutes, the carrying out of performance and the distribution of rewards;

- relationships between means and ends, and actions and motives;
- reconciliation of conflicts of interest.

It is further necessary to identify the nature of those legitimate interests. If the organisation is not profitable and/or effective it will close (or be closed down). The first duty, therefore, to staff and customers, is to ensure long-term permanence. This only occurs where there exists a fundamental integrity of relationships and activities, and where this extends to all dealings with every stakeholder. From this arises the confidence that is the foundation of the ability to conduct activities over the long term. Ethical concerns therefore pervade all aspects of organisation activities and performance.

13.2 Survival

Survival becomes the main ethical duty of the organisation, to its staff, customers, communities and other stakeholders. For this to happen over the long term, a long-term view must be taken of all that this means. For businesses and companies, profits must be made – over the long term; for public services, this means effectiveness – over the long term. This is the basis on which confidence and an enduring and continuous positive relationship with customers (or service users) is built and developed. This is also the only ground on which an effective and satisfactory organisation for the staff is to be created.

Short-term views, expediency and the need for triumphs all detract from this. In particular, there is a serious problem in this area with some public services. For example, the output of education can take 15–20 years to become apparent. Health and social services have similar extreme long-term requirements and commitments. Yet those responsible for their direction (both service chiefs and cabinet ministers) need to be able to show instant results to be presented to the electorate or to the selection panel for their next job.

This is not wholly confined to services. For example, pressures from bankers and other financial backers in some sectors (especially loan makers) lead to companies being forced or strongly encouraged to sell assets during lean periods in order to keep up repayments or show a superficial cash surplus over the immediate period. This happened with the UK construction industry over the early 1990s when there was a great decline in work brought on by recession and general loss of confidence. Short-term cash gain was made through the sale of assets (especially land banks). Long-term survival was threatened because these assets would not be present when any upturn in confidence and activity came about.

However, this again has to be balanced with matters of general confidence and expectation. If backers expect to see a series of short-term positive results then these have to be produced, especially if backing may be withdrawn if these are not forthcoming or do not meet expectations. This implies re-educating backers into the long-term view. It also means seeking out others who are disposed to take the long-term view.

13.3 Relationships with employees

This refers to the nature of participation and involvement, and the point of view from which this is approached. Basic integrity in employee relations stems from the view taken of the employees, their reasons for working in the organisation, their reasons for being hired to work in the organisation and the absolute levels of esteem in which they are held.

Confrontational or adversarial styles of employee relations are always founded on mistrust and reinforced by offensive and defensive positions adopted by the two sides concerning particular issues. The phrase 'the two sides' confirms and underlines this. Resources are consumed in this way to the detriment both of organisation performance and also of resource utilisation (those used in these ways cannot be put to better use elsewhere). This form of employee relations is therefore unethical. On the other hand, greater or full participation and involvement is only ethical if the point of view adopted is itself honest: that is, if a genuine view of respect and identity is taken. This will become apparent – or not – in the continuity and enduring nature of this relationship. It is underlined by the volume, quality and relevance of information made available to the staff, the means by which problems are addressed and resolved, the prevalence of equality of treatment and opportunity, and the development of staff.

It also refers to the attention to the standards set to which employees are to conform and the reasoning and logic behind this. It covers all aspects of the traditional personnel area: recruitment and selection, induction, performance appraisal, pay and reward, promotion and other opportunities for development and advancement. Above all, at its core, lies equality of treatment for everyone.

13.4 Responsibilities and obligations to staff

The general responsibilities and obligations to staff consist of providing work, remaining in existence, equality and fairness of treatment, compliance with the law and the specific regulations of training and development. The basis on which this is established consists of the following.

1 Acknowledging the range of pressures and priorities that exist in the lives of everyone, including health, family, social, ethical, religious pressures, as well as those related to work. The outcome of this is understanding, rather than interference or imposition. It sets the relationship between work organisations and people in context. It indicates areas where stresses and strains are likely to arise. It indicates the relationship between organisation and individual priorities, where these coincide and where they diverge. It indicates areas for accommodation and for regulation.

2 Acknowledgement of extreme human concerns. This refers to personal crises, such as serious illness, death, bereavement, divorce, drink and drug problems. The concern is to ensure that the organisation gives every possible support to people facing these issues so that a productive and profitable relationship is maintained even through such times. Individuals can and should referred to

outside professional support services and agencies for these matters with the full backing of the organisation. However, organisations do not have the right to pry into peoples' personal affairs. Individuals may be referred for counselling or other expert help and advice if they give their consent unless the matter is adversely affecting their work performance beyond a fair and reasonable extent, or where they constitute a real or potential threat or danger to their colleagues or the activities of the organisation. Problems related to drug or alcohol use or addiction always fall into the latter category and are therefore always a matter of direct concern. Organisations set absolute standards of handling and using equipment, carrying out activities and dealing with the public. Addiction and abuse problems directly affect each of these. The individual must therefore be removed from these situations and supported through rehabilitation.

3   Confidentiality and integrity in all dealings with staff. This is the cornerstone on which all effective staff relationships are built. Where confidences are not kept, where sensitive personal and occupational information becomes public property, the relationship is tainted and often destroyed. Confidentiality also encourages people to be frank, open and honest themselves, and this leads to a genuine understanding of issues much more quickly. It also enables managers and supervisors to address their matters of concern – for example, declines in standards of performance and behaviour – directly and immediately they are observed. The following approaches may be adopted:

(a) **ice-breaking** – using one issue as the means of breaking into a wider area to identify the real nature of problems and causes for concern;
(b) **drawing out and understanding** – based on a general discussion, often conducted from the employee's point of view and leading to an understanding of his perspective;
(c) **confrontation** – the direct presentation of the matters of concern.

Whichever is used at first, the three inter-relate. By using each approach in turn, a full understanding may eventually be achieved and effective proposals formulated (see Figure 13.1).

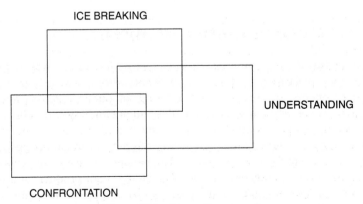

Figure 13.1   Causes for concern

4 Support for individuals when either they or the workplace identify that there are problems. In most cases, this is to ensure that people are not penalised as a result of the pressures and strains indicated above. Support should only be withdrawn by the organisation where the individual is compromising the total relationship or the quality of activities. When this happens, the organisation has to consider the integrity of the relationship between itself and all of the staff. Part of this support therefore means creating the conditions in which individuals are able to confront issues knowing that help is available and that they are not to be penalised, and neither will their concerns become matters of public knowledge.

5 Respect for individuals based on the value of their contribution to the organisation. If they bring no value, they should not be there in the first place. Ideally, therefore, the fact of their employment (in whatever capacity) equates to high and distinctive value; and where it does not, stress and conflict invariably occur. This respect extends to all aspects of the relationship. It includes attention to the current job, future prospects, continuity of working relations, creation of suitable working environments, creation and maintenance of effective occupational and personal relationships, creation and maintenance of effective management and supervisory styles.

The traditional or adversarial view of this approach to responsibilities and obligations was that it was soft and unproductive, and diverted attention away from production and output. Organisations could not afford to be 'nice' to their employees while there was a job to be done.

The reverse of this is much closer to the truth. The acknowledgement, recognition and understanding of the full nature and range of complexities and conflicting pressures on individuals is the first step towards effective and profitable activities. By engaging on a basis of honesty, confidentiality, trust, support and integrity – rather than coercion, confrontation, dishonesty and duplicity – a long-term positive relationship can be established. The interests of organisation and individual are bound up with each other, especially over the long term. Ultimately, therefore, the interests coincide. A critical part of this approach is concerned with creating the basis on which this can be built.

13.5 Relationships with customers

This is the basis of the commercial or service provision and it concerns respect and the value placed on customers and clients. From this springs the drive for product quality, presentation and offering; of public relations and other customer management and service activities and of handling complaints.

It also impinges on the staff. Where staff know that high standards of customer service and top quality products are being offered, the relationship between organisation and staff is also reinforced. The converse is also true: where these standards are low or falling, or where it is known that poor products and services are being offered, the integrity of the relationship between organisation and staff is also compromised.

This impacts on all production, output and sales activities, especially in terms of attention to product quality, the terms under which it is offered, its uses and availability and recognition of the levels of satisfaction that are required by the customers. In the long term, if this is not present, confidence is lost. While it is possible to identify areas where short-term gain has been made without integrity (for example, in the sale of building products, home improvements, life assurance and pensions, poor quality Christmas presents), there is no (or reduced) likelihood of repeat business occurring. This also fails to satisfy either the long-term criteria or the requirement of confidence on the part of the employees; above all, there is no integrity of relationship. This way of conducting business is therefore unethical.

This also refers to attention to the marketing activities undertaken and the point of view adopted. Creative and imaginative presentation is highly desirable as long as this underlines (and does not misrepresent) the quality, desirability and image of the particular product or organisation. Again, where integrity is missing, the relationship is invariably short term and terminated with loss of confidence in the organisation and loss of regard for its products and services. This applies to all aspects of marketing, such as promotion and advertising, packaging and presentation, direct sales and distribution.

These are the main relationships upon which successful and effective organisational performance is built and developed. They should be under-pinned by the following.

■ Corporate governance and direction

This is the position adopted by the organisation that is apparent from its policies, aims and objectives and the means established by which these are to be achieved. In this context the extent of honesty and integrity are immediately apparent. This is reinforced by the clarity and realism of overall purpose, the basic approach taken to customers, markets and staff, and management style; and underlined by the rules, systems and procedures that are put in place to support all of this, and the ways in which these are presented, delivered and implemented.

■ Stakeholders

Attention to the relative position of stakeholders is based on the recognition that some – especially staff, customers and owners – are more critical than others (for example, the local community pressure groups and vested interests). Each has its own position and is worthy of being dealt with from the point of view of honesty and integrity, and is worthy also of respect and esteem. However, organisations will not normally accommodate a peripheral interest at the expense of the core purpose, although they will (or may) do this if it can be successfully integrated. The best organisations seek ways forward which are capable of integrating the peripheral interest with that of the core.

■ Resources

There are ethical implications for resource utilisation. Profligacy is wasteful and therefore wrong, even where constraints are not apparent. It is also unsatisfactory, normally leading to a general loss of care and consideration. It is also off-putting to customers: for example, those customers visiting luxurious offices may well come to the conclusion that a good part of the business that is being conducted is being used for expensive furnishings rather than business performance and effectiveness. In general, therefore, it is bad business.

A useful equivalent in public service terms may also be drawn. This is the propensity – very often driven by managers and directors – to use up the year's budget in time for the year ending (usually February and March because of the end of the financial year on 1 April). Resources that have been managed and constrained for 9 or 10 months suddenly therefore become expendable; this is reinforced if there is no prospect of carrying the resources forward to the following year. The result is that departments affected in this way engage in any activities or purchases that are guaranteed to use up the resources.

On the other hand, resource constraints lead to choices and priorities. This leads, in turn, to the consideration of who should receive resources and who should not, and why. An ethical assessment will look at organisational aims and objectives. Other elements include establishing whether everything is to be attempted in the knowledge that it will probably fall short of full success and effectiveness (common in public services); or whether resources will be concentrated on that which can be completed fully at the expense of that which cannot.

Resource constraints also lead to resource battles in many cases, and this compounds the issue. Problems especially arise when resources are seen to be distributed on the basis of favour and expediency as distinct from operational necessity; or for head office functions at the expense of outlying and often front-line activities.

The ethical line is therefore to maximise and optimise resources in the pursuit of objectives. This is based on the judgement and integrity of those responsible, taking the point of view of what is best for the organisation and its long-term future.

■ Conduct

This is the basis on which all relationships are founded. The key is the attitude adopted by staff to each other and the organisation to its people. It is underlined by establishing standards of conduct and enforcing them, so that a clear distinction is made between what is acceptable and what is not. Everyone is held in confidence, respect and esteem. This is, in turn, underlined by the nature, emphasis and application of the rules and regulations.

■ Professional standards

This is attention to the quality of staff, the ways in which they apply their particular trades and expertise, and the expectations and requirements that are placed on them by the organisation. These standards are to apply to everyone. There is no reason why ostensibly unskilled or simple tasks and jobs are not to be carried out to the highest possible quality. This is supported by the organisation's commitment to provide the correct working environment, equipment, style of supervision; and by the standards of respect, trust and esteem referred to above. Absolute standards are present and upheld where each of these elements is present; and where one falls short, this may lead to the beginnings of questioning the integrity of the relationship. Where the shortfall is allowed to persist, professional standards inevitably fall in all areas. There is, moreover, a loss of self-worth all round and those with distinctive trades or professions retreat into being a professional or expert practitioner (as distinct from an organisation practitioner) and may seek employment elsewhere where these standards are known (or perceived) to be higher.

■ The law

Compliance with the law may or may not be ethical: this again depends on the attitude and standpoint adopted. Organisations are known to hide behind the law in certain circumstances, especially where legal standards are lower than the absolutes that are known to be required.

This applies especially to waste disposal and discharges, and the relationship between the organisation and its environment. It occurs also in all dealings with staff: the right to disclosure of information, and right to time off work, to breaks, to maternity leave; and to minimum levels of redundancy notice and pay. Organisations comply with the law because they have to and not because they know that this is the right approach to take.

Organisations should nevertheless comply with the law. Not to do so questions, and is likely to destroy, their total integrity and honesty, and the standards which have been set. Condoning acts that are against the law (even encouraging them) also destroys integrity, especially if one of the perpetrators is promoted or receives advancement as a direct result.

■ Health and safety

Health and safety at work is covered by the law and it is also a distinctive element in its own right, simply because it is such a fundamental reflection of respect for people (and especially lack of respect for people). The problem lies in the organisation's acceptance of its responsibility to take an absolute view of its environment, technology and other equipment, its procedures and practices, its staff and any other persons who visit or use its premises; acknowledging the entirety of things that can go wrong; and designing each element so that nothing can go wrong.

This is a continuous responsibility and requires reaction as and when new knowledge becomes available.

For example, asbestos was used during the period 1930–60 as an effective fireproofing material in buildings, and construction workers worked with it in the same way as any other material. When it became apparent that it caused skin disease and also that the dust that it produced was harmful to the lungs, protective clothing, including breathing protection, became obligatory. The best organisations went out and bought the correct equipment and insisted that their staff used it; and when the equipment was improved, went out and bought it again. Other organisations either phased the equipment in, or made it available to the staff to use if they wanted to, or simply rejected the evidence.

13.6 Conclusions

The ethical approach is not altruistic or charitable, but rather a key concept of effective long-term organisational and business performance. The commitment to the staff is absolutely positive. This does not mean any guarantee of lifetime employment, but it does mean recognising obligations and ensuring that staff, in turn, recognise their obligations. These obligations are to develop, participate and be involved; to be flexible, dynamic and responsive. The commitment of the staff to organisation, and organisation to staff, is mutual. This also extends to problem areas – especially the handling of discipline, grievance and dismissal issues and redundancy and redeployment – and the continuity of this commitment when these matters have to be addressed.

Organisations must structure decision-making processes in ways that consider the range and legitimacy of ethical pressures. This also means understanding where the greater good and the true interests of the organisation lie, and adopting realistic steps in the pursuit of this. An ethical assessment will consider the position of staff, the nature and inter-relationship of activities, product and service ranges, mixes and balances, relationships with the community and the environment (see Figure 13.2).

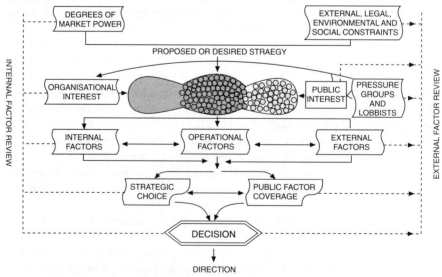

Figure 13.2 Decision-making model including ethical considerations

Organisations are not families, friendly societies or clubs. By setting their own values and standards and relating these to long-term effectiveness they become distinctive. They are almost certain to be at variance from those that are, and would be, held by natural families and clubs. Problems that arise are clouded therefore where the organisation does indeed perceive itself to be 'a big happy family': families are able to forgive prodigal children, and organisations may not be able to afford to do so if they are to maintain long-term standards or if substantial damage has been done to customer relations, for example. Organisations exist to provide effective products and services for customers while families and clubs exist to provide comfort, society and warmth. These elements are by-products; they are not the core.

Organisations are not obliged to provide employment at all except insofar as they need the work carried out. They will select and hire people for this on the basis of capabilities and qualities. They have no obligation to take staff from the ranks of the unemployed (though they may choose to do so). They have no obligation to locate for all eternity in particular areas (though again they may choose to do so).

Organisations that pursue high ethical standards are not religious institutions, and neither do they have any obligation to reflect any prevailing local traditions, values, customs, prejudices or religion.

Japanese organisations setting up in the UK were, and remain, successful precisely because of this. Rather than trying to integrate their activities with the traditions of their locations, they brought very distinctive and positive values with which people who came to work for them were required to identify.

Organisations must distinguish between right and wrong. Lying, cheating, stealing, bribery and corruption are always wrong and can never be ethically justified.

This has to be set in the context of the ways in which business is conducted in certain sectors and parts of the world. If a contract is only to be secured by offering a bribe, the relationship is corrupted and based on contempt. If and when prevailing views change, the total relationship between organisation and customer is likely to be called into question and any scandal or adverse publicity that emerges invariably affects confidence. It is in any case extremely stressful for individuals to have to work in this way, or indeed to connive or conspire with any overt wrong doing (though this may clearly be accommodated if the organisation institutionalises such matters, protects individuals who are taken to court or accepts responsibility for every outcome).

▾ 14 Culture

14.1 Introduction

Organisation culture is an amalgam and summary of the ways in which activities are conducted and standards and values adopted. It encompasses the climate or atmosphere surrounding the organisation, prevailing attitudes within it, standards, morale, strength of feelings towards it and the general levels of goodwill present.

It is an essential feature of effective organisation creation and performance. It arises from a mixture of the following elements.

1 **History and tradition:** the origins of the organisation; the aims and objectives of the first owners and managers, and their philosophy and values; the value in which these are currently held; the ways in which they have developed.

2 **Nature of activities:** historical and traditional, and also current and envisaged; this includes reference to the general state of success and effectiveness, and the balance of activities (steady-state, innovative, crisis).

3 **Technology:** the relationship between technology and the workforce, work design, organisation and structure; alienative factors and steps taken to get over these; levels of technological stability and change; levels of expertise, stability and change.

4 **Past, present and future:** the importance of the past in relation to current and proposed activities; special pressures (especially struggles and glories) of the past; the extent to which the organisation 'is living' in the past, present or future, and the pressures and constraints that are brought about as a result.

5 **Purposes, priorities and attention:** in relation to performance, staff, customers, the community and environment; and to progress and development.

6 **Size:** and the degrees of formalisation and structure that this brings. Larger organisations are much more likely to have a proliferation of divisions, supervisory structures, reporting relationships, rules, processes and procedures tending to cause communication difficulties, inter-departmental rivalries and problems with coordination and control.

7 **Location:** geographical location, the constraints and opportunities afforded through choosing to be, for example, in urban centres, edge of town or rural areas. This also includes recognising and considering prevailing local, national and sectoral traditions and values.

8 **Management style:** the stance adopted by the organisation in managing and supervising its people; the stance required by the people of managers and

supervisors; the general relationships between people and organisation and the nature of superior–subordinate relations.

This is the context of organisation culture. A simple way of defining organisation culture is:

'The ways in which things are done here'.

Culture is formed from the collection of traditions, values, policies, beliefs and attitudes that prevail throughout the organisation.

Specific pressures are also present.

14.2 External pressures on organisation culture

■ Reputation

This must be seen from all points of view. The organisation may go into a given location for commercial advantage but with preconceived ideas or prejudices (which may either be positive or negative). The organisation may bring with it a particular reputation (again, positive or negative) and this may be in relation to itself or the sector which it represents and within which it operates. There may be wider questions of prejudice, fear and anxiety to be overcome as the organisation tries to live up to (or live down to) its reputation. Areas that have had bad experiences of multinational activities in the past, for example, may be anxious about the next influx.

■ Legal

All organisations have to work within the laws of their locations. These exert pressure on production methods, waste disposal, health and safety, marketing and selling, contractual arrangements, staff management, human resources, industrial relations and equality (or otherwise) of opportunity and access, community relations, organisational and professional insurance, and the reporting of results.

Pressures are compounded when the organisation operates in many countries and under diverse legal codes. Balances have to be found in these cases to ensure that, as far as possible, everyone who works for the organisation does so on terms that transcend the varying legal constraints. Organisations are therefore obliged to set absolute standards that more than meet particular legal minima. Moreover, the phrase 'we comply with the law' invariably gives the message that 'the only reason that we set these standards is because we have to' and that the organisation has therefore been pressured into these standards rather than achieving them because it believes that they are right. It calls into question not just the organisation's attitude to the law, but also its wider general attitudes, values and standards.

■ Ethical

Ethical pressures arise from the nature of work carried out and from the standards and customs of the communities in which the organisation operates.

There are also general ethical pressures on many activities concerned that are covered by the law.

Again, the ideal response of any organisation is to put itself beyond reproach so that these pressures are accommodated and leave the way clear for developing productive and harmonious relationships with all concerned.

Examples of ethical pressures are as follows.

1 **Activities:** most activities carry some form of commitment and others are imposed on their staff by organisations. For example, medical staff have commitments to their patients; commercial services staff have commitments to their customers; public servants have commitments to their clients.

2 **Sectors:** again, there is a universal commitment not to supply shoddy goods and services, but rather to provide products of integrity. Some sectors have specific additional problems with this (for example, tobacco, alcohol, armaments and medical research).

3 **Waste disposal:** the onus is clearly on organisations to make adequate arrangements to clear up any mess made by their processes. Some areas and countries have lower standards for this. Organisations assess the convenience of dumping of rubbish, and balance this against absolute standards of right and wrong, and any loss of reputation that might occur in the future if their waste leads to some form of contamination.

4 **Equal opportunities, staff management, industrial relations and health and safety:** high standards of practice in each of these areas are marks of respect and care for staff, customers and communities. Their absence or variations in them lead, apart from anything else, to feelings of distrust and loss of confidence, and therefore to demotivation of the staff.

5 **Results reporting:** the pressure here is in the presentation. Ideally, this should be done in ways that can be understood by anyone who has an interest or stake in the organisation and, indeed, anyone else who would like to know how it is performing. Again, obfuscation tends to lead to those taking an interest to look for hidden meanings and agenda.

14.3 Internal pressures on organisation culture

These are as follows.

1 The interaction between the desired culture and the organisation's structures and systems. Serious misfit between these leads to stress and frustration and also to customer dissatisfaction and staff demotivation.

2 The expectations and aspirations of staff, the extent to which these are realistic and can be satisfied within the organisation. This becomes a serious issue when the nature of the organisation changes and prevailing expectations can no longer be accommodated. Problems also arise when the organisation makes promises that it cannot keep.

3 Management and supervisory style: the extent to which this is supportive, suitable to the purpose and generally acceptable to the staff.

4 The qualities and expertise of the staff, and the extent to which this divides

their loyalties. Many staff will have professional and trade union memberships, continuous professional development requirements and career expectations, as well as holding down positions and carrying out tasks within organisations. In many cases – and especially when general dissatisfaction is present – people tend to take refuge in their profession or occupation, or their trade union.

5 Technology and the extent to which it impacts on the ways in which work is designed, structured and carried out.

6 Working customs, traditions and practices including restrictive practices, work divisions, specialisation and allocation, unionisation and other means of representation; and the attitudes and approaches adopted by both organisation and staff towards each other, whether flexible and cooperative, or adversarial, and the degrees of openness.

7 The extent to which continuity of employment is feasible; or, conversely, uncertainties about future prospects for work and employment. This includes degrees of flexibility, the extent and prevalence of employee and skills development, learning subcultures and the wider attitude of both staff and organisation to this. It also affects reward packages.

8 Internal approaches and attitudes to the legal and ethical issues indicated; the extent of genuine commitment to equality of opportunity and access for all staff; whether or not different grades have different values placed on them; standards of dealings with staff, customers, communities, suppliers and distributors.

9 The presence of pride and commitment in the organisation, its work and its reputation; standards of general well-being; the extent of mutual respect.

10 Communication methods and systems, the nature of language used, the presence/absence of hidden agendas.

11 Physical and psychological distance between functions, departments, divisions and positions in the organisation and its hierarchies.

■ The cultural web

The cultural web is an alternative way of looking at the internal pressures upon organisation culture. People draw heavily on points of reference which are built up over periods of time and which are especially important at internal organisational level. The beliefs and assumptions that comprise this fall within the following boundaries.

1 The routine ways that members of the organisation behave towards each other and that link different parts of the organisation and which comprise 'the way that things are done'. These, at their best, lubricate the working of the organisation and may provide distinctive and beneficial organisational competency. However, they can also represent a 'taken for granted' attitude about how things should happen that can be extremely difficult to change.

2 The rituals of organisational life such as training programmes, promotion and assessment point to what is important in the organisation, reinforce 'the way we do things round here' and signal what is actually valued.

3   The stories told by members of the organisation to each other, to outsiders and to new recruits, embed the present organisation in its history and flag up important events and personalities.
4   The more symbolic aspects of organisation such as logos, offices, cars and titles, or the type of language and terminology commonly used.
5   The control systems, measures and reward systems emphasise what is actually important and focus attention and activity.
6   Power structures are also likely to be associated insofar as the most powerful groupings are likely to be the ones most associated with what is actually valued.
7   The formal organisation structure and the more informal ways in which the organisation works are likely to reflect these power structures and, again, to delineate important relationships and emphasise required levels of performance (Johnson and Scholes, 1992).

14.4 Cultural influences

Geert Hofstede (1980) carried out studies that identified cultural similarities and difference among the 116 000 staff of IBM located in 40 countries. He identified four basic dimensions of national culture and the differences in their emphases and importance in the various countries.

1   **Power-Distance**: the extent to which power and influence is distributed across the society; the extent to which this is acceptable to the members of the society; access to sources of power and influence; and the physical and psychological distance that exists between people and the sources of power and influence.
2   **Uncertainty Avoidance**: the extent to which people prefer order and certainty, or uncertainty and ambiguity; and the extent to which they feel comfortable or threatened by the presence or absence of each.
3   **Individualism-Collectivism**: the extent to which individuals are expected or expect to take care of themselves; the extent to which a common good is perceived and the tendency and willingness to work towards this.
4   **Masculinity-Femininity**: the distinction between masculine values (the acquisition of money, wealth, fortune, success, ambition, possessions), and the feminine (sensitivity, care, concern, attention to the needs of others, quality of life), and the value, importance, mix and prevalence of each.

■ Power-distance

The study looked at the extent to which managers and supervisors were encouraged or expected to exercise power and to take it upon themselves to provide order and discipline. In some cases – for example, Spain – this expectation was very high. Relationships between superior and subordinate were based on low levels of mutual trust and low levels of participation and involvement. Employees would accept orders and direction on the understanding that the superior carried full responsibility, authority and accountability. Elsewhere – for example, Australia and Holland – people expected to be consulted and to participate in decision-making. They expected to be kept regularly and fully informed of progress, and had much greater need for general equality and honesty of approach. They would feel free to question superiors about why particular courses of action were necessary, rather than simply accepting that they were.

■ Uncertainty avoidance

People with a high propensity for uncertainty avoidance (that is, those that wished for high degrees of certainty) tended to require much greater volumes of rules, regulations and guidance for all aspects of work. They sought stability and conformity, and were intolerant of dissenters. Uncertainty caused stress, strain, conflicts and disputes. Stress could be avoided by working hard, following the company line, and adhering to and complying with required ways of behaviour. Where uncertainty avoidance was lower, these forms of stress were less apparent; there was less attention paid to rules and less emphasis placed on conformity and adherence.

■ Individualism-collectivism

The concern here was to establish the relative position of individual achievement in terms of that of the organisation, and also the wider contribution to society and the community. For example, in the UK and USA overwhelming emphasis was placed on individual performance and achievement. This has implications for membership of teams and groups and the creation of effective teams and groups in such locations. It also indicates the extent of likelihood of divergence of purpose between the organisation and individuals. Where collectivism was higher, there was also a much greater emphasis on harmony, loyalty, support and productive interaction, and much greater attention to organisational performance and also to the position of the organisation and its wider environment, and its contribution to society as well as the achievement of its own desired results.

■ Masculinity-femininity

This considered the value placed on different achievements. Cultures with high degrees of masculinity set great store by the achievement of material possessions and rewards. Those with high degrees of femininity saw success in terms of quality of life, general state of the community, individual and collective well-being, the provision of essential services, the ability to support the whole society and to provide means of social security.

The work emphasises the importance of cultural factors and differences in all areas and aspects of organisational behaviour. It indicates both the strength and interaction of cultural pressures. Moreover, it indicates the source and nature of particular values, particular drives and barriers and blockages, and behavioural issues and problem areas that all organisations need to consider. Above all, it illustrates the relative strength of some of the main cultural and social pressures that are brought to bear on all organisations in all situations.

■ Summary

These pressures indicate the context in which organisation culture is founded. Culture is present in all organisations. It is either positive, which tends to attract people, or negative, tending to repel people (which people tend to reject). It may also be designed, emergent or informal, as explained below.

❒ Designed

Designed cultures are shaped by those responsible for organisational direction and results and created in the pursuit of this. This involves setting the standards of attitudes, values, behaviour and belief that everyone is required to subscribe to as a condition of joining the organisation. Policies are produced so that everyone knows where they stand, and these are under-pinned by extensive induction and orientation programmes and training schemes. Procedures and sanctions are there to ensure that these standards continue to be met. Organisations with very specific cultures are not all things to all people: many, indeed, make a virtue of their particular approach of 'many are called but few are chosen'. High levels of internalisation of shared values are required.

Other perceptions emerge from this. Feelings of confidence trust and respect are created. Individual response to the level of organisation commitment that is evident in this approach tends to be high.

❒ Emergent

This is where the culture is formed by the staff (and staff groups) rather than directed by the organisation. The result is that people think, believe and act according to the pressures and priorities of their peers and pursue their own agenda. This is clearly fraught with difficulties and dangers; organisations that allow this to happen will succeed only if the aims and objectives of the staff coincide absolutely with its own.

It leads to the staff setting their own informal procedures and sanctions, or operating in ways that suit their own purposes rather than those of the organisation. Individuals and groups, again, are not all things to all people; they may (and do) reject those who refuse to abide by the norms and values that they have set for themselves.

❒ Informal

Subcultures exist in all organisations. They relate to membership of different groups and vary between these (for example, in the state of openness of dealings between members). Subcultures become more destructive when they operate contrary to absolute standards. Forms of this are set out below.

1 The canteen culture, whereby the shared values adopted are those of groups that gather away from the work situations and in such places as the washroom or canteen;

2 Elites and cliques, whereby strength and primacy is present in some groups at the expense of others. This leads to over-mightiness. It affects operations when the elites and cliques are able to command resources, carry out projects and gain prestige at the expense of others; to lobby effectively for resources at the expense of others; and to gain favour at the expense of others;

3 Work regulation, whereby the volume and quality of work is regulated by the group for its own ends rather than those of the organisation; and when it sets and works to its own targets which are at variance with those of the organisation.

4 Informal norming, whereby individuals are pressurised to adopt the attitudes and values of those around them rather than those of the organisation. This occurs most when the organisation's own norms are not sufficiently strong or structured to remove the local or group pressure.

14.5 Archetype cultures

The following archetypes may be distinguished.

■ Power culture

This is where the key relationship exists between the person who wields power and influence, and those who work for her. It depends on the figure at the centre, the source of power. Everyone else draws their strength, influence and confidence from this centre and requires its continued support to ensure prosperity and operational viability. The relationship is normally terminated when there is a loss of confidence on the part of the person at the centre of power with those who work for them. Individuals generate power cultures when they attract those who have faith in them and who wish to be involved with them.

The main problem that a power culture must face is that of size. As it grows and diversifies, it becomes difficult for the person at the centre to sustain continued high levels of influence. There is also the problem of permanence, of what happens when the person at the centre of power passes out of the organisation. In situations where he has generated the ideas, energy, identity and strength of the situation, a void is left when he leaves or dies.

The structural form of the power culture may be seen as like a spider's web (see Figure 14.1). The main relationship between the subordinates is with the centre.

■ People/person culture

People/person culture exists for the people in it: for example, where a group has decided that it is in its own over-riding interest to band or form together and produce an organisation for its own benefit. This may be found in certain research groups; university departments; family firms; and companies started by groups of friends where the first coming together is generated by the people involved rather than the matter in hand. The key relationship is therefore

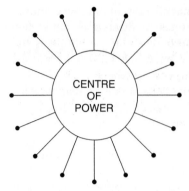

The **key relationship** is with the centre or source of power, hence no joining lines between the 'spokes'.

The **key issue** is the continuation of confidence and reciprocity between the two.

Figure 14.1 Power culture + structure: The Wheel

The **key relationship** is between the people; what binds them is their **intrinsic** common interest. Hierarchy and structure may evolve incidentally; they will also be driven by this intrinsic common interest.

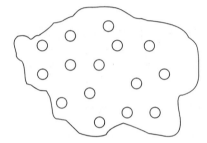

Figure 14.2 People/person culture + structure: The Mass

between people, so what binds them is their intrinsic common interest. Hierarchy and structure may evolve, but these too will be driven by this intrinsic common interest.

■ Task culture

Task cultures are to be found in project teams; marketing groups and marketing-oriented organisations. The emphases are on getting the job completed, keeping customers and clients satisfied, and responding to and identifying new market opportunities. Such cultures are flexible, adaptable and dynamic. They accommodate the movements of staff necessary to ensure effective project and development teams and continued innovation; and concurrent human activities such as secondments, project responsibility and short-term contracts. They are driven by customer satisfaction. They operate most effectively in prosperous, dynamic and confident environments and markets. They may also generate opportunities and niche activities in these and create new openings. Their success lies in their continued ability to operate in this way.

■ Role culture

Role cultures are found where organisations have gained a combination of size, permanence and departmentalisation, and where the ordering of activities,

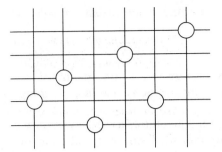

The **key relationship** here is with the task. The form of organisation is therefore fluid and elastic.

The **structure** is often also described as a MATRIX or GRID; none of these gives a full configuration as the essence is the dynamics of the form, and the structure necessary to ensure this.

Figure 14.3 Task culture + structure: The Net

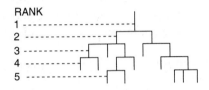

RANK
1
2
3
4
5

The **key relationship** is b ased on authority and the superior–subordinate style of relationships
The **key purposes** are order, stability, permanence and efficiency.

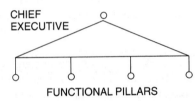

CHIEF
EXECUTIVE

FUNCTIONAL PILLARS

The 'Greek Temple' format delineates function as well as authority.

Figure 14.4 Role culture + structure: The Pyramid or Temple

preservation of knowledge, experience and stability are both important and present.

The key relationship is based on authority and the superior–subordinate style of relationships. The key purposes are order, stability, permanence and efficiency (see Figure 14.4).

Role cultures operate most effectively where the wider environment is steady and a degree of permanence is envisaged.

14.6 Other aspects of organisational culture

Other features of organisational culture may be distinguished.

1 **Relationships with the environment:** including the ways in which the organisation copes with uncertainty and turbulence; the ways on which the

organisation seeks to influence the environment; the extent to which it behaves proactively or reactively.

2 **History and tradition:** the extent to which the organisation's histories and traditions are a barrier or a facilitator of progress; the extent to which the organisation values and worships its past histories and traditions; key influences on current activities and beliefs; the position of key interest groups (for example, trade unions).

3 **The internal relationship balance:** the mixture and effectiveness of power, status, hierarchy, authority, responsibility, individualism, group cohesion; the general relationship mixture of task/social/development.

4 **Rites and rituals:** these are the punctuation marks of organisation operations. They include: pay negotiations; internal and external job application means and methods; disciplinary, grievance and dismissal procedures; rewards; individual, group, departmental and divisional publicity; training and development activities; parties and celebrations; key appointments and dismissals; socialisation and integration of people into new roles, activities and responsibilities.

5 **Routines and habits:** these are the formal, semi-formal and informal ways of working and interaction that people generate for themselves (or which the organisation generates for them) to make comfortable the non-operational aspects of working life. They develop around the absolutes – attendance times, work requirements, authority and reporting relationships – and include regular meetings, regular tasks, forms of address between members of the organisation and groups, pay days, holidays and some trainee development activities.

6 **Badges and status symbols:** these are the marks of esteem conferred by organisations on their people. They are a combination of location (near to or away from the corridors of power for example); possessions (cars, technology, personal departments); job titles (reflecting a combination of ability, influence and occupation); and position in the hierarchy pecking order.

The effects of rites, rituals, routines, habits, badges and status symbols all lie in the value that the organisation places on them and the degree of esteem in which they are held by the members of staff. There is no point in offering anything, or in undertaking any form of cultural activity if a negligible or negative response is received. In general, therefore, these forms of culture development both anticipate people's expectations and seek to reinforce them and to meet them.

It is essential also to recognise the influence of different aspects of organisation design and operation:

- technology influences work arrangements and groupings, physical layout and the nature of the people employed;
- structure and hierarchy influence personal and professional interactions, personal and professional ambitions and aspirations;
- rules, regulations and systems influence attitudes and behaviour (positively or negatively) depending on how they are drawn up and operated and on their particular focus;
- leadership provides the key point of identity for everyone else, from which

people establish their own perceptions of the organisation's general standards;
- management style influences the general feelings of well-being of everyone else, and sets standards of attitudes and behaviour as well as performance;
- managerial demands and the ways in which these are made also influence attitudes and behaviour;
- hierarchical and divisional relations and interactions influence the nature of performance, attention to achievement and the value placed on achievements; this also applies to functional activities.

Where the need for culture change or development is apparent interventions can be made in each or all of these.

14.7 Conclusions

Effective organisation cultures are positive and designed rather than emergent. They must be capable of gaining commitment to purpose, the ways in which this is pursued and the standards adopted by everyone. Cultures are a summary and reflection of the aims and objectives, and values, held. Where this is not apparent, different groups and individuals form their own aims and objectives and adopt their own values; and where these are at variance with overall purpose, or negative in some way, they are dysfunctional and may become destructive.

For this to be effective, a strong mutual sense of loyalty and acceptance between organisation and people is essential. Employees exert positive effort on behalf of the organisation, making a personal as well as professional or occupational commitment. The reverse of this – the organisation's commitment to its people – is also essential. A strong sense of identity towards the organisation and its purposes and values is required, and this happens when these are clear and positive. Any commitment made by people to organisations (or anything else) is voluntary and personal, and can be changed or withdrawn. The best organisations produce cultures that are capable of generating this. They create the desire among their people to join, remain with and progress, recognising their mutuality of interest and the benefits available to everyone.

▼ 15 Technology

15.1 Introduction

All organisations use some form of technology and equipment in pursuit of their business and this has a basic and critical impact on the nature, design, structure and conduct of work. Technology also has implications for compartmentalisation, functionalisation and specialisation. Departments and divisions are created around the equipment used, whether for production, communications, information or control. It impacts on the physical environment because particular processes determine the layout and format in which work is conducted and the proximity of individuals and groups to each other. It therefore becomes a factor to be recognised in the creation of supervisory and managerial functions and activities.

Again, there is a historic background. Forms of technology and equipment were used in the construction of the great buildings, temples and monuments of the ancient world. Most of this was unmechanised, often requiring armies of people to move heavy blocks of wood and stone into place. Roman war galleys – fighting ships – used slave-driven banks of oars for propulsion and direction and to manoeuvre into fighting positions. In each of these cases a basic technology existed and was exploited, but using human, rather than mechanised energy, to make it effective. In each case, also, the task requirements meant that forms of organisation were required; and while in many cases the labour was composed of slaves, these nevertheless had to be sufficiently interested, motivated and directed to ensure that the product or output was both effective and of the required quality.

The relationship between people and technology in organisations and organised groups has therefore long been established and recognised. The effects of technology upon organisational behaviour become increasingly apparent, however. This is especially true in the current environment of constant technological development and change.

The relationship between technology and organisational behaviour may be considered under the following headings.

1 **Approaches to production:** scientific management and its effects on production and behaviour; studies of groups in different working situations; the use of work groups in production.
2 **Levels and types of technology:** the effects of the size, scope and scale of operations; the use of production lines; the effects of mechanisation and

automation on individuals and groups. This also extends to information technology.

3 **Organisational requirements:** the maximisation/optimisation of production; attention to standardisation, quality, speed, reliability and consistency of output.

4 **Human and behavioural implications:** boredom and alienation; health and safety and occupational health; stresses and strains; job and task division.

Organisational technology consists of:

- hardware (the capital equipment), such as computers, screens, robots, process machines;
- software: the packages needed to energise and direct the hardware profitably and effectively.

It also includes the following inter-related elements.

1 Production technology and equipment which may be largely manual or mechanised, requiring human expertise, energy and input to make it effective and productive.

2 Largely automated technology designed to produce products (or components of products) to uniform standards of quality, appearance and performance. In these cases the human input is often chiefly confined to switching the process on and off and monitoring (watching) the output flow. This includes production robotics and computerised manufacturing.

3 Support function technology: including computer-aided design, desktop printing and publishing, purchasing, stock room, storage and ordering systems.

4 Information systems: for the input, storage, retrieval, output and presentation of data in ways suitable to those using it; and the production of data for purposes of control, monitoring, evaluation and decision-making.

5 Specialised: for example, health equipment includes scanners, monitors, emergency equipment, laser technology for surgery and healing, heart, lung, organ and pulse monitoring equipment.

6 Generic: off-the-shelf computerised production and information systems that are of value to a wide range of organisations and activities.

7 Access to, and use of, the Internet: in some cases as a part of core business; in others as a means of accessing a great range of conformation.

All organisational technology is developed and improved along the following lines:

- that which is to be used in future supersedes that which was used in the past, either by improving quality or volume of output, or by reducing the time and resources (including human) taken to produce the existing levels;
- that which is to be used in the future has a greater variety of uses and applications than the existing and may lead to the ability to gain entry into new markets and sectors, thus helping to secure the future of the organisation;
- fashion: everyone else in the given sector is using a particular form of technology and there is pressure to conform;

- the organisation itself has an accurate assessment of the nature of the technology required to produce its products to the required volume, quality and deadline and commissions the design and manufacture of the equipment to do this;
- organisations and the technology that they use must be capable of harmonisation with the given culture, values, attitudes, skills and qualities;
- items of technology must increasingly be capable of integration and inter-relationship with each other.

15.2 Size and scale of production

A variety of different scales of production and expertise may be identified and it is now necessary to define these. Each has behavioural implications.

Joan Woodward studied the impact of technology and behaviour on each other in a wide range of manufacturing organisations in Essex in the 1950s. From this work there has emerged a widely used classification of sizes and scales of production.

1. **Unit:** the production of individual, unique or specialised items. Resources are gathered together to produce these in response to demand and orders. To be successful in this a variety of conditions must exist. The technology and equipment used must be specialised. The expertise available must be both highly specialist in the given field and flexible, adaptable and responsive to individual demands. There must be commitment to quality and attention to detail to the particular demands of customers. Scheduling and patterns of work will be flexible.

Most unit work is carried out by small organisations. Those who work in them must, in turn, be flexible in their attitude and approach to work. Many people involved in unit production bring with them high levels of technical expertise and this has to be integrated into effective output.

2. **Mass production:** the design of mass production operations was and remains based on the scientific management principles first developed by Taylor in the late nineteenth century. Work is broken down into simple and progressive operations. Large volumes are standardised and regular output is therefore produced. Automated and computerised production technologies are now widely used for this. The result has been to increase quality, volume, speed and reliability of output.

Mass production requires high and continuing levels of investment in production technology of work premises. It also requires investment in the determination and management of scheduling, storage, marketing, sales and delivery and the organisation and training of the workforce. This normally means the employment of a wide range of distinctive, professional or semi-professional functional specialists and experts, and the creation of departments and divisions reflecting this. The contribution of each and their interaction with each other has to be managed and harmonised. Areas of conflict become apparent between the departments and divisions. There is also often the need to reconcile organisational priorities and directions with the demands of individuals to progress and develop their professional and technical expertise and their careers.

3. **Batch production:** this exists between the unit and mass scales of production. It draws features from each: the specialist quality output and the flexibility and responsiveness of the small producer, combined with the production standardisation from larger scales of activities. A batch is therefore a quantity large enough to require substantial technological investment in its production. This is limited by the size of demand for the product and one only of a range of outputs that a batch producer makes.

Organisations engaged in batch products require distinctive and appropriate technology and equipment and the expertise to use it effectively. They also need staff to be able to carry out the support functions indicated (for example, marketing sales, personnel) whether or not these are constituted into formalised departments.

4. **Flow production:** this is related to mass production in scale, but applies to areas of activity where the output is a continuous stream or flow, such as oil, petrol, chemicals, steel and plastic extrusion. The investment in technology is by far the greatest charge on organisations in these sectors. Input and expertise has to be scheduled in order to ensure a steady and correct flow of raw materials into the production and output processes. The second priority is in the maintenance of the equipment used in order that there are as few breakdowns and stoppages as possible because the other critical level of charge comes from shutting down the processes and then restarting them.

For example, switching off a steel furnace normally means that it has to be relined with the fireproof heat retention and energy generation elements that are used to produce the extreme levels of temperature required. These cannot accommodate cooling off after they have been operational, which means substantial maintenance and refitting has to be accommodated if a shutdown occurs.

In flow production organisations, high levels of technology and process expertise therefore exist. Support functions have to be recreated, harmonised and reintegrated.

This gives a general indication of the managerial and organisational behavioural issues that arise as the result of the adoption of particular types and scales of production and the technology used. There are implications for work division and allocation, work patterns, styles and methods of management, and supervision of operations. There are also production and operational pressures on those who actually conduct the organisation's primary activities.

15.3 Expertise

As with technology and equipment, different levels of expertise may be distinguished.

■ Professional

The original professions were medicine, soldiering, priesthood and the law. They distinguished themselves from other occupations as follows.

1 They set their own entry barriers, normally in the form of pre-required levels of education or training, that those who aspired to the profession had to have in order to be eligible for consideration for entry. This also limited the numbers in the profession and helped to keep reward levels relatively high.
2 They were self-regulating. There was a distinctive body of knowledge, skills and expertise required to be learned that was determined by the profession itself. The profession also set its own standards of expertise and integrity. It required those who came into it to follow courses of study and practice in order to achieve these standards. It also took responsibility for the disciplining and regulation of members' activities. Constitutions, councils or gatherings of elders or senior members of the profession were responsible for this.
3 They required regular updating and training to be undertaken to ensure that the service and expertise offered was current.
4 They set their own levels of pay and reward. For soldiering this normally meant participating in the spoils of victory. For medicine reward levels were based on the nature of the ailment being treated and the need of the patient to live. For the law this was based on the nature of the clients being represented and the charges that had been levelled against them. For the priest this was based on the respect and love in which he (and it was usually a man) was held by his congregation.
5 They carried a distinctive and high level of status and esteem. Professions were deemed positive and worthwhile by those who went into them. They were also held in high regard and respect by the rest of society.
6 They carried a commitment to serve, to provide the highest possible quality and level of service to those for whom they worked. They would do this regardless of whoever employed them or came to them for their services.
7 They had a loyalty to their profession itself, and to the other members of it.

Other occupations also aspire to professional status. These include teaching, social work, nursing, accountancy, building, construction, civil and chemical engineering. Most of these require some formal training and expertise in order to be able to practise, though none of them are entirely self-regulating. There are also limitations on the ability of individuals in these occupations to command reward levels.

Other occupations still have developed themselves with the purpose of establishing a general body of expertise that the best practitioners in the sectors should have. These include personnel, marketing, general management, commodity sales and brokerage, central and local government, retail, travel and tourism.

■ Technological

The basis of this is historically similar to that of the professions. Particular trades – for example, wheelwright, cooper, carpenter – required the acquisition of specialist skills and knowledge. They also had periods of articles or apprenticeship which meant that individuals had to be attached to someone already working in the trade to learn the expertise and its applications, and to undertake on-the-job training. The time scales involved – sometimes as long as seven years – also constituted an entry barrier.

Much of this still remains current today. Some engineering occupations, mechanics, cooks and catering, building and construction trades all require formalised qualifications and periods of on-the-job training if individuals are to be able to maximise the potential of their expertise.

In summary, at best, high standards of commitment loyalty, expertise, training and development are both offered and expected. These have great implications for those who manage people from professionalised and expert occupations and for the organisations in which they work. In each case, the individuals concerned have a dual loyalty: to their profession or expertise, and to their organisation. This expertise is marketable and may be offered or sold to the organisation that makes 'the best bid'. This clearly concerns salary; it is likely also to include job interest, challenge, opportunities for development, the need for continuous training and updating.

The contribution of expertise also needs to be valued by organisations and their managers. There is no point, for example, in hiring experts (in whatever field) and then giving them tasks for which their skills are not particularly required. This is a waste of organisational resources and leads to frustration on the part of the individual concerned.

The need, therefore, is to assess the interaction between organisation, technology and expertise in order to be able to draw up effective methods of work that are both satisfactory and challenging to the experts and professionals involved, and also successfully and profitably integrated with the organisation's drives and purposes.

It is apparent from all this that there is a range of conflicting pressures that must be considered:

- the scientific management and organisation of activities demands the standardisation and ordering of work in the interests of efficiency, speed and volume of output;
- outputs of the scale and scope of production dictate that the flow, mass and (to an extent) batch types of activity require this standardisation;
- professional and technical staff require variety, development and the opportunity to progress and enhance their work and expertise;
- everyone, whatever their occupation, has basic human needs of self-esteem, self-respect and self-worth.

The need is therefore, to be able to address and reconcile these issues.

The specific effects of developments, improvements and automation of technology seen in isolation are:

- to remove any specific contribution made by operators to the quality and individuality of production, whether real or perceived;
- to dilute or remove understanding of the production processes used and to remove any direct individual contribution that is made;
- to de-skill operations: operators become button pushers, machine minders

and (when breakdowns occur) telephone users summoning specialist assistance;
- to create a feeling of distance – alienation – between the work and the people who carry it out;
- to create frustration which occurs, perhaps when equipment is available but the expertise to use it is not; or when the equipment is not available but the expertise is; or when both are available but the organisation chooses not to have it available to use.

The result is again to underline feelings of low self-esteem and worth and to encourage boredom and dissatisfaction (and sew the seeds of conflict).

15.4 Alienation

Alienation is the term used to describe the following feelings.

1 Powerlessness – the inability to influence work conditions, work volume, quality, speed and direction.
2 Meaninglessness – the inability to recognise the individual contribution made to the total output of work.
3 Isolation – which may be either physical or psychological. The physical factors arising from work organisation require that people are located in ways that allow for little human interaction and feelings of mutual identity and interest. The psychological factors are influenced by the physical. They also include psychological distance from supervisors, management and the rest of the organisation.
4 Low feelings of self-esteem and self-worth arising from the lack of value (real or perceived) placed on staff by the organisation and its managers.
5 Loss of identity with the organisation and its work, the inability to say with pride 'I work for organisation X.' This is reinforced by the physical and personal commitment made by the individual to the organisation in terms of time, skill and effort which does not bring with it the psychological rewards.
6 Lack of prospects, change or advancement for the future – feelings of being stuck or trapped in a situation purely for economic gain.
7 General rejection – based on adversarial, managerial and supervisory styles and lack of meaningful communications, participation and involvement. This is increased by physical factors such as poor working conditions and environment.
8 Lack of equality – especially where the organisation is seen or perceived to differentiate between different types and grades of staff to the benefit of some and detriment of others.

Alienation is the major fundamental cause of conflicts and disputes at places of work. It is potentially present in all work situations. Those who design and construct organisations need to be aware of it in their own particular situations and to take steps to ensure that ideally it can be eliminated, or at least kept to a minimum and its effects offset by other advantages.

15.5 Effects of technological advances

Some further conclusions concerning the effects of technology upon worker morale may now be drawn.

1 Pay, at whatever level it is set, does nothing to alleviate any boredom or monotony inherent in the work itself. It may make it more bearable in the short to medium term. In many cases also, bonus systems are not within the control of the individual operator. Operators may work to their full capacity, only to see their bonus fail because of factors further down the production process.

2 Insecurity (and, related to this, the threat of insecurity and job loss) may be used as a coercive management tool to try to bully the work out.

3 Poor working conditions, especially those that include extremes of temperature and noise, discomfort, lack of human content and warmth, all contribute to poor morale.

4 Low status and esteem is generated through feelings of being 'only a cog in the machine'. This leads to feelings of futility and impotence on the part of the operator. It is from this that feelings of hostility towards the organisation start to emerge. This also leads to increases in strikes, grievances and disputes.

5 Mental health was identified as a feature by the 'Kornhauser' Studies, the results of which were published in 1965. Arthur Kornhauser studied car assembly workers at Ford, General Motors and Chrysler in Detroit, USA. A major conclusion was that basic assembly line work led to job dissatisfaction which, in turn, led to low levels of mental health. This became apparent in the low self-esteem of the workers who also exhibited anxiety, life dissatisfaction and despair, and hostility to others.

6 Adversarial and confrontational styles of work supervision also contribute to alienation and dissatisfaction. This style of supervision tends to be perpetuated even by those who have been promoted from among the ranks of operators. This is partly because it is all that they know and partly because of the pressure to conform that is exerted by the existing supervisory group. It is also apparent that supervisors themselves become alienated because of pressures from their managers and also because of feelings of hostility towards them from the workers.

Approaches to the problems of dissatisfaction and alienation have taken three basic forms:

- attention to the work;
- attention to the working environment;
- attention to the people.

■ Attention to the work

Attention to the work has taken a variety of forms.

1 Job enrichment and enlargement, in which operators have their capabilities extended to include a range of operations. In some cases this has meant

becoming responsible (with a group of others) for the entire production process in autonomous work groups.

2 Job rotation, in which operators are regularly rotated around different work stations and activities, making a different contribution to the whole.

3 Empowerment, in which the operator accepts responsibility for her own supervision of quality control as well as for the work itself.

Each of these also partly addresses some of the psychological and behavioural aspects of dissatisfaction and alienation. It is worth noting also the experience of an electronics firm quoted by Handy (1993) as follows: 'Production went up only slightly but, more important from their point of view, quality was very high without the need for quality control experts, absenteeism and turnover went down to low levels, production flexibility was greatly increased and the job satisfaction of employees was higher.'

Attention to the work is a continuous process. Today's adventure becomes tomorrow's steady state and the monotony of the day after. There is a great propensity for development to occur in current production systems because of technological advances and also because the globalisation of competition has led organisations to seek new fields and new ways in which to operate.

There is clearly a mutual obligation in all of this for the organisation to provide continuous training and development and for the individual to accept and undergo it. Without this, effective organisation and job development cannot take place.

The question of pay has also to be considered. If work enrichment is followed successfully, the outcome should be a highly skilled, highly motivated and well-paid workforce.

■ Multi-skilling and flexibility

Some versions of job enrichment and enlargement have sought to develop 'the fully flexible workforce' by ensuring that all those in a particular work group are capable of carrying out each of the activities required. This is a basic and integral job requirement. The obligation is placed on the organisation to provide increased levels and volumes of training and development and also to recognise and reward the additional value that the member of staff brings by being capable and flexible.

■ Autonomous work groups

The general attraction of autonomous work groups is that they appear to address both the operational and psychological factors. The giving of autonomy in deciding the allocation of work, organisation and production, attention to quality and output based on broad performance targets (for example, 'to produce X amount of product Y by deadline Z') leaves the group itself to arrange and determine how these are to be achieved. This involves:

- participation in determining and allocating the work, scheduling of priorities and activities, and meeting preferences, and gaining commitment to meeting the targets;

- responsibility in ensuring that the broad targets are met, and that stages along the total schedule are reached also;
- esteem, in that a complete output is seen at the end of activities with which the individual member of staff can identify;
- spirit and harmony, in that the contribution of everyone involved can be seen and valued.

For autonomous working groups to be successful, high levels of skill and flexibility are required. Production technology and processes must be structured to meet behavioural, as well as operational, needs. Individual and group training and development is essential in all aspects of the work. The process is also greatly enhanced if the group is able to participate (or at least be consulted) on the target-setting activities and to set its own means of quality control and assurance.

■ Attention to the environment

Attention to the work environment is now a vastly wider field. It stems from the recognition that people bring their full range of needs to work with them and that the more of these that are met, the lower the levels of personal dissatisfaction likely to arise. Basic and adequate levels of comfort are required. The opportunity to sit down at the workstation (unless this cannot, for over-riding operational reasons, be provided) should always be offered. Temperature is to be controlled and extremes of heat and cold avoided or managed. Pot plants, the radio, pictures on the walls are all allowed and encouraged (and in some cases provided) wherever possible. Good quality furniture, decor and furnishings in all places of work reinforce the perceptions of value that organisations place on their staff; conversely bad quality or decrepit furnishings and tatty decor tend to lead to feelings of being expected and exalted.

■ Attention to the people

The view taken here is that dissatisfaction and alienation are lessened if the behavioural causes are attacked. Extreme proponents of this point of view go a stage further, taking the view that if you genuinely respect and value people, they will do anything for you.

This approach may be taken in different ways. The aim is always to arrive at the point at which individuals know that they are valued for the contribution that they bring to the organisation and that this extends to all occupations.

Attention to people is a key point of inquiry of the 'Excellence' studies. It is central to the philosophy and ways of working of many high performing organisations. The main features are:

1 Setting absolute standards of honesty, integrity, expectations of performance, quality of output, attitudes, values and ethics to which all those coming to work must aspire and conform.
2 Recognising that problems are inherent in all jobs and organising the work

based around a philosophy of fairness and evenness that requires everyone to share in the problem areas and unattractive tasks.

3 Setting absolute organisational standards for managing the staff. These are based on high levels of integrity, support, equality, training and development. Pay and reward levels tend to be high in return for high quality work. Pay and reward methods are honest, clear and unambiguous. Communications between organisation and staff, and the general information flows, are regular, continuous and open.

Rather than addressing the causes of alienation, or taking action to minimise their effects, these are removed altogether. Also removed are factors that differentiate between levels and standards of employee – for example, executive dining rooms and individual car parking spaces – to emphasise equality in both personal and occupational terms.

In some cases, this has extended to the structure and ownership of the organisation. For example, employees have become part-owners through company equity schemes (in the case of US Air, the majority shareholding is held by the staff). In others a proportion of pay is linked to the organisation's financial performance and the percentage of profits paid out to the staff. In the best cases this is paid as a percentage of individual salary so that everybody receives the same proportion of reward. This again underlines equality of treatment, contribution and value.

Whichever view is taken, the desired outcome is the reconciliation of the organisational and operational drives with the technology and equipment that is to be used, and the effects of these on the staff. The ability to do this stems from a recognition and understanding of the influences of the technology, both operational and behavioural. Each approach addresses this issue from differing points of view. It also provides a level of understanding of the underlying causes of conflict and dissatisfaction inherent in any work situation.

15.6 Conclusions

Overall, therefore, it is very difficult to under-state the importance of attention to technology and its effects on organisational behaviour. In all circumstances, it affects organisation and work design and structure and therefore working relationships, patterns of supervision, control and management style. It also affects the wider strategic and contextual views adopted.

The key lies in the choice and effective usage of technology. This involves attention to volume and quality of production and output, the skills and qualities required to operate it effectively, and the quality of input and operation. Specific equipment must also be capable of harmonisation and integration with other technology that exists and is used.

Attention to investment, levels and frequency of investment and attitudes to investment also have to change. The best organisations concentrate on purpose, quality and suitability, as well as cost, durability and returns. Investing in technology and equipment is a consequence of engaging in particular activities.

Technological change, advance and innovation is also part of the equa organisations must be prepared to adopt, adjust, and even sacrifice, curre equipment if and when others in the sector find better ways of doing things and better equipment to use. Again, there are implications for the skills, qualities and expertise required.

The impact of technology on organisational behaviour and performance is all-pervasive. This is both direct and indirect. It directly affects the size, nature and design of the environment and premises, the numbers of people required and their capabilities. It is also the focus around which support functions, processes and practices are devised and grouped. Furthermore, it directly affects the behaviour, motivation and morale of individuals and groups.

16 Organisation structure and design

16.1 Introduction

Organisation structures reflect the aims and objectives, the size and complexity of the undertaking, the nature of the expertise to be used, the preferred management and supervisory style and the means of coordination and control. Whatever arises as the result must be flexible, dynamic and responsive to market and environment conditions and pressures. It must provide effective and suitable channels of communication and decision-making processes; and provide also for the creation of professional and productive relationships between individuals and groups. Departments, divisions and functions are created as required to pursue aims and objectives, together with the means and methods by which they are coordinated and harmonised.

Structure also creates a combination of permanence and order. This is required to provide continuity for the organisation itself, and to generate the required levels of confidence and expectation in customers. It is also necessary to provide staff with (as far as possible) a settled and orderly working life. Means must also be found of ensuring the permanence and continuity of the organisation itself as people join or leave.

Organisations are designed and structured in order to:

- ensure efficiency and effectiveness of activities in accordance with the organisation's stated targets;
- divide and allocate work, responsibility and authority;
- establish working relationships and operating mechanisms;
- establish patterns of management and supervision;
- establish the means by which work is to be controlled;
- establish the means of retaining experience, knowledge and expertise;
- indicate areas of responsibility, authority and accountability;
- meet the expectations of those involved;
- provide the basis of a fair and equitable reward system.

The general factors affecting organisation structure are as listed below.

1 The nature of work to be carried out and the implications of this. Unit, batch, mass and flow scales of production all bring clear indications of the types of organisation required, as do the commercial and public service equivalents;

job definitions, volumes of production, storage of components, raw materials and finished goods; the means of distribution, both inwards and outwards; the type of support functions and control mechanisms.

2 Technology and equipment, and the expertise, premises and environment needed to use it effectively; its maintenance; its useful life cycle; its replacement and the effect of new equipment on existing structures and work methods.

3 The desired culture and style of the organisation and all that this means (it affects the general approach to organisation management; nature and spans of control; the attitudes and values that are established; reporting relationships between superiors and subordinates and across functions; staff relationships).

4 The location of the organisation; its relationships with its local communities; any strong local traditions (for example, of unionisation, or not); particular ways of working; specific activities, skills and expertise.

5 Aims and objectives strategy; flexibility, dynamism, responsiveness, or rigidity and conformity in relation to staff, customers and the community; customer relations; stakeholder relations.

16.2 Structural forms

■ Tall structures

There are many different levels or ranks within the total. There is a long hierarchical and psychological distance between top and bottom. Tall structures bring with them complex reporting relationships, operating and support systems, promotion and career paths, and differentiated job titles. Spans of control (see Figures 16.1 and 16.2) tend to be small. The proportion of staff with some form of supervisory responsibility tends to be high in relation to the whole organisation.

■ Flat structures

There are few different levels or ranks within the total. Jobs tend to be concentrated at lower levels. There is a short hierarchical distance between top and bottom; this may reduce the psychological distance or it may not. Lower-level jobs often carry responsibilities of quality control, volume and deadline targets. Spans of control tend to be large. The proportion of staff with some form of supervisory responsibility (other than for their own work) tends to be small in relation to the whole organisation. Career paths by promotion are limited; but this may be replaced by the opportunity for functional and expertise development, and involvement in a variety of different projects. Reward structures may not be as apparent as those offered alongside progress through a tall hierarchy. Reporting relationships tend to be simpler and more direct. There is a reduced likelihood of distortion and barriers to communications in a flat structure compared with a tall one simply because there are fewer channels for messages to pass through.

1. *SIMPLE*

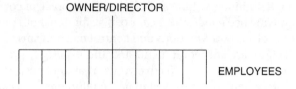

2. *LINEAR STAFF*

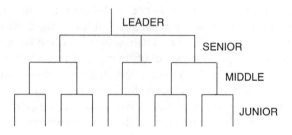

3. *FUNCTIONAL*

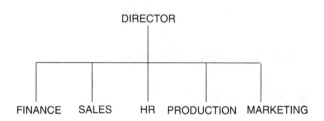

4. *DIVISIONAL*

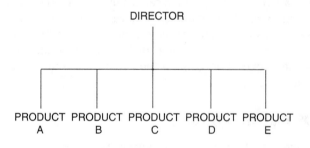

5. *DISPERSED*

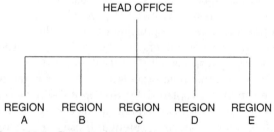

Figure 16.1   Organisation structures

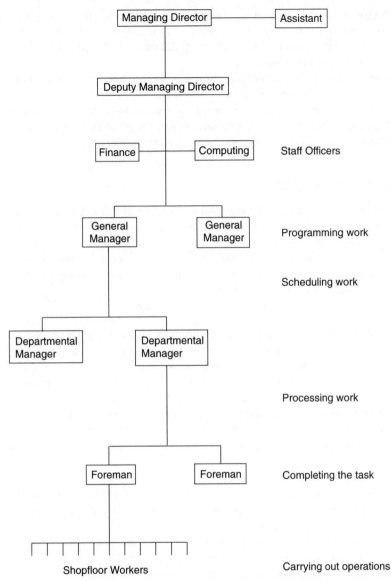

Figure 16.2 Traditional organisational model

16.3 Centralisation and decentralisation

■ Centralised structures

Centralisation is generally an authority relationship between those in overall control of the organisation and the rest of its staff. The tighter the control exerted at the centre, the greater the degree of centralisation. An organisation may therefore operate in a wide range of activities and locations, or the majority of the staff may work away from these locations and the majority of work carried out in them also; however, top management may still retain tight control over the ways in which activities are conducted.

The great advantage of centralisation is that top management remains fully aware of the operational as well as strategic issues and concerns. There is relatively little likelihood that senior managers will become detached from the actual organisation performance, or retain illusions of continuing excellence and high achievement, for example, where the reality is very different.

■ Decentralisation

The converse is to delegate or decentralise. The role and function of the centre is therefore to maintain a watching brief, to monitor and evaluate progress and to concern itself with strategic rather than operational issues. The operations themselves are designed and allocated in accordance with overall aims and objectives, and the departments, divisions and functions are given the necessary resources and authority to achieve them.

The advantages of decentralisation are set out below.

1 The speeding-up of operational decisions enabling these to be taken at the point at which they are required, rather than having to refer every matter (or a high proportion) back to head office.
2 It enables local management to respond to local conditions and demands, and to build up a local reputation for the overall organisation.
3 It contributes to organisation and staff development through ensuring that problems and issues are dealt with at the point at which they arise. This helps and enables organisations to identify and develop potential for the future.
4 By the same token, it also contributes to staff motivation and morale. The exercising of responsibility and authority, and other opportunities for development, are more likely to filter through to all staff levels in a decentralised organisation.
5 It enables organisations to get their structures and systems right. Reporting relationships between functions and the centre still have to be designed for effectiveness; activities have to be planned and coordinated.
6 Consistency of treatment for both staff and customers has to be ensured across all functions and locations. However great the level of autonomy also afforded to departments, divisions and functions, they must still contribute to the greater good of the whole organisation; they are not personal or professional fiefdoms.
7 It encourages an organisation to continually assess the well of its talent, its strength and its depth. This is, above all, at managerial and supervisory levels; the greater the decentralisation, the more likely this is to be important at all levels. It is also essential in the identification and development of professional and other forms of expertise.

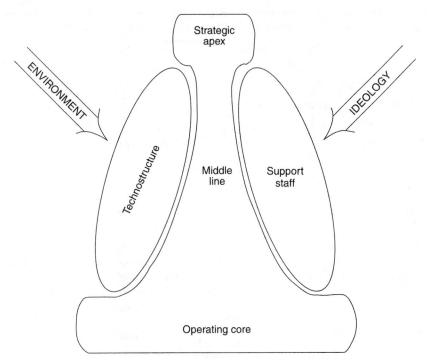

Figure 16.3 The Mintzberg model of organisations

■ The role and function of Head Office

Head offices in all but the simplest structures have responsibility for planning, coordinating and controlling the functions of the rest of the organisation; translating strategy into operations; and monitoring, reviewing and evaluating performance from all points of view (volume, quality, standards and satisfaction).

Whether a relatively centralised or decentralised form of organisation is adopted, it is essential never to lose sight of this key range of activities. The problem lies in how they should be carried out and not in what should be done.

In large, complex and sophisticated organisations – public, private and multinational – the head office is likely to be physically distant from the main areas of operations and this brings problems of communications systems and reporting relationships. Equally important, however, is the problem of psychological distance and remoteness. This occurs when the head office itself becomes a complex and sophisticated entity. This often leads to conflict between personal and organisational objectives, infighting, and concentrations of resources on head office functions rather than operational effectiveness. This is exacerbated when jobs at head office are, or are perceived to be, better careers and more likely to lead to personal opportunities than those in the field. In many cases the head office becomes so remote that it loses any understanding of the reality of activities. Cocooned by the resources that it commands for its own

Table 16.1 Principles of organisation structure: a summary

| | Operational constraints | | Key features | |
	Environment	Internal	Structure	Activities
Simple structure	Simple/ dynamic Hostile	Small Young Simple tasks CEO control	Direction + Strategy	Direct supervision
Teachnocracy	Simple/static Conformist	Old Large Regulated tasks Technocrat control	Technostructure	Standardisation of work
Professional bureaucracy	Complex/ static	Complex systems Professional control	Operational expertise Professional practice	Standardisation of skills
Divisionalised bureaucracy	Simple/static Diversity Hostile	Old Very large Divisible tasks Middle-line control	Autonomy Reporting relationships	Standardisation of outputs Sophisticated supervision
Ad hocracy	Complex/ dynamic Committed	Often young Complex tasks Expert control	Operational Expertise	Mutual adjustment
Missionary	Simple/static Committed	Middle-aged Often 'enclaves' Simple systems Ideological control	Ideology Standards	Policy, norms, Standards
Network organisation	Dynamic Committed	Young Reformed	Operational expertise Technostructure	Networking

Source: Based on Mintzberg (1979); Johnson and Scholes (1994).

functions, it preserves the illusion of excellence and dynamism often in the face of overwhelming evidence to the contrary.

■ Spans of control

'Span of control' refers to the number of subordinates who report directly to a single superior, and for whose work that person is responsible.

Spans of control are defined in a broad to narrow spectrum. The narrower the span, the greater the number of supervisors required by the organisation in total. A workforce of 40, with spans of control of 4 (1 supervisor per 4 staff), needs 10 supervisors. The same workforce with a span of control of 10 only needs 4 supervisors. If the principle is then developed as a hierarchy, it can be seen that, in the first case, additional staff will be needed to supervise the supervisors (see Figure 16.5).

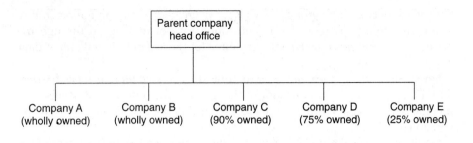

Advantages	Disadvantages
• Low central overheads • Offsetting of individual business losses • Availability of cheaper finance for individual businesses • Spreading of risk for holding company • Ease of divestment for holding company • Facilitates decentralisation	• Risk for individual business of divestment by holding company • Unavailability of skills at group level to assist individual businesses • Lack of synergy • Difficulties of centralised control

Figure 16.4 Holding company structure

Figure 16.5 Spans of control: 1

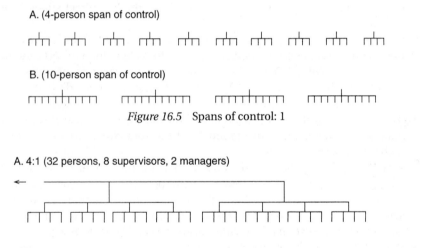

Figure 16.6 Spans of control: 2

If this principle is followed in larger organisations, layers of management and hierarchy can be removed by increasing spans of control. An organisation of 4000 staff would remove about 800 managers and supervisors by changing its spans of control from 4 to 1 to 8 to 1 (see Figure 16.6).

The matter does require additional consideration, however. Narrow spans of control normally mean a tighter cohesion and a closer working relationship between supervisor and group. They also give greater promotion opportunities. There are more jobs, more levels and more ways of moving up through the organisation, and this may be a driving force for those within it and one of their key expectations.

On the other hand, the complex structures thus created tend to act as barriers and blockages to communications: the greater the number of levels that messages have to pass through, the more likely they are to become distorted and corrupted.

On the face of it, there is therefore a trade off between the effectiveness of the organisation and the satisfaction of staff expectations through the availability of promotion channels. Assuming that the effectiveness of the organisation is paramount, means should be sought to enable expectations to be set and met in ways that contribute to this. The absolute effectiveness of the promotion channels should therefore be measured in this way and, where necessary, different means of meeting staff expectations found.

Attention must be paid to operational factors. These are:

- the ability of management to produce results with spans of a certain size;
- the ability of the subordinates to produce results within these spans (in general, the greater the level of expertise held, the less direct supervision is required);
- the expectations of relative autonomy of the subordinates; for example, professional and highly trained staff expect to be left alone to carry out tasks as they see fit, while other types (for example, retail cashiers) need the ability to call on the supervisor whenever problems, such as difficulties with customers, arise;
- the expectations of the organisation and the nature and degree of supervision necessary to meet these, or the ability of the staff concerned to meet these without close supervision;
- specific responsibilities of supervisors that are present in some situations which give the supervisor a direct reason for being there other than to monitor the work that is being carried out (the most common examples are related to safety – for example, on construction sites and in oil refineries – and in shops and supermarkets to handle customers, queries and complaints);
- the nature of the work itself, the similarity or diversity of the tasks and functions, its simplicity or complexity;
- the location of the work, whether it is concentrated in one place or in several different parts of one building or site, or whether it is geographically diverse (subspans are normally created where the location is diversified, even if ultimate responsibility remains with one individual and boundaries of autonomy are ascribed to one person and group in the particular location);
- the extent of necessity and ability to coordinate the work of each group with all the others in the organisation; to coordinate and harmonise the work of the individuals in the group, and to relate this to the demands of the organisation;
- the organisation's own perspective: the extent to which it believes that close supervision, direct control and constant monitoring are necessary and desirable.

■ Hierarchies

Spans of control create hierarchies. These reflect the level, quality and expertise of those involved and also the degree of supervision and responsibility of those in particular positions. These are under-pinned by job titles that indicate both levels of position held in hierarchy and also the nature and mix of expertise and responsibility.

Hierarchies are a familiar feature of all aspects of life. To turn a previous example around, if someone complains at the supermarket checkout and satisfaction is not forthcoming from the cashier, the person then asks to see the supervisor. If there is still no satisfaction then the manager will be called for; to be followed, if necessary, by a letter or approach to the CE. At each point, therefore, the approach is to the next person up the hierarchy in the hope/expectation that she will be able to resolve the matter in hand.

Hierarchies form the organisational basis of public institutions, both for the ordering and management of services – national, military, civil and social – and also as points of reference for those who need to use them. Hierarchies tend to be formed or to emerge in all organisations for these purposes, and because it is a familiar structural form. From an organisational behaviour point of view, it also acts as the means of coordinating and integrating the activities of departments, divisions, groups, functions and individuals that have been separated out for the purposes of efficient and effective working.

16.4 Mechanistic and organic structures

Work carried out by T. Burns and G. M. Stalker in the 1950s identified distinctive variations in the components of organisation structure. These were affected by the nature of the work, the technology used, the rate and nature of change taking place, the stability or volatility of markets, and the nature and expertise of the staff. Their conclusion was that there were two distinctive forms of management system: mechanistic and organic.

■ Mechanistic systems

1 Degree of specialisation: very high, with specialised divisions and differentiation of tasks based on precise job descriptions and pursued on an operational rather than strategic basis.
2 Degree of standardisation: very high, with work methods prescribed and ordered.
3 Orientation of members: operational, attention to means and processes.
4 Conflict resolution: by the superior, and using procedures and channels.
5 Obligations: precisely defined, written into each role.
6 Authority: based on hierarchy, reporting relationships, strictly delineated limitations; includes the setting of work standards and targets.
7 Communication: also based on hierarchy; patterns and interactions tend to be vertical; the content of communications tends towards instructions, directions and orders.

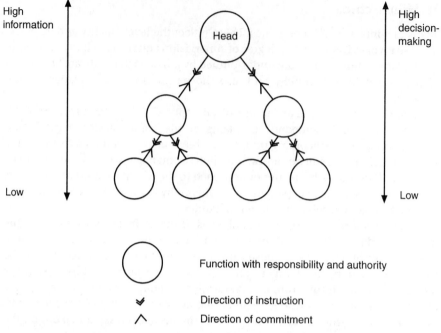

High information — High — Low

High decision-making — High — Low

Head

○ Function with responsibility and authority

⋁ Direction of instruction

⋀ Direction of commitment

Figure 16.7 Organisation structures: mechanistic
Source: Lawrence (1984: after Burns and Stalker).

8 Loyalty: is to the organisation, based on obedience to superiors.
9 Status: from job title and the job held in the organisation.

■ Organic systems

1 Degree of specialisation: low, little specialisation, few boundaries and divisions, low differentiation, no restrictive practices, work pursued on task and strategic basis.
2 Degree of standardisation: low, individual, interactive.
3 Orientation of members: towards aims and objectives, achievement, customer and personal satisfaction.
4 Conflict resolution: through interaction, discussion and debate.
5 Obligations: to task, output and satisfaction.
6 Authority: based on expertise, networks, availability, and accessibility.
7 Communication: based on strategic and operational need rather than hierarchy; lateral as well as vertical; content is based on advice, information, illumination and enlightenment.
8 Loyalty: to task and group as well as organisation.
9 Status: from personal contribution, results and achievements.

The two systems are presented as polar opposites. However, Burns and Stalker found that individual organisations could accommodate both forms within their

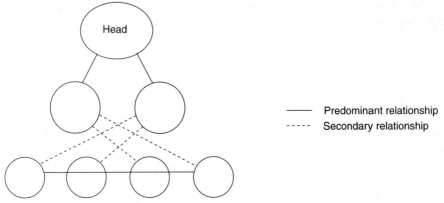

Figure 16.8 Organisation structures: organic/organismic
Source: Lawrence (1984: after Burns and Stalker).

different divisions and operations and that this worked well in some circumstances. They also found that organisations could move from one to the other.

Burns and Stalker favoured neither one system nor the other. The important thing was to ensure that what was designed and introduced was appropriate in the circumstances. However, approaches tending towards mechanistic systems are likely to be more appropriate when the organisation uses long-standing technology to conduct activities in stable and steady markets, rather than in a highly volatile, changing and turbulent situation.

■ Reporting relationships

Again, in the line relationship, these are clear; and again, they become clouded where the functional activities are carried out across departments and divisions. This also leads to questions of workload priority where, for example, an urgent job is required for one department and an important one for another.

Forms of informal authority may also impact. For example, the CEO may want a general request dealt with, the production manager an important request, and the finance assistant an urgent request.

■ Service relationships

These exist outside the line, functional, authority, control and reporting relationships indicated. Service departments gain and maintain their reason for being through the quality and value of the general contribution that they make to the work of others. There is no absolute obligation on the part of the rest of the organisation to avail itself of these services.

Service functions therefore gain an understanding of the requirements of the rest of the organisation for their activities. What is provided is a combination of service expertise, presented in ways useful to the receiving departments. This is enhanced and developed by making specific requests for the service in question in order to gain information or solve problems.

■ Core and peripheral organisations

These forms of structure are based on a total reappraisal of objectives and activities with the view to establishing where the strategic core lies, what is needed to sustain this and where, when and why additional support and resources are required.

The essential is the core. The rest is the peripheral and may be seen as a shamrock or propeller (see Figure 16.9). This may be viewed in the following ways.

1 Professional and technical services and expertise, drawn in to solve problems; to design and improve work methods and practices; to manage change and act as catalysts and agents for change. All of these functions are conducted by outsiders on a contracted basis and the areas include: marketing, public

(a) *The Shamrock Model*

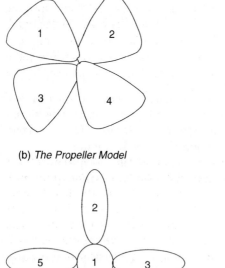

1. The core

2. Specialists

3. Seasonal staff

4. Staff on retainers for pressures and emergencies

(b) *The Propeller Model*

1. The core
2. Specialists
3. Subcontractors
4. Research and development
5. Seasonal staff

Figure 16.9   Core and peripheral

relations, human resource management, industrial relations, supplies, research and development, process and operations management and distribution.

2 Subcontracting of services such as facilities and environment management, maintenance, catering, cleaning and security. These are distinctive forms of expertise in their own right, and therefore best left to expert organisations. This form of subcontracting is now very highly developed across all sectors and all parts of the world as organisations seek to concentrate on their given expertise and minimise areas of non-contributory activity.

3 Operational pressures, in which staff are retained to be available at peaks (daily, periodical or seasonal) and otherwise not present. This has contributed to both the increase in part time, flexible and core hours patterns of employment, and also to the retention of the services of workforce agencies, who specialise in providing particular volumes of expertise in this way.

4 Outworking (often home working), in which staff work at alternative locations including home, avoiding the need for expensive and extensive facilities. This also enables those involved to combine work with other activities (parenting, study, working for other organisations). For this, people may be paid a retainer to ensure their continued obligation of loyalty. They may be well paid, or even over-paid to compensate for periods when there is no work. They may be retained on regular and distinctive patterns of employment (normally short time or part time).

The benefits lie in the need and ability to maximise resources and optimise staff utilisation. Rather than structuring the workforce to be available generally, the requirement for expertise and nature of operations is worked out in advance and the organisation structured from this point of view. All activities that are to be carried out on a steady-state daily basis are integrated into the core. The rest are contracted or retained in one of the forms indicated.

■ Project groups and teams

The creation of project groups is less disruptive if they are drawn from within one division. Where it is drawn from a range of different functions, problems arise when the work of the particular groups impacts and conflicts with that of other functions involved. Again, problems of authority and functional relationship may arise; and again, there are questions of priority and workloads to be considered. The work of the group may be dearer to the heart of one contributing department than others. Some individuals may also be much more enthusiastic about participating than others.

Many of the problems of organisation structure stem from the term used: structure. In all other cases in life, structures are perceived to give a combination of stability, permanence and rigidity, and this is also what those in organisations ostensibly seek. The need for structural permanence, however, springs from the ability that this provides to those who use the structure for other purposes and this is the context within which organisation structures should be seen.

16.5 Bureaucracy

Bureaucracy means 'government by office'. The basis of the concept lies in the need to give organisations their own life, permanence and stability and to retain the fund of expertise and precedent that is built up over their period of existence, rather than being dependent on the personal knowledge of individuals. It also prescribes areas of authority and expertise and formalises the ways in which these are divided.

Every activity is therefore broken down into jobs, offices or positions. Each is formally described and its position in relation to the rest is determined and established. Each is given its own combination of expertise and authority, and its position in the organisation's hierarchy. The whole is then circumscribed by rules and regulations, indicating the relationship between each position, the bounds within which the office holder is to operate and the wider general standards by which people are to act and behave.

Bureaucracy therefore has the following characteristics:

1 **Specialisation:** each position has a clearly defined sphere of competence and activity.
2 **Hierarchy:** a firmly ordered system of supervision and subordination in which lower offices accept direction from those higher up.
3 **Rules:** the organisation follows general rules which are more or less stable, more or less comprehensive and which can be learned by everyone.
4 **Impersonality:** impersonality is the spirit in which the ideal functionary conducts business. Everyone is subject to equality of treatment. The official has no partiality or favouritism, either for subordinates or customers.
5 **Appointments:** people are selected for office on the basis of their expertise and qualifications. They are appointed, and not elected or brought into the organisation as a matter of favour.
6 **Full-time:** officials are employed on a full-time basis and this is reflected in the nature and volume of work.
7 **Careers:** the job constitutes part of a career path. There are systems of promotion based on a combination of seniority and achievement.
8 **Separation:** bureaucracy separates official and functional activity as something distinct from private life. Wages and salaries are paid in return for the work. An obligation is placed on the organisation to provide all necessary equipment and facilities.
9 **Permanence:** the expertise of the organisation is retained in a system of files so that achievements, precedent and previous activities can be referred to. For each recorded transaction a copy or note is kept for the files.

This approach offers guidelines and patterns for the organisation and distribution of work and the structuring of organisations. It also ensures impersonality and permanence above the particular contributions of individuals. Bureaucracies in this form have sprung up all over the world, and in all sectors and industries. Many people believe that this is the only suitable structural form for large and sophisticated organisations; and that in any case the principles of retention and impersonality need to apply to all organisations, however small.

▮ Problems of bureaucracy

The main problem lies in the maze of offices and functions created, and their interactions and relationships. At worst, this leads to proliferation of papers, systems and procedures that govern every aspect of work and which, in turn, require monitoring and supervision.

From an internal point of view, this causes chains of command and communication to become clogged up and overloaded. Matters often have to be referred through several tiers for decision and then handed back to the originator.

Comprehensive sets of rules invariably do not cover every eventuality. The more they set out to do this, the more likely anomalies and contradictions are to occur. This leads to the need to refer matters again for decision, and so leads to delays and frustration.

Bureaucracies tend towards tall hierarchical structures and top-heaviness. Too many offices are either procedural or non-productive. Pressure is exerted on those who work at the front line, both from customers and clients, and also from the higher ranks supervising them.

Bureaucracies are stable and permanent; the converse of this is inert. They tend to greatest efficiency and effectiveness when working in a stable work environment with relative permanent operations, technology and markets. Long-established bureaucracies are often themselves barriers to change and development (whatever the feelings of the jobholders within them) when these become necessary.

Bureaucracies are not customer-friendly. They work best in this respect when the demands of the customer are regular and universal. Problems arise when this is not the case and when individual sets of circumstances have to be taken into account. Again, this causes frustration if decisions are not readily available.

▮ Rules and regulations

These are created to support structures and practices, to establish general standards of behaviour, and to provide boundaries for operations, activities and functions.

The simpler the rules, the more likely they are to be understood, accepted and followed. The drive is therefore away from long and complex manuals designed to cover every eventuality (this is, in any case, impossible) and towards much shorter, crisper and clearer guidelines that set general and absolute standards.

The benefits of the simple approach lie in the ability of all concerned to take a flexible and judgemental view of problems and situations as they arise. Energies are not spent on searching exhaustively for precedent, or in interrupting different clauses according to the point of view adopted. The onus is placed on managers and supervisors to set standards of fairness and equality: this has to be done anyway, whatever the complexity or otherwise of the rulebook. The manager's task is to exercise judgement and deal directly with problems, however, rather than search out and administer the appropriate rule or clause.

The organisation itself must have some degree of permanence in order that confidence in it can be generated on the part of both customers and staff. The relationships that are built on that permanence are always based on a combination of expectations, continuity and satisfaction, and this is only achieved if the organisation is flexible and progressive enough to develop itself and its staff to ensure that this happens. Structure therefore becomes a basis for their development just as a house, for example, becomes the basis of personal comfort and satisfaction to the owner or user: the structure is stable, the opportunities and usage afforded almost infinitely variable. What is required therefore is a genuine understanding and realisation of the purpose of structure and the opportunities afforded by an adequately and effectively structured organisation. Functions, ranks, hierarchies, bureaucracy and relations are not ends in themselves, and neither are they required *per se*. They are components to be combined and used in ways suitable to, and supportive of, the stated purposes.

16.6 Conclusions

Organisations are designed for particular purposes and circumstances and, when these change, the structure should move on also. The concept of organisation structure has come full circle, from the position of having a structure and seeking uses for it, to having a purpose and seeking the means and order for pursuing it effectively.

Related to this is the expense of carrying sophisticated support functions, hierarchies and administrative superstructures. It is also often very difficult to coordinate and harmonise these with the organisation's main purposes. They tend to generate lives of their own – aims and objectives, results areas, systems and reporting relationships – which are both time- and resource-consumptive, often out of all proportion to the actual purpose served or envisaged.

It is clearly necessary that organisations retain their permanence and their knowledge and expertise, in spite of the comings and goings of the staff. It is also necessary to coordinate and control activities, operations and resources. Most of the principles indicated therefore remain sound. However, the creation of bureaucracies, human structures and pyramids, ranks and hierarchies, administrative systems and reporting relationships in the pursuit of permanence and order is not conducive to effective performance, clarity of purpose or optimum resource usage.

▶ **17** Change

17.1 Introduction

Current political and economic turbulence, the globalisation of business and competition have called into question all the hitherto accepted ways of organising and conducting affairs, making products and delivering services. This has been fuelled by advances in all forms of technology such as production, service, consumer and information. There is a much greater capacity for producing products more quickly, more uniformly and to higher standards of quality and reliability. The result of this has been to transform consumer expectations. With the ever-greater choices afforded by the internationalisation of activities, no organisation, company, industry or sector is immune from these pressures.

It is clear that much of the order and stability of the 1950s and 1960s was brought about by what has turned out to be a global dominance–dependency relationship: the dominance of manufacturing and production by Western industrialised nations serving ever-expanding and almost guaranteed markets. The entry of organisations from the Pacific Rim into this area with advanced technology and attention to product quality and reliability has transformed the scene. There are now more organisations from more countries competing for the same markets.

Those responsible for designing organisations therefore have to create the conditions in which change is a fact of life. This consists of fostering attitudes of flexibility, dynamism and responsiveness; seeking structures and cultures that are positive and organic; and developing the human resource to its maximum capacity. It also includes providing space and resources for creative and high-quality individuals and groups to pursue projects and other developments, and to continually develop and improve skills, knowledge, qualities, processes and practices. Innovation, development and change have to be accepted and valued in the future, just as order and steadiness were in the past.

17.2 Changing the status quo

Changing the status quo is a process. It is not enough to destroy the existing order (however desirable that might be); that simply causes chaos. It is also not enough simply to take the first step towards changes to dissolve the old order; this should be done with a long-term plan in mind. The process must have a view of 'from and to' in order to be effective. People will not willingly step off the kerb of a pavement if they do not, or cannot, see how far down it is to the road; much less will they willingly follow major disruptions to any part of their lives, including work, if they cannot see where this is supposed to lead.

The 'change from' part of the process therefore requires the recognition of the behavioural and psychological barriers that will present themselves when the change is first proposed (see Figure 17.1). The 'change to' part is to create knowledge, understanding and acceptance by those involved, and to present the desired result in terms of the benefits, enhancement and enrichments to working life that are to accrue (see Figure 17.2).

■ Change catalysts

Catalysts are events – often crises or dramas – that cause organisations to question the wider situation. They may also take the form of a technological advance, changes in ownership, function or activity, or the activities of a competitor.

In each case the outcome is the appraisal of the current position as unsatisfactory and the determination to do something about it.

■ Change agents

Change agents are those who energise, direct and drive the processes. They include key appointments, people brought in to give particular emphases; such as outsiders (where the need is for acceptable or where the views of the insiders are unacceptable for some reason), or distinctive experts, who bring confidence and credibility, understanding and acceptability by virtue of their level of skill or knowledge.

17.3 Drives for change

The need for organisational change is created by the following.

■ Changes in ownership

These may come about through takeovers, mergers, acquisitions; through the privatisation of public services; through changes in the balance of shared

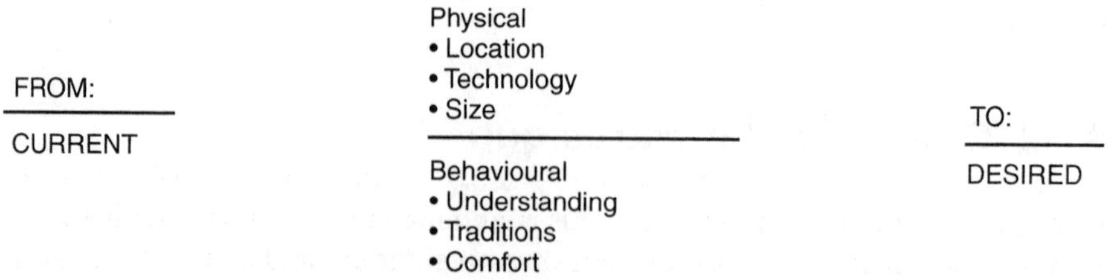

FROM:
_____
CURRENT

Physical
• Location
• Technology
• Size
_____
Behavioural
• Understanding
• Traditions
• Comfort

TO:
_____
DESIRED

Figure 17.1 Barriers

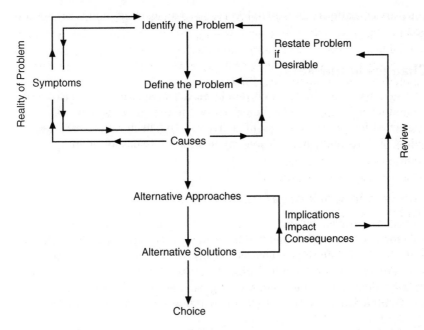

Purpose: to ensure that a rigorous and disciplined approach is recognised and understood as being necessary in all situations; or that it is adopted.

Points for consideration throughtout the process must include: the context and nature of it, when it is occurring; where it is occurring; why; its impact on the rest of the organisation, department or division, the extent to which it can be avoided; the extent to which it can be controlled; the consequences and opportunities of not tackling it (which is always a choice).

Figure 17.2   Simple change model

ownership. In each case the new owners will normally bring their own views on the present and desired performance of the organisation, and this invariably affects many of the other areas indicated below.

■ Changes in management style

Such changes are driven by a general organisational recognition that the current approach is not right. This is normally accompanied by training developments and familiarisation programmes and briefings for all staff. It may also lead to some restructuring of patterns of supervision, allocations of responsibility and divisions of work.

■ Changes in technology

These are driven by the need to improve product, volume and quality and to maintain and improve the given competitive position. This normally leads to retraining, redeployment, transfers; and also, often, to redundancies. It may also lead to the redesign and restructuring of the work environment and, again, is likely to affect patterns of supervision and management and work group cohesion.

■ Changes in markets

Changes in markets are driven by current levels of activities in relation to desired or required levels. This may also be driven by the need to seek new outlets for existing activities or new ranges of activities. The likely effects are (again) retraining and redeployment. There may also be issues of identity to be overcome.

■ Changes in work organisation

Here, change is driven by the need to improve production and output, and enhance the working environment. This normally means the creation of flexible patterns of work, offering increased levels of responsibility, broadening, enlarging and enhancing individual jobs. This, in turn, has the purpose of leading to increased identity with the organisation, greater levels of commitment, greater levels of volume and quality of output, and better wages and salaries for the staff.

■ Changes in structure

These are driven by assessments which conclude that the current structure is not as effective as it might be. This is normally arrived at by identifying blockages – in production, output, systems and communications – and relating these to structural factors. Restructuring will therefore be designed to ensure that these are removed. Restructuring also covers work practices. They may also include changes in work organisation as, for example, with the move from production lines to work groups at Saab and Volvo.

■ Changes in culture, value, attitudes and beliefs

Here again, such changes are driven by the fact that these are inappropriate or not contributing fully and effectively to the organisation and situation. This is addressed through major communications, retraining, redeployment, organisation and personnel development and enhanced by other related activities, such as the changes in technology structure and work patterns indicated.

■ Obsolescence

This change may be driven by the entry of a new player into the sector who has found radical new ways of operating that are much more effective than the status quo. Others either have to make the same shift or else reposition their existing activities (or cease business).

The usual immediate effect is to destabilise the whole sector, while all players come to terms with the new ways of working. This form of change has occurred throughout the car and electrical goods industries driven by the Japanese approach and ways of working.

Obsolescence may also be brought about by government action: for example, the sudden placing of legal restrictions or taxation charges on particular products and activities may cause people to turn away from them, leaving the organisations hitherto involved highly at risk.

Obsolescence in one organisation also occurs when others come along with substitute products and services. This is then taken up by the customers of the first organisation, again leaving it vulnerable.

In each case, obsolescence may come about very suddenly. It may also be due to circumstances over which the organisation has little or no control.

■ Managerial drives

These come about as the result of concerns by managers that the status quo will not serve the organisation forever. These are often hard to accept when the organisation is ostensibly going along extremely effectively and profitably; and harder still when this is allied to high levels of motivation, commitment and identity. These drives question and address each of the areas indicated. They come from within the organisation rather than outside. They are also likely to come from the point of view of taking preventative action rather than having to respond to crises.

■ Performance indicators and outputs

The assessment of these by managers leads to drives for change if either the operational or behavioural indicators give cause for concern. In these cases, the causes of each will be assessed and addressed. They, in turn, lead to change programmes that remedy the total performance of the whole organisation and the contribution of each department, division and function.

Performance indicators may be divided up as follows.

1 **Strategic:** related to successful and effective performance over the lifetime of an organisation.
2 **Operational:** related to the success and profitability of products and services; product mixes and portfolios; productivity and output.
3 **Specific:** including organisational income or profit per member of staff, per customer, per offering, per outlet, per square foot; returns on investment; density/frequency of usage; longevity of usage; speed of response; product durability and longevity of usage; volume and quality targets.
4 **Behavioural:** related to the perceptual and staff management aspects; desired and prevailing attitudes and values; the extent of strikes, disputes, absenteeism, labour turnover and accidents; harmony/discord, cooperation/conflict; the general aura of well-being.
5 **Confidence:** the relationship between the organisation and its environment, its backers, its stakeholders, its customers, its communities.
6 **Ethical:** the absolute standards of behaviour and performance that the

organisation sets for itself and their acceptance in their markets and communities.

These form the basis on which organisation performance may be analysed, and they help to pin-point its strengths, weaknesses and areas for concern.

■ Continuous improvement and development

The drive here stems from the recognition that there is no such thing as the perfect organisation and that the environment within which it operates is continuously fluctuating and changing. New and improved methods of work and constant attention to the behaviour and functioning of the individuals and groups therefore become key features of all effective organisations. The logical conclusion is therefore that everything is subject to potential change, and that even if something is seen and known to work extremely effectively, it may still be improved if the right means can be found.

The approach to continuous improvement and development is therefore as much about attitude and state of mind as it is operational. As such it needs feeding, supporting and nurturing to ensure that everyone involved adopts the approach. The desired output is a combination of flexibility, dynamism, responsiveness, proactivity and pioneering, leading to enhanced business performance and greater levels of personal identity with, and commitment to, the organisation.

■ Dissatisfaction with the status quo

Whatever the apparent strength of the familiarity, comfort and vested interest barriers, general and overwhelming dissatisfaction has to be changed. This is normally mainly behavioural, though the outputs of high levels of dissatisfaction are likely to be found in poor volumes, quality of products and increasing levels of customer complaints.

■ Crises and conflicts

Where an organisation is perpetually in crisis, radically different ways of working and patterns of behaviour are required and must be sought.

■ Lack of clear direction

In this case the situation is analysed and the clarity of purpose sought and established. This, again, is likely to lead to changes in attitudes, values and beliefs (indeed, it is often likely to fill a void in these). It also normally leads to the establishment of absolute standards of behaviour and performance.

■ Taking control

This is especially essential when there are powerful of well against vested interests, over-mighty departments, divisions, groups and subjects, and other lobbies and influences (for example, trade unions and consumer groups).

These drives stem from a combination of organisational effectiveness and behaviour. They reinforce the point made at the outset that neither can be achieved in isolation from the other. Any change programme that arises must address both; achieving effective results is only possible if the staff are also committed to the chosen direction.

Reasons for organisational change normally fall into one of these categories. Each also has present most of the drives indicated above, though the actual emphasis and mixture of these varies between and within organisations.

A summary framework may now be drawn up.

Why change:	What are the reasons and the drives; what are the barriers; what are the desired outcomes?
What to change:	Technology, jobs, structure, style, attitudes, values, beliefs, culture.
How to change:	What is the route to be followed between the present and what is required?
When to change:	What is the deadline for implementation and when must interim activities be completed?
Who to change:	Retraining, redeployment, redundancy; job titles and descriptions; areas of responsibility; areas of activity; changing aspirations, expectations, hopes and fears.
What to change to:	Benefits and consequences; advantages and disadvantages; for the organisation and for all concerned.

17.4 The change process

The process by which particular changes are to be achieved arrives from assessment of the components of the framework and elements indicated above. There are certain essentials.

1 Organisation commitment must be absolute.
2 Aims and objectives are to be clearly stated in terms that all affected understand.
3 Resources are required for all aspects of the process and each of the activities conducted in its pursuit.
4 Continuous monitoring, review and evaluation processes are to be conducted in the name of those responsible for designing and implementing the change programme.
5 Recognition that the expectations, hopes, fears and aspirations of all affected will themselves be changed, and that these require understanding and satisfaction.
6 Recognition that the process itself will generate its own life; that it will bring opportunities and problems that are not apparent at the outset; and that part

of the successful management of change lies in assessing these as they arise and having the capacity to take whatever steps are necessary as the result.

7 The process requires leadership and direction, and general and specific responsibilities allocated to everyone.

8 Recognition that the unfreezing of the status quo is potentially destabilising and leads to chaos if it is not a part of the complete process and targeted as such.

9 General organisation support is required for all those affected. This is necessary in the form of communications, counselling, empathy based on an understanding of the situation of those involved; and also in providing retraining, redeployment, time off to look for alternatives.

10 Recognition that change is not an end in itself and that it will lead to further opportunities.

■ Changing unsatisfactory attitudes

Unsatisfactory attitudes generally take the form of being negative or indifferent or not positive enough. Negative attitudes especially arise as the result of a lack of clarity of purpose and where the organisation has paid insufficient attention to the standards of behaviour, performance and output that are required.

Negative attitudes may also arise as the result of the influence of different groups and individuals. This occurs when these groups and individuals have some cause for dissatisfaction and seek to influence others as the result. A form of siege mentality may develop (a negative form of group-think in organisational behaviour terms).

Negative attitudes also develop alongside work structuring and the organisation and management style that has been devised to support it, and where this is alienative based on status differentials, lack of respect and esteem and absence of equality of treatment.

■ Ideal and desired attitudes

These are always positive and reflect the levels of commitment and demeanour necessary to productive and harmonious performance. The necessity is therefore to recognise the desired ideal and the current state so that a path from one to the other may be found.

Processes of attitude formation are then to be engaged with the stated purpose of achieving the ideal.

■ Responsibility

The first part of this involves accepting that change is to take place and also accepting the responsibility that goes with this. It has then to be addressed in the same way as any other change. Strategies are devised with the goal of achieving the desired attitudes and with monitoring, review and evaluation processes established to ensure that the changes taking place are those required, and also to monitor the rate at which change is taking place and its effects on organisation performance.

■ Barriers

The main barriers to attitude change are set out below.

1 Prior and current commitments – occurring where people are unwilling to change because they have invested energy and expertise in the status quo and perceive or understand it to be working well and in their own interests.
2 Ego-protection – occurring where people are unwilling to admit that there is something wrong with the situation and especially that they have made mistakes or committed themselves to faulty courses of action.
3 Value defence – occurring where there is a strong group or individual identity with prevailing values, whether or not these are effective and successful from the organisation's point of view.
4 Lack of information – this is where people will not change their attitudes because they do not see it as being in their interests to do so, because of a lack of information in relation to the imperfections of the status quo and because there is insufficient information made available about the purpose of the required and desired changes.
5 Fear – this is, above all, fear of the unknown and engages defensive and protectionist attitudes on the part of those involved.
6 Influence of individuals – occurring especially where strong and dominant personalities tell others that the desired change is not required or that it is to be punitive or coercive (or negative or detrimental in some other way). This is reinforced if the particular individual has a history or reputation for having been right about these things in the past.
7 Influence of groups – the influences here are similar to those of particular individuals. People have a strong tendency to conform to group-think and group norms. This is exacerbated if the group in question has high status or reputation. The group also has influence if the individual has taken a conscious decision to join it (such as with a trade union or professional association). In these cases the stated views of the group in relation to a particular situation are perceived to have a high degree of substance and credibility, and again this is enhanced if a group has a history of having been right about such matters in the past.

■ Drives for attitude change

Radical changes in attitude will only take place if each of these aspects is addressed effectively. The means of achieving this therefore involve the following elements.

1 Addressing prior and current commitments as stepping stones on the path of progress rather than seeking to deny or destroy them, and recognising and valuing the level of commitment that individuals have placed on these. If that

has been largely related to self-interest then means must be found of harmonising this with the commitment to the organisation that is now required.

2 Addressing ego-protection from the point of view of ensuring, again, that what has been done was not of the order of fatal or mortal error (unless it was based on vanity, arrogance or incompetence). More positive still, recognition again must be given for the value and effectiveness of whatever was done and achieved in the past; and, where this is minimal or lacking, it may still be represented as a stepping stone.

3 Addressing values from the point of view of building on the past and present rather than destroying it; this is likely to be most effective where the organisation repositions or restates its shared values and other absolute standards of policy and behaviour at the same time, taking active and positive steps to ensure that these are accepted and adopted (and that any sanctions used are given to those who do not, or will not, respond positively).

4 Overhauling channels of communication to ensure that what is put out is of quality and value, as well as volume, and to address the basic problem of ignorance that is the barrier here.

5 Addressing fear from the twin standpoint that it is a barrier to attitude change and that it can also be used to change attitudes. Fear as a barrier normally constitutes fear of the unknown and is thus largely addressed by the attention to the channels of communication activities indicated above. Fear as a drive for attitude change has to strike the balance between stating, on the one hand, that the status quo can no longer go on, with the converse, on the other, that something that is too threatening simply leads to a negative response (normally rejection). This is compounded by the fact that too little emphasis on the fear factor means that people perceive that there is nothing to be fearful of.

17.5 Other factors in the management of change

■ Co-opting

This is the process of getting highly influential groups and individuals involved in the change process. Those who defend the status quo and the prevailing attitudes and values are invited to participate in the drive for change, to suggest and devise means by which the changes required can be implemented successfully, while at the same time having regard to their own needs.

■ Use of operational change

Operational changes are also used to affect attitudes by emphasising and enhancing the opportunities that are to become available to staff as the result. This is part of the process of addressing the fear and ignorance elements. A relationship between the future ways of working and the general interest of those affected is defined. This is likely not to be an end in itself. Opportunities for training, occupational variety and redeployment normally have to be offered alongside operational change if new attitudes are to be formed effectively.

■ Use of technological change

Changes in all organisation technology – operational, production and information – invariably lead to attitude change because of the need to be retrained in order to be able to use the new equipment effectively. The result is the development of new outlooks as well as skills and knowledge, enhancement and proficiency, opening up new horizons, possibilities and potential.

■ Restructuring

Coopting, operational and technological change may all lead to, and contribute to, restructuring. The process can also be used to break up resistant groups and departments, as well as addressing operational effectiveness. It is also often possible to redefine relationships with trade unions and professional bodies and associations during restructuring on the grounds that, while the old ways may have been suitable in the past, they are no longer relevant to the new style of organisation.

■ Cooperating with the inevitable

If something is certain to happen, if the decision to change has already been taken, there is no point – and no honesty – in giving any other impression. Indeed, to do so is detrimental to the quality of future relationships. It also contributes to any prevailing negative attitudes. People who are given to understand that they have some say in matters, and then subsequently find that this is not so, generate feelings of mistrust and of negativity towards the organisation.

Positive attitudes are generated in response to the inevitable by presenting the benefits of the new situation, by dealing with negative aspects in open and straightforward ways and by reinforcing each with necessary activities. Above all, this means attention to communications and the ways in which these are delivered and presented. It also means giving organisation support to groups and individuals who are to feel particular effects – especially negative effects such as job loss – in the form of retraining and redeployment where possible. This should always be supported in terms of counselling, help, support and advice. It demonstrates respect and esteem for the staff. It acknowledges their past contribution and is a mark of value. It is also of benefit to those who remain, even if they have not been directly affected by the changes, because it proves the organisation's care, concern and respect for all staff.

■ Letting go

Prevailing attitudes – both positive and negative – are familiar and therefore comfortable. Part of the process of changing attitudes is therefore concerned with generating acceptance of, and comfort with, the new. It may be possible to gain a general acceptance that the new is highly desirable, but the old has still to be left behind; people have still to 'let it go'.

Again, the likelihood of this is greater the greater the level of direct and active involvement taken by the organisation and generated in the people. The value and quality of communications and counselling, attention to groups and individuals, reinforcement of respect and esteem is critical. The overall need is to persuade people to adopt and internalise the required attitudes and to let go of the old because it is in their interests to do so, as they will be better served by the new than the old.

■ Consultation

Consultations will begin to take place at the point at which proposals for change become clear. The purpose is to ensure that initial familiarity with the idea is generated as quickly as possible (a form of ice-breaking).

Subjecting proposals to a wider audience is also likely to ensure that any absolute objections are raised as early as possible. This, in turn, identifies the nature and location (and the likely strength) of potential lobbies and vested interests. It may also draw in concerned responses with real problems that nobody had hitherto considered.

Consultation will therefore be as wide as possible, drawing everyone involved (and any representative bodies such as trade unions and professional associations) into the process. It is the first step towards identity, internalisation, ownership – and acceptance – by all concerned.

■ Participation

Genuine participation in the determination of change is unlikely. In most situations this is the key task and responsibility of top managers. Participation in the implementation of change is essential. The process will be much smoother and more effective if what is proposed is accepted and internalised by those directly concerned. These are the direct results of effective participation. Participation in change is also conducted through all the instruments available within the organisation: staff meetings, briefing groups, work improvement groups, quality circles and quality assurance groups, any trade unions and other staff representative committees. The role of each is to accept and adopt the change processes, give them life and energy and ensure that everybody is involved.

■ Facilitation

This is the provision of specialist and directed support to groups and individuals through the process. It is especially important if there is to be a major restructuring or if redundancies, redeployments and retraining are to take place. Those affected in these ways have special needs and anxieties that must be supported.

There may also be problems with 'pockets of resistance'. Individuals and groups that refuse to accept the proposals need special counselling and additional support.

Specific individual problems may also need to be addressed in this way, such as the provision of company transport to enable people to get to a new location not on public transport routes.

■ Organisation development

The establishment of programmes of organisation development, learning cultures and programmes of continuous development and improvement both create and reinforce the environment within which changes take place. In these situations participation in the programmes is normally an absolute requirement. Skills and knowledge are therefore changed and developed first. This leads to changes in behaviour, expectations and aspirations; and in turn, again, prevailing styles, relationships, attitudes and values are affected.

This is reinforced through the use of quality circles, work improvement groups, briefing groups and targeted group and staff meetings.

17.6 Conclusions

In every change effort and programme there are winners and losers. Attention needs to be paid to the losers as well as to the winners. This is especially important for long-serving employees who came into the organisation under one set of circumstances and who are now being required to adapt to others, or even face the fact that their skills, qualities and expertise are no longer required. It should always be remembered that their contribution was valuable in the past and this should form the basis of the attitude adopted towards them for the future, whether or not they are to be kept on.

All change processes and programmes require wholehearted organisation commitment, supported with adequate levels of resource and time.

Successful change only comes about where managers successfully energise and drive each of the elements indicated. They key issue therefore is for organisations to adopt attitudes of flexibility, dynamism, responsiveness and positiveness, and the drive is to maximise output and resource usage. Change is a process; it is also a state of mind (just as order and steadiness were in the past).

It therefore requires active involvement and direct and positive participation rather than simple acquiescence, and this should apply to everyone. Hierarchical progressions, steady jobs and administrative functions and their historic output of satisfactory performance and results are all being questioned, and often abolished, in the pursuit of direct contribution to performance and continued improvement and development.

Above all, the role of managers and supervisors must change from the operation of systems and procedures to the development of expertise, skills, knowledge and qualities in their people. The new manager will be a leader, director, developer and coach of the human resource, and the creator of conditions in which this can be successful. This, above all, is why an understanding of the behaviour of organisations and those who work in them is so valuable.

▼ Bibliography

J.H. Adair (1975) *Action-Centred Leadership*, Cambridge University Press.

J.H. Adair (1986) *Effective Team Building*, Gower.

I. Adams, S. Hamil and A. Carruthers (1990) *The Future of Organizations*, Free Press.

M. Argyle (1989) *The Social Psychology of Work*, Penguin.

C. Argyris (1957) *Personality and Organisations*, Harper & Row.

M. Armstrong (1993) *Personnel Management*, Prentice-Hall.

M.K. Ash (1985) *On People Management*, McDonald.

R.M. Belbin (1986) *Superteams*, Prentice-Hall.

E.H. Berne (1984) *Games People Play*, Penguin.

D. Biddle and R. Evenden (1989) *Human Aspects of Management*, IPM.

R. Blake and J. Mouton (1986) *The New Managerial Grid*, Gulf.

E. de Bono (1984) *Lateral Thinking for Managers*, Pelican.

T. Burns and G.M. Stalker (1968) *The Management of Innovation*, Tavistock.

D. Carnegie (1936) *How to Win Friends and Influence People*, Simon & Schuster.

S. Caulkin (1995) 'Hooked on High Tech', *Business International*.

C.R. Christensen (1980) *Business Policy*, Irwin.

G.A. Cole (1994) *Management Theory and Practice*, DPP.

D. Drennan (1992) *Transforming Company Culture*, McGraw-Hill.

P.F. Drucker (1955) *Management by Objectives*, Prentice-Hall.

P.F. Drucker (1986a) *Drucker on Management*, Prentice-Hall.

P.F. Drucker (1986b) *The Practice of Management*, Prentice-Hall.

P.F. Drucker (1988) *The Effective Executive*, Fontana.

P.F. Drucker (1990) *Frontiers of Management*, Heinemann.

P.F. Drucker (1993a) *The Ecological Vision*, Transaction.

P.F. Drucker (1993b) *The Post-Capitalist Society*, HarperCollins.

G. Egan (1994) 'Cultivate your Culture', *Management Today* (April).

A. Etzioni (1964) *Power in Organisations*, Free Press.

F.E. Fiedler (1967) *A Theory of Leadership Effectiveness*, McGraw-Hill.

J. French and B. Raven (1959) 'The Bases of Social Power', in D. Cartwright (ed.), *Studies in Social Power*, University of Michigan.

N. Glass (1996) *Chaos, Conflict and Management*, European Management Journal.

W. Goldsmith and D. Clutterbuck (1990) *The Winning Streak*, Penguin.

J.H. Goldthorpe *et al.* (1968) *The Affluent Worker*, Vol. 3, Cambridge University Press.

C.T. Goodworth (1920) *Recruitment and Selection*, Cove.

C.B. Handy (1984) *The Future of Work*, Penguin.

C.B. Handy (1988) *The Age of Unreason*, Penguin.

C.B. Handy (1991) *The Gods of Management*, Penguin.

C.B. Handy (1992) *The Empty Raincoat*, Penguin.

C.B. Handy (1993) *Understanding Organisations* (first published 1990), Penguin.

C.B. Handy (1995) *Beyond Certainty*, Macmillan.

C.B. Handy *et al.* (1981) *Making Managers*, Penguin.

P. Harris and R. Moran (1991) *Managing Cultural Differences*, Gulf.

F. Herzberg (1960) *Work and the Nature of Man*, Granada.

F. Herzberg *et al.* (1959) *The Motivation to Work*, Chapman & Hall.

P. Honey and A. Mumford (1986) *Preferences in Learning Styles*, Peter Honey.

A. Huczynski and D. Buchanan (1993) *Organizational Behaviour*, McGraw-Hill.

G. Hofstede (1980) *Culture's Consequences*, Sage.

A. Jay (1967) *Management and Machiavelli*, Holt, Rinehart & Winston.

G. Johnson and K. Scholdes (1994) *Exploring Corporate Strategy*, PHI.

D. Katz and R.L. Kahn (1978) *The Social Psychology of Organisations*, Wiley.

D.A. Kolb (1985) *Experience and the Source of Learning and Development*, Prentice-Hall.

P.A. Lawrence (1984) *Insight into Management*, Macmillan.

R.S. Lessem (1987) *Intrapreneurship*, Wildwood.

R. Likert (1961) *New Patterns of Management*, McGraw-Hill.

R. Likert (1967) *The Human Organisation*, McGraw-Hill.

B. Livy (1987) *Corporate Personnel Management*, Pitman.

F. Luthans (1989) *Organisational Behaviour*, McGraw-Hill.

D.C. McClelland (1988) *Human Motivation*, Cambridge University Press.

D. McGregor (1961) *The Human Side of Enterprise*, Harper & Row.

N. Machiavelli (1993) *The Prince*, Penguin Classics.

A. Maslow (1987) *Motivation and Personality* (first published 1960), Harper & Row.

H. Mintzberg (1974) *Management*, PHI.

A. Morita (1987) *Made in Japan: The Sony Story*, Collins.

W.G. Ouchi (1981) *Theory Z*, Avon.

H. Owen (1985) *Myth Transformation and Change*, Collins.

D.S. Payne and D.A. Pugh (1990) *Principles of Organisation*, Penguin.

T. Peters and N. Austin (1986) *A Passion for Excellence*, Collins.

R. Pettinger (1997) *Introduction to Management*, Macmillan.

R. Pettinger (1998) *Managing the Flexible Workforce*, Cassell.

C. Rogers (1947) 'Observations in the Organization of Personality', *American Psychologist*, vol. 2.

E. Schein (1988) *Organisational Psychology*, Prentice-Hall.

R. Semler (1992) *Maverick*, Free Press.

E. Sternberg (1995) *Just Business*, Warner.

R. Stewart (1996) *Employee Development*, IPD.

B. Tuckman (1965) *Effective Working Groups*, McGraw-Hill.

V. Vroom (1964) *Work and Motivation*, Wiley.

D. Walton and A. McKersie (1965) *A Behavioural Theory of Labour Negotiations*, McGraw-Hill.

P. Wickens (1992) *The Road to Nissan*, Collins.

J. Woodward (1970) *Industrial Organisation: Behaviour and Control*, Oxford University Press.

Index